IN HITLER'S
BUNKER

IN HITLER'S BUNKER

A Boy Soldier's Eyewitness Account
of the Fürher's Last Days

Armin D. Lehmann with Tim Carroll

THE LYONS PRESS
Guilford, Connecticut
An imprint of the Globe Pequot Press

The Lyons Press is an imprint of The Globe Pequot Press.

10   8   6   4   2   1   3   5   7   9

ISBN 1-59228-578-3

This edition of the UK original title *In Hitler's Bunker* is published by arrangement
with Mainstream Publishing Co. Ltd., 7 Albany Street, Edinburgh EH 1 3UG.
www.mainstreampublishing.com

Printed in the United States of America

Library of Congress Cataloging-in-Publication Data is available on file.

Contents

		7
		9
16 January 1945		15
	Bad Omens	25
	War	35
EE	First Blood	48
R	First Love	64
	Happy Birthday, Führer	75
	Hitler and His Women	87
N	Hitler's Children	101
T	Madness in the Führerbunker	112
	The Last Goodbyes	122
CHAPTER TEN	Into the Führerbunker	135
CHAPTER ELEVEN	The Mad House	147
CHAPTER TWELVE	The Final Betrayal	156
CHAPTER THIRTEEN	Marriage	168
CHAPTER FOURTEEN	*Götterdämmerung*	175
CHAPTER FIFTEEN	Murder in the Bunker	187
CHAPTER SIXTEEN	Break-out	198
CHAPTER SEVENTEEN	The Ghost of Adolf Hitler	207
Epilogue		217
Index		222

Foreword

IN HITLER'S BUNKER IS BASED ON Armin Dieter Lehmann's account of growing up in Nazi Germany, fighting as a Hitler Youth against the Russians and ending the last days of the war serving in Adolf Hitler's bunker beneath the Berlin Chancellery Garden. Lehmann's narrative is compelling because it tells through the eyes of an innocent the story of the Nazi regime's genesis and subsequent nemesis. They were the youthful eyes that were dazzled by the visions of power and glory that Nazism seemed to offer a humiliated people. They were the uncritical eyes that witnessed the brutality of the Nazi regime without pausing to question its rectitude. They were eyes that remained blinded to the truth even as the shaky edifice of Hitler's Third Reich crashed down before them. It was only after his beloved Führer finally killed himself that Lehmann eventually opened his eyes and realised his childhood had been stolen.

Lehmann grew up in Silesia and went to school in Breslau where his father was in the SS. In the last days of the war he saw action against the Red Army outside Breslau. By a stroke of fate he was subsequently taken to Berlin to serve as the courier to Artur Axmann, the leader of the Hitler Youth. Axmann is virtually unknown outside Germany, but he was a pivotal figure in the Nazi hierarchy in the last years of the war, and became one of Hitler's closest confidants in his final hours. He had been promoted to Hitler's inner circle by virtue of his offer to sacrifice every last Hitler Youth in the defence of the Führer and the Fatherland.

As Axmann's courier Lehmann worked in the bunker complex beneath the Reich Chancellery where Hitler spent his last days. The experience brought the 16-year-old boy into contact with some of the most notorious Nazis of Hitler's regime, including the Führer himself. Lehmann was by Axmann's side as the drama of Hitler's last days unfolded. In Axmann's biography, the former Reich Youth leader recalled how Eva Braun had been impressed by the dedication of his *Melder* (courier), Armin Lehmann, whom she met in the bunker.

Axmann was a fanatical Nazi until his dying day. Lehmann has come to have a radically different perspective on life, and became a pacifist, appalled at the atrocities that the Nazis inflicted on mind and body. Lehmann's own memoir, *Hitler's Last Courier*, is a highly personal effort to explore his upbringing in a fanatical Nazi family. It was an effort that Lehmann himself admits he found difficult and his memories proved to be far from perfect. His memories do not always coincide with established history. Whenever possible I have checked the facts, but sometimes the facts have proved elusive. *In Hitler's Bunker*, which is based on Armin's memoir, is partly the story of Lehmann's early life, and partly a historical account of those last days in the bunker.

Tim Carroll

Introduction

There is only victory or annihilation. Know no bounds in your hatred of the enemy. It is your duty to watch when others tire, to stand when others weaken. Your greatest honour is your unshakeable fidelity to Adolf Hitler.

– Artur Axmann, Leader of the Hitler Youth, April 1945

IT WAS WITH WORDS SUCH AS these that the Third Reich's Hitler Youth Leader, Artur Axmann, exhorted ten-year-old boys and girls being sworn into the Hitler Youth in Berlin on the eve of Adolf Hitler's last birthday. The children were being inducted in the junior echelons of the movement, the *Jungvolk* (young folk) and *Jungmädel* (young maidens). I was looking on, then aged 16, a member of the Hitler Youth Volkssturm (literally: people's storm). The *Volkssturm* was the Home Defence Force of old men and young boys hastily assembled in the dying days of the war. Every able-bodied male between the ages of 16 and 55 was ordered to put on whatever uniform he could find (anything from postmen's uniforms to firemen's uniforms) and fight for the Fatherland. The Russians called us 'totals' – because we were the result of total war. The Wehrmacht called us 'stew' – because we were a mixture of old meat and green vegetables.

However, I had recently distinguished myself in battle and had even been awarded the Iron Cross II (Second Class). The Hitler Youth Leader, Artur Axmann, at 32, was the youngest of the senior Nazis around Hitler. But his influence within Hitler's inner circle was growing daily towards the end of the war as he pledged that the Hitler Youth movement would fight to the death for the Führer and the Fatherland. In Hitler's last days, Axmann was one of only a handful of Nazis, including Hitler's private secretary Martin Bormann and the cynical Propaganda Minister Joseph Goebbels, who enjoyed the Führer's absolute trust and confidence. Axmann had personally selected me to be presented to Hitler on the occasion of his 56th birthday at a ceremony in the Reich Chancellery in Berlin, partly because of my recent distinction in fighting the Russians, but partly, I suspect, because my role in my Hitler Youth unit was as a Melder (a courier). Hitler had won his Iron Cross as a courier in the First World War. I think that Axmann saw that as a lucky sign of some sort.

At that moment our Führer could do with every bit of luck he could get. As I watched Axmann I did not realise it but victory for the Allies was no longer in doubt. Germany was being overrun from every direction. City after city was being turned into ash under a ferocious Allied bombing campaign unprecedented in its intensity.

I, along with several hundred other teenage soldiers of the Hitler Youth Volkssturm, was among the last who would serve Hitler's regime in Berlin – in the much-vaunted *Zitadelle* (citadel) of the Führer's last redoubt – in the dying days of the war. I didn't know it at the time, but I would soon be serving as a courier in his bunker beneath the Chancellery. It was an experience that would bring me into contact with some of the most notorious Nazis of the time, as well as some of the most decent soldiers and civilians struggling to cope with the death wish Hitler had imposed upon all Germans. Facing total defeat, the Führer was now willing to sacrifice everything and everybody, including even the youngest and most innocent of German lives. (It wasn't just males either. The Bund *Deutscher Mädel* – the German Girls' Legion, or BDM – was the female section of the Hitler Youth. They too sacrificed their lives for the Führer.)

I did not realise at the time that Germany faced total defeat. I still believed in the myth of our 'miracle weapons' that was widely circulated before the end of the war. I had no comprehension of the sheer evil that was at the heart of the Nazi regime. Yet I was prepared to lay down my life for Hitler in defence of the Fatherland and the noble ideals of the National Socialist movement. I was elated at the prospect of greeting Hitler the following morning on his 56th (and last) birthday. To comprehend why anybody can have been so thoroughly taken in by such a deception, one must understand a little about my background.

I was four years old when Adolf Hitler became Reich Chancellor of a coalition cabinet in Germany. It was 30 January 1933. Later, this historic date became known as *die Machtergreifung* (the Seizure of Might). Absolute power, as history has taught us, often brings about primal chaos. But in Hitler's case it went beyond that. His absolute control over the minds of countless individuals created a living hell that destroyed the lives of millions of people in a human catastrophe too enormous to comprehend.

But it wasn't like that in the beginning. It all started with promises of a better life. My grandfather, for example, an old guard Nazi Party member and an early follower of Hitler, was convinced that a fast economic recovery would come about because of Hitler. It did. He was also sure that Germany would be avenged for the Treaty of Versailles. It was. My father believed in Hitler as well. He not only became a member of the National Socialist Workers' Party, as thousands did, and joined the SS, he also turned into a fanatical disciple of what he looked upon as the new order needed to restore Germany to the glory it deserved.

My father was an authoritarian so perhaps it is understandable that he admired the new regime. But my mother was as loving and caring a soul as you could possibly imagine. She too admired Adolf Hitler. She too thought Adolf Hitler had been anointed by God to lead Germany to its historic destiny as the greatest nation on earth. Most Germans did. It may come as a shock, or maybe a mild surprise, to many people, but women were among Hitler's most ardent followers. My mother adored him.

I grew up in the woods of Lower Silesia, very close to the Polish border, and very far away from the thriving metropolitan areas of Europe. It was a sheltered existence and, looking back, it seems to me to have been almost medieval in its outlook. As a young boy I witnessed, with a great sense of excitement, the first rally and torchlight procession of Nazi storm-trooper units. When I was ten I saw Hitler for the first time at a gathering in Breslau. His hold over his audience was hypnotic. The Nazis, like the Jesuits, knew the secret of capturing the body and soul of an individual: get them when they are young. Under Adolf Hitler's regime, children were taught that their parents might have raised them, but they belonged to the nation.

If it is hard to accept that any civilised person would believe such a notion, the case of the future leader of the Hitler Youth should be examined. Baldur von Schirach was the predecessor of Artur Axmann. Under him the infant Nazi youth movement thrived and the cult of the Führer thrived. But von Schirach was no barbarian. He came from a highly cultivated bourgeois family from Weimar, the literary capital of Germany. He was a poet and a song-writer. (And he would play an important role in my life as the years unfolded.) His family were left destitute by the First World War. His father was unemployed. His army officer brother committed suicide because he felt his career had been ruined by Versailles. Baldur von Schirach became a Nazi. On the first occasion he saw Hitler, he was so moved he wrote a poem.

The Hitler Youth was just one of many quasi-military associations that blossomed in Germany in the 1920s and 1930s. I became an enthusiastic youth leader and follower of this exciting new order. At the age of ten, I became a cub scout in the junior section of the Hitler Youth, the Jungvolk. Within two years I was in charge of my own 30-member unit. We were taught that Germans were members of a superior race, destined to dominate the inferior and weak. We were Aryans and Aryans were superior to all others, particularly Jews. Jews, we were taught, were parasites. I went on to fight ferociously for my Führer and the Fatherland, almost to the death. Eventually, fighting on the streets of Berlin in the very last days of the war, I would win the Iron Cross I (First Class) to complement my Iron Cross II (Second Class).

I was a fanatical Nazi. I was devoted to Hitler. I would have died for him, and I nearly did, several times, as a fighter against the Red Army and as a courier in the last days of his life. They were the days that would turn out to be the most strange, extraordinary – and banal – of his remarkable existence. They were the days that witnessed his sudden and unexpected marriage to Eva Braun, his mistress, whom few people had ever heard of. They were the days that saw the Führer take his own life in circumstances that are still shrouded in mystery and myth. They were the days that saw his mythmaker-in-chief, Joseph Goebbels, end his own existence, after his wife Magda, the unanointed 'First Lady' of the Third Reich, slaughtered her six children in the bunker.

I was in the citadel when all this happened. Not once did I lose faith in Adolf Hitler. Not even after he had put a gun to his head and blown his brains out, thus abandoning the German people he had urged to fight to the death. Not once did I question my allegiance to the obviously insane creed of his Nazi Party. Even as I ducked and dived Allied bullets outside the bunker, and could see before my own eyes how the edifice of his absurd Thousand-Year Reich was crashing down around me: not once did I doubt that we Germans were right and our enemies were wrong.

In those last days of madness in the Führerbunker I witnessed just how seedy and self-serving almost all of Hitler's henchmen were. Those that were not bad were simply mad and were seemingly prepared to carry on sacrificing innocent blood for a cause that had been lost years ago. I could see all this before my eyes. Yet my belief structure only collapsed after Hitler's suicide. Then my survival instincts kicked in. When the Americans interrogated me after our defeat, I could not believe what they told me about concentration camps and my beloved leader's Final Solution. But how could I not when the evidence was there before my eyes? Why did I not open my eyes just briefly to try and see?

I have spent my lifetime since trying to find the answer to that question. I hope this book goes some way towards an explanation.

Armin Dieter Lehmann,
Waldport, Oregon,
United States.
June 2003.

Berlin, 16 January 1945

ON THE AFTERNOON OF 16 JANUARY 1945, Adolf Hitler left his official Berlin residence in Berlin's neo-baroque Old Reich Chancellery for the last time. In the relentless Allied bombing that was reducing central Berlin to rubble, the ornate apartment on the first floor of the Old Chancellery was no longer deemed safe for the Führer. The building stretched along the Wilhemsstrasse, still one of the most attractive boulevards of Berlin, although not for much longer. Dating back to before Bismarck's time, the Old Reich Chancellery had been the Führer's home since he came to power in 1933. On many occasions the Führer had stood on its small balcony acknowledging the tumultuous applause of the crowds in Wilhelmplatz below. It was from that balcony that Hitler and his air Reich Marshal Hermann Göring acknowledged the wildly cheering crowds after their return in triumph from France in 1940. Now, except for the one wing that survived almost intact, little remained of the building other than its elegant façade. Its interior had been almost entirely burnt out by bombs and incendiaries. By the dawn of 1945 there were no longer any cheering crowds to greet Adolf Hitler.

Perhaps taking leave of the Old Chancellery building was the least of Hitler's disappointments. He had once told his protégé Albert Speer that his official residence was fit only for 'a soap factory'. That bleak afternoon of January 1945, Hitler walked along the long labyrinth of corridors and hallways that connected the Old Reich Chancellery to the New Reich Chancellery, the new seat of government that was supposed to symbolise everything that was great about the new Germany he had wrought out of the old. It was built on his orders by Speer in 1938. The Führer's instructions had been to create a building on such a monumental scale that every visitor would be struck by the grandeur and might of the Third Reich. Speer had not failed him. The New Reich Chancellery was a vast, low building stretching an entire city block. It was a grandiose statement of Teutonic might built to last the thousand years that the Third Reich was destined to endure. Neo-Roman in its allusions, the New Reich Chancellery boasted the brutal lines and proportions that projected the iron will of Hitler's uncompromising National Socialist creed. Walking up the wide steps of the main entrance on Voss Strasse, visitors were dwarfed by four enormous columns, above them a huge eagle, its wings outstretched, its claws bearing the swastika symbol. At the entrance Arno Breker's statue of a muscular, nude sword-bearer greeted new arrivals.

Albert Speer's New Reich Chancellery was a potent symbol of the National Socialist movement and the powerful grip it had exerted on Germany. But by 1945, even it had become a victim of the Allied campaign of aerial retribution that had been visited upon the Reich capital, for once giving Hitler a taste of the Nazis' own barbarous medicine. The Chancellery no longer looked as if it was going to last the full thousand years. Several direct hits had left parts of the long roof collapsed. The walls were blackened by smoke from the many conflagrations that had ravaged the city. Many of the windows had been blown in. The sheer weight of the construction had meant that Speer's creation had withstood the bombardment better than most of the other office blocks and apartment buildings of Berlin, but it was a ghostly shadow of its former self.

Inside this vast monument to his overweening power, Hitler's magnificent office, measuring 400 metres square, was remarkably unscathed. The thick, sumptuous carpets and cool, grey, silk floor-to-ceiling curtains had been maintained in impeccable condition by an army of orderlies and servants. Despite the deprivations of the world outside, the plump armchairs and sofas were as plush and plumped as those of the luxurious hotel lobby Hitler's study resembled. But 16 January 1945 would be the last day that the Führer would sit behind his enormous polished desk. After supervising the collection of those papers that he would require in his new, slightly more modest quarters, Hitler began to shuffle his way out of the room across the thick carpet and along the hallways that would lead him to his last, less ostentatious, home. When the Nazis had come to power in 1933 Hitler had sworn never to leave the Reich Chancellery voluntarily. He vowed that no power in the world would drive him out. It was yet another promise he had failed to live up to.

The Führer was by now a chronically ill man. He looked more like 70 than his 55 years. His neatly trimmed brown hair had turned into uneven strands of greasy grey. His once-blue eyes were now palely opaque. He had long worn reading glasses in private. But his aides now could not help but notice how he seemingly found it difficult to pick out his surroundings even in broad daylight. His haggard frame and shoulders were stooped, and he occasionally appeared to be bent double. He had been in bad health for much of the last years of war. But his condition had deteriorated rapidly after the assassination attempt of the previous 20 July, when Colonel Claus von Stauffenberg placed a briefcase stuffed with explosives under the conference room table of his East Prussian bunker. The explosion killed four members of the 24 staff, seriously injuring half of them. Hitler was badly hurt, his trousers shredded in the explosion, but he had somehow survived. It reinforced in the Führer and his supporters the belief that he was somehow divinely protected, and that Providence had destined him to lead the German people until all his noble ambitions for them had been achieved.

The explosion, however, had also burst his eardrums, leaving him with a deteriorating sense of balance. His left arm had been badly damaged and he found it difficult to control its movements. He had long suffered from stomach cramps and now they plagued him even more. His skin was visibly discoloured. His voice, once powerful and energetic, was now little more than a whisper. Hitler was surviving on a cocktail of drugs supplied by his personal physician Dr Theodor Morell. (Although there were those around the Führer who believed that pain from the medicine itself was damaging his health even further.)

The building Hitler now walked through had undergone a similar transformation. It had been stripped of most ornamentation when the bombing began. The magnificent tapestries and carpets, the splendid works of art, many of them looted from Nazi-occupied countries, had been moved into storage. Now the New Reich Chancellery was a cold and dismal place. Dust and cement from crumbling masonry were sprinkled over the once-spotless marbled floors. The grand reception hall with its sparkling chandeliers was famed for being twice as long as Palace of Versailles' Hall of Mirrors. But now it was little more than a gloomy, echoing cavern of cracking walls and crumbling masonry.

On the ground floor of the Chancellery his Praetorian Guard, the *Leibstandarte* Adolf Hitler (LAH – Leibstandarte means bodyguard), stood to attention in their smart black uniforms, white gloves and swastika armbands. The LAH was an elite SS division and the only division to carry the Führer's name in full. It accompanied Hitler wherever he went and had its permanent barracks in the grounds of the Reich Chancellery. But the men of the LAH no longer strutted across the hub of a Nazi empire that stretched from the Channel Islands in the west to the Caucasus in the east, and from the Sahara in the south to the Norwegian

Arctic in the north. No longer were their Nazi jackboots trampling over the oppressed peoples of Europe. Very soon they would be on the receiving end of a mighty military assault that would crush them into oblivion just as the Nazis had annihilated so many other people. Soon, the Third Reich would extend hardly beyond the other side of the Tiergarten (Berlin's Zoo).

That January of 1945 the Führer's masterful Propaganda Minister Joseph Goebbels had written that Hitler was the 'man of the millennium'. But when Hitler arrived in Berlin in the early hours of 16 January it was without fanfare. His train slipped quietly into the main station, and his car drove him to the Old Reich Chancellery in the pitch darkness of the night. He had left his last field headquarters at Adlerhorst amid the drooping pine forests of the Masurian Lakes, having realised that the battle in the west was futile and every effort had to be directed to the Eastern Front. His arrival in Berlin went unannounced and most Berliners would not realise the Führer was in the city until a Reich Radio announcement towards the very end of the war. By then, most of them just wanted him to go, and the quicker, the better.

Hitler was now embarking on the last journey of his life. And as history was sucking him remorselessly down into the annals of its darkest days, so Hitler was descending into the bowels of the building that had been such a potent symbol of everything he stood for. Leaving the official rooms above, Hitler walked past the command post of the LAH, now permanently situated in the basement of the Chancellery and now under the command of SS Brigadeführer Wilhelm Mohnke. Mohnke would play a pivotal role in the drama of the last days of Hitler. With the Führer was Heinz Linge, his ever-attendant valet, and Hans Rattenhuber, his head of security, along with several RSD (*der Reichssicherheitsdienst*, Reich security service) guards.

The Führer's personal protection was divided between two distinct corps, which both held SS ranks. The RSD was under the command of Rattenhuber. They were trained police detectives and shadowed Hitler wherever he went. Members of the RSD had to be tried and trusted Nazis of pure German descent. The RSD had different units assigned to each Nazi leader. Hitler's was Dienstselle 1, which was composed of trained detectives from Heinrich Himmler's criminal police. The FBK (*Führerbegleitkommando*), his honour guards, were drawn from the ranks of the LAH. A squad of about 40 men, they not only guarded the entrances to wherever the Führer was, but acted as couriers, valets and orderlies.

Rattenhuber and Linge would be by Hitler's side virtually every moment until the very end of his life. Shortly to follow Hitler was his team of four secretaries, who would also be in the Führer's presence for much of the trying time to come. Two of them, Traudl Junge and Gerda Christian, refused to leave his side, even when he implored them to do so. The other two, Christa Schroeder and Johanna Wolf, had to be ordered to leave by the Führer. Such was the loyalty Hitler commanded. Eventually the small party arrived at the inauspicious surroundings of the Chancellery kitchens. From there they made their way down some steps to the capacious pantry of Hitler's butler-cum-major *domo* Artur Kannenberg.

With its shelves groaning with fine food the likes of which most Berliners had not seen for six years, Kannenberg's pantry had never been wanting. Hitler was, of course, a vegetarian and a strict non-drinker. In these – his last – days he rarely touched anything but clear soup and mashed potatoes, perhaps the occasional spaghetti dish with tossed salad washed down with his personal physician's concoction of pills. But the Reich Chancellery pantries and cellars never lacked for the finest food – caviar, the best kind of fresh salami, tinned *sauerbraten* (sour roast beef) and *wurst* (sausage). Kannenberg's shelves were stocked with seemingly endless crates of French wine and champagne. Germany was starving. But those at the top of the Nazi feeding chain had never gone without the very best of luxury food.

Next Hitler was ushered through an unobtrusive but heavy door along one side of the pantry. Behind it was a short row of hard concrete steps leading downwards and into a grey, featureless corridor beyond. Those that knew of this secret passageway called it *der Kannenberggang* (the Kannenberg Alley). Halfway along the dimly lit corridor Hitler met two FBK guards bearing machine guns and wearing smart field-grey uniforms. The FBK were the SS honour guards that protected the official buildings that the Führer occupied. They stood at the threshold of a huge reinforced steel door. Jumping sharply to attention, the FBK men saluted the Führer as he passed through the entrance. Since the assassination plot these guards were under instructions to confiscate the sidearms of even the most senior officers. Their briefcases were always searched. Even Hitler's secretaries were subject to the humiliation of having their handbags examined.

Hitler was taking the first steps into the Führerbunker, an eerie subterranean world that would witness the dying moments of the Third Reich. It was an artificial underground existence that few of his senior staff and generals enjoyed. But it was one that the Führer seemed perfectly acclimatised to. Increasingly, as the war had gone against him, Hitler had shunned the daylight, preferring to fight his battles from a series of bunkers. Ominously, the Führerbunker was the 13th such structure he had occupied. It would be a strange upside-down world in which this tyrant who had been responsible for the slaughter of millions would be referred to affectionately as *der Chef* (the chief) by his orderlies, secretaries and attendants. The man who had thrust Europe to the very edge of a new Dark Age would be regarded as a good boss, a kind and paternal man who liked nothing better than playing with his dog.

Hitler had every reason to seek refuge. His Thousand-Year Third Reich had actually only lasted twelve, and was collapsing before Hitler's own blurred eyes. The Americans came by day, the mighty Eighth Air Force's Liberators and silver Flying Fortresses appearing like little angels of death over Germany. The RAF (Royal Air Force) came by night, the growl of the Wellington and Lancaster bombers by now a familiar and dreaded midnight overture in many once-proud cities. Hundreds and thousands of tonnes of bombs and perhaps even more lethal incendiaries had been dropped on Germany in a sustained and merciless attack. The fearful assault from the air had regularly seen formations of 1,000 or even 1,500 American and British heavy bombers over German skies. Within a month of Hitler's descent into the bunker would come one of the most devastating air attacks of them all: the destruction of Dresden. Now central Berlin was increasingly becoming the focal point of this implacable assault from the sky.

The German surface navy, to all intents and purposes, had long-since ceased to exist. The navy's operations were now limited to its valiant U-Boat fleet that was increasingly starved of fuel and harried from the air by British Hunter aircraft and in the sea by surface vessels. On land, the British, French and American armies were advancing rapidly across the west and into the German heartland. In the south the British and Americans were storming up the peninsula of Italy. Most ominously of all, the Russians were advancing on a broad front from the east and were poised for a giant pincer movement that threatened to completely encircle Berlin. It was the Russians that the Germans, and Hitler, feared most. Such was the barbarism that the Nazis had inflicted upon the Russians, few people in Germany were under any illusions about what the Red Army had in store for them. There were contingency plans to fly Hitler and his entourage out to the Berchtesgaden in the Bavarian Alps where Hitler's Berghof mountaintop retreat stood over the vast underground complex of the National Redoubt. But it was never seriously an option for the Führer. As Albert Speer would point out in a few months' time, if the Führer was to die in the style to which he had become accustomed, it would be better amid the full Wagnerian splendour of a Berlin bloodbath, rather than the gentle Alpine surroundings of his 'weekend bungalow'.

To the very end Hitler would rouse his acolytes with stirring talk of the impending Nazi counter-offensive that would hurl the invaders back to where they came from. But his actions on that January afternoon as he took to his bunker spoke louder than words. He would never see the sun rise or fall over Berlin again. In fact, over the next three months, Hitler would emerge from time to time from what became known as the Führerbunker. He would sometimes take lunch with his secretaries in his old official dining-room. But the once grand room echoed with emptiness now, and the view over the Chancellery Garden was of a rubble- and debris-strewn wasteland pockmarked with bomb craters.

The Führer could be forgiven for being despondent – but he was far from it. Over the next few weeks he would insist on returning to the cellars of the New Reich Chancellery to inspect an elaborate architectural model. It was of the spectacular city he had long dreamed of building on the foundations of Linz, the pretty Austrian town on the Danube that he had adopted as his 'home'. (He had actually been born in a village nearby.) Even as Berlin crumbled and Russian artillery pounded the Reich Chancellery, Hitler would ponder over the blueprints for Grand Linz, checking the proportions of the buildings and poring over the plans. He must surely have known by now that his dream would never be realised. But so much of Hitler's rise to power had been based on fantasies and myths which turned out to be little more than the chimera of a deluded mind that exercised an extraordinary grip over so many other deluded minds.

The bunker was not a bunker at all but an air raid shelter intended for nothing more than temporary refuge, although it was a fairly elaborate, strong and more than usually comfortable air raid shelter at that. It didn't have a sophisticated communications centre to speak of, just a small telephone switchboard operated by one man, SS Sergeant Rochus Misch, and a radio that depended for its functioning on an aerial suspended over the bunker by a gas balloon. At the very end Hitler ended up relying on couriers to relay his messages over to the Party Chancellery on the other side of Wilhelmsstrasse, where there was a navy radio facility that had all the naval and Party ciphers.

Nevertheless his glorified air raid shelter was never referred to as anything but a bunker. The Führer had several other underground complexes available to him in the Berlin area that were of far more sturdy construction and contained the modern communications equipment needed to run a war. Joseph Goebbels had a luxuriously appointed bunker at his Propaganda Ministry on Wilhelmplatz. Hitler's private secretary Martin Bormann had a reinforced air raid shelter in the cellar of the Party Chancellery. There was a vast double bunker complex at Zossen, 35 kilometres to the south, home of the Reich's supreme military command. His military commanders were constantly urging him to decamp to Zossen. And his air Reich Marshal Hermann Göring had two Luftwaffe bunkers, one not far away in Berlin, the other at Gatow airfield on the outskirts of Berlin. But after the von Stauffenberg assassination plot Hitler no longer trusted his regular military officers, and after the repeated failures of the Luftwaffe, Göring was beginning to be regarded as something of a buffoon by the Führer. Hitler preferred the safety of his modest little shelter that was guarded by the loyal LAH.

There were actually two bunkers beneath the Chancellery Garden. Together they were a self-contained complex with their own heating and lighting provided by a generator. Fresh water was acquired from an artesian well 20 metres beneath the ground. There were kitchens, toilets, store-rooms and bedrooms. The first bunker lay not far beneath the surface of the ground. This was known to everyone as the *Vorbunker* or upper bunker. It was a simple oblong shape, centred around a room that was little more than a wide corridor with a dozen or so small rooms either side housing kitchens, storerooms and quarters for servants or Hitler's aides. That room was known as the *Gemeinschaftsraum* (common room or public room) and was also referred to as the canteen corridor or dining passageway. The walls were painted dull shades of grey or brown or were simply bare concrete. The ceilings were low. The lighting was oppressively dim. It was into this central dining passageway that Hitler now walked.

At first the dining passageway was mainly for the more junior staff, who rarely ventured into the lower bunker. But it was the centre for bunker gossip and idle chatter as orderlies and guards rested between shifts. Most of the staff who would work in the Führerbunker were old hands from the early days of Hitler's rise to power. Much of the time they spent talking about the good old days of Munich and their time at Hitler's mountain retreat at Berchtesgaden. On Hitler's left as he entered the upper bunker was the tiny kitchen and scullery overseen by his dietician Constanze Manziarly. An Austrian woman in her 20s, Manziarly maintained the Führer's strict vegetarian diet and would often dine alone with him. On the right of the corridors were some bedrooms and living quarters. All the rooms were very small, a little bigger than three metres by three. When Hitler entered the bunker in January they were empty. But they would become the home to Magda Goebbels and her six children, and the dining passageway would become their playroom.

The Führer would then have walked to the end of this short corridor, perhaps no more than four or five metres or so, and passed another door that led beyond to a rectangular turn of concrete steps that descended further into the gloom below. At the bottom of the steps was another complement of FBK guards and another watertight door. This was the entrance to the lower bunker. (This, technically, was the Führerbunker, but most of the staff referred to the two bunkers as one and the same thing.)

The lower bunker was some 15 metres or more beneath the Chancellery Garden. Its reinforced concrete walls were at least 2 metres thick. The ceiling was an additional 4 metres of reinforced concrete topped with tonnes of soft alluvial sand to absorb the impact of any direct hits from shells or bombs. Deep down in the Führerbunker the rooms were of similar proportions to the upper bunker and arranged in a similarly neat and simple fashion. Some of the walls of the lower bunker glistened a little with dampness, having had reinforcement work done on them in a hurry only recently.

Like the upper bunker there was a wide central corridor. The first part of this passageway served as a *Vorzimmerlage*, a waiting ante-room (confusingly it was also referred to as a *Warteraum*, a waiting-room, or as *der Durchgang*, the hallway). This hallway waiting-room was the only 'public' part of the lower bunker. It played host to all those visitors who had business with the Führer in private. There was a red carpet on the floor, and elegant upright chairs that had been brought from the Chancellery above, along with paintings on the walls to create an air of civility. The waiting-room would play host to the many senior Nazis and generals who would come to and from the bunker over the next three months. Usually they would be greeted there by a *Teewagen* (trolley) generously laden with fresh sandwiches (typically, *Aufschnitt*, a variety of open sandwiches) prepared by Manziarly. There was a small toilet for guests just off the waiting-room. Orderlies kept this room impeccably clean, as they did all the facilities in the Führer's private quarters.

At the end of the waiting-room was a thin partition wall and door that led to an identically sized room, with a large table in the middle. This was Hitler's main conference room to which he would summon his generals every day to assess the increasingly bleak military situation. There was so little space that they all had to stand up, sometimes for hours on end, in the oppressive heat. Their discomfiture would not be helped by their Führer's furious demands as to why his armies were not counter-attacking the Russian forces. The answer was that the armies did not exist any more. But nobody had the guts to tell him, and their field positions remained tacked on the map on the table in front of them.

On the right of the corridor was a set of six or so rooms, housing the power plant that fuelled the lighting and ventilation, the telephone switchboard and a doctor's surgery for Hitler's personal physician Dr Theodor Morell. Hitler's secretaries and Martin Bormann's secretaries would also use some of these rooms, sometimes working in a little drawing-room to the right, at other times squashing themselves between the doctor's treatment room and Rochus Misch's telephone switchboard. Hitler's secretaries used the special Führer typewriters that printed oversized letters that he could read without his spectacles.

To the left of the corridor was Hitler's private domain. His living quarters below ground were a sharp contrast to the elegance of the Old Reich Chancellery. On a door off the conference corridor, he had a sitting-room (or an ante-room), no more than 3 metres by 4, with a couch, coffee-table and three chairs. There was a large safe to which he entrusted his most important documents, including his A4-sized sturdily bound appointments diary. This room led to his study, which was an equally small room, frugally furnished except for a portrait of Frederick the Great. The Führer would gain great comfort from staring at this portrait, sometimes with nothing more than a candle to provide illumination. Beyond that was his bedroom with one single bed. From Hitler's living-room and study, he had access to a tiny bathroom and a further bed-sitting room that would be occupied by his mistress, Eva Braun. Her room was dominated by a sturdy oak dressing-table that Albert Speer had designed for her in 1938. The letters 'EB' were inscribed in a four-leaf-clover pattern.

At the other end of the conference corridor was another so-called ante-room. But this was little more than a concrete shell and more sparsely furnished than the waiting ante-room. It led to two different sets of steps. The first, to the left, led to an unfinished watchtower that rose above the Chancellery Garden above. The second were four very steep flights of concrete steps that led to the emergency entrance above. This emerged in an ugly concrete pillbox in the grounds of the Chancellery Garden and was again manned by Hitler's own FBK guards. They stood behind another large steel door, which was beneath a small canopy that faced the Chancellery Garden. The pillbox was entirely covered by thick *Zeltplanen* (patterned ground sheets used for camouflage).

Close to the door was a dog run where Hitler would occasionally emerge in the night to give his pet Alsatian, Blondi, a walk. Hitler would say that taking Blondi for a walk was the most relaxing thing he could do. And Goebbels once wrote, mischievously perhaps, that Blondi was probably the only living soul who had ever truly loved Hitler.

This, then, was the scene of Hitler's last stand, a plain and banal setting in which the Führer who had consigned so many millions to a fiery hell would finally be engulfed in the flames of his own eternal damnation.

⁘ CHAPTER ONE ⁘

Bad Omens

THE OMENS HAD NOT BEEN GOOD. When my mother was pregnant with me, we lived in Waldtrudering, a suburb of Munich near Heinrich Himmler's chicken farm. The future Reichsführer of the SS, who had once been a salesman for a firm of fertiliser manufacturers, set up the poultry farm in Waldtrudering after marrying his wife Marga in 1927. He proved to be not as good at raising chickens as he would later prove to be at organising the slaughter of millions of Jews, but the chicken farm became something of an 'alternative lifestyle' Mecca for followers of the Nazi Party. Himmler had all sorts of cranky obsessions ranging from philosophical mysticism to the occult and clairvoyance. He rarely did anything without consulting his horoscope. Marga Himmler was the same, and there was a bakery in Waldtrudering where a clairvoyant predicted people's futures for them. My mother once found herself with Mrs Himmler at one of these sessions, just before I was born. She naturally wanted to know what sex I would be. And both my mother and Marga Himmler were anxious to know how Germany would prosper if Adolf Hitler came to power. The clairvoyant told mother that I would be a girl. This distressed her greatly because she knew my father would not want his first-born to be a female. And if Hitler came to power the clairvoyant predicted the Himmler and Lehmann families would both find great prosperity and Germany would flourish for a thousand years. This greatly heartened both women. My mother was relieved some weeks later when the first prophecy turned out to be entirely wrong. I arrived in the world on 23 May 1928, a healthy baby boy. Whether that compensated for the fact that the second prophecy would turn out to be equally wrong is another question.

As a four year old at the time of Hitler's seizure of power in 1933, I knew little of Germany before the Reich. It would only be a slight exaggeration to say that Hitler and Nazism dominated almost every facet of my youthful existence. I had been born in Munich, the cradle of the Nazi Party. But I grew up mostly in the quiet rural surroundings of Silesia. It was actually not far from Berlin by today's standards but may as well have been on a different planet in those days. We lived in a succession of homes, an early one in the forest, and our lore was the lore of country folk going back a century or more. It was only when my father joined Himmler's *Schutz Staffel* (SS, meaning protection guard) that we returned to living in an urban environment, in Breslau where he worked for the Reich Radio station, part of Joseph Goebbels' propaganda machine.

But that was later. My earliest, and happiest, memories were of the countryside and forests. My early childhood was like something out of *Grimm's Fairy Tales*. I had three sisters, Anje, Ute and Dörte, whom I adored, and later there would be two brothers, Wulf and Ulrich, and another sister, Angela. The Nazis actively encouraged Germany's women to breed. It was regarded as their patriotic duty to provide new children for the state. There were a variety of incentives to procreate and badges awarded for the more children one had. My mother was awarded the Mothers' Cross and assigned a maid in return for bearing her children. My grandfather was friends with the family of the woman who married Martin Bormann, the future Reichsleiter. Gerda Bormann had ten children, the first named Adolf, after Hitler, his godfather. 'Poor woman,' my grandmother used to say at the thought of Gerda spending so much of her adult life being pregnant.

At one stage we lived in a beautiful *Schloss* (castle) surrounded by nothing but woods for many kilometres. It was actually more of a manor house arranged around a walled courtyard. But we weren't well off. It belonged to an army officer who was posted away from home. We only had part of it. Then we moved deeper into the forest. All my earliest memories are of picking berries with my mother, or walking in the woods with my beloved dogs. My favourite was Sonja, a lean, reddish-brown Irish setter. We also had two pointers, Troll and Treff.

For a while I had a pet deer. It turned up one afternoon in our courtyard. The first I heard was a gentle ring of a bell. I went to the window to look outside and saw it – a buck with antlers. The small bell dangled on a golden-looking collar around his neck. At first, I wondered if I was dreaming. Never had I seen a live deer so close, right in our yard, and never one with a collar and a gilded one at that. I went outside. The deer looked at me, unruffled. It did not run away. I reached out and petted it. Even our dogs didn't chase the deer away. It all seemed so strange. From then on the deer became part of my 'family'.

I loved my mother and my grandparents. My grandfather, who lived with us, was a kindly old man, full of wisdom and knowledge. He had two passions: steam railways – a childish enthusiasm and a great invention of his era – and *Friedrich der Grosse*. Frederick the Great was his idol as he was, I would discover, to very many Germans, not least Adolf Hitler. As a boy the future Prussian king was despised by his father as an effeminate aesthete. But as Frederick the Great he surprised everyone with his great leadership. He was a benevolent monarch who promoted, with great foresight, far-reaching social reforms. The notion of Frederick the Great's importance weighed upon my grandfather's mind like nothing else. My grandfather used to recite to me the King's speech to his generals before the battle of Leuthen on 4 December 1757. It was a rousing, invigorating speech in which Frederick instilled in his men the courage to attack an enemy nearly twice as strong and well entrenched on higher ground. At the end of the speech the King proclaimed: 'By this hour tomorrow, we shall have defeated the enemy, or we shall not see another again.' The legend of Frederick the Great would be invoked time and time again by the Nazis, particularly by Joseph Goebbels, the Party's mythmaker-in-chief, and particularly as Germany's enemies grew in strength and size. I loved my grandfather dearly. He never seemed annoyed by any question I had for him, and he always responded in a way that was understandable to my young mind. He kindled in me a lasting desire for knowledge.

On the other hand I had a very ambiguous relationship with my father. He was a bully and thought me a weakling. I tried to please him but I failed him constantly. My very earliest memory was when I was being cradled by my mother in the front seat of my grandfather's car. I must have been three years old. My father was driving. We were on a trip in the countryside. I suddenly started to cry as children do. I don't know why but it clearly irritated my father. He demanded that I shut up. I didn't. He stopped the car and got out. Opening the door on my mother's side, he tried to tear me out of her arms, but she wouldn't let go of me. There were tears and anguish in her eyes too. So Father just pulled the two of us out of the car. Then he got back in the car, slammed the door and drove off. The car disappeared. I kept sobbing, gasping for air and remained, panic-stricken, where he had put me down. Eventually he came back.

'Now you know what happens to boys who cry!' he roared at me.

I tried to stop but couldn't. I kept on weeping. My mother held me closer and closer, trying to muffle my sobs. Now his anger turned towards her. 'If you can't make him stop crying, I'll drive off again!' And that's what he did. We had to make our own way back. Father had a hard heart. I was a disappointment to him throughout my, and his, life. He used to regularly whip me for telling lies and for even the smallest infractions.

I loved my grandmother. She was always doing things that annoyed Father. She liked to boast about the blue blood in her family. I think she was only distantly related to the aristocracy but she took great pride in her copy of the *Almanach de Gotha* (the bible of European nobility; it was of great snob value to appear in it). Grandmother always consulted it whenever a new name came up either in conversation or in the newspapers. When Hitler appointed Joachim von Ribbentrop as Foreign Secretary my grandmother sniffed that he was 'nothing more than a champagne salesman'. 'Ssh!' she said contemptuously. 'He's only *new* nobility.'

'For God's sake keep quiet!' my father said under his breath as if anyone could be listening.

Comments like that used to irritate my father. I think he thought grandmother would get him into trouble with the Party. The aristocracy weren't entirely fashionable in Nazi times. They were seen as the natural class enemies of the National Socialists, although there were exceptions. While he boasted about almost anything else, Father didn't mention our supposedly illustrious ancestors.

Father was a car salesman and part-time driving instructor. He and Grandfather had actually owned a Mercedes Benz dealership once. But within a year of them taking it over it was insolvent. Father blamed the failure on a Jewish businessman who, he claimed, had swindled him. He never explained exactly how, but he insisted to his dying days that the Jew cheated him.

One day, I heard my grandmother scolding my father: 'Jews are human beings too.'

I did not grasp what the conversation was all about. I had never met a Jewish person. When I asked my grandmother what the argument had been all about, she would only say, 'I can't talk about it.' It was not until the *Kristallnacht* (Crystal Night, or the Night of Broken Glass) several years later that I became aware of the fate of Jews in Germany. The argument had been about my father's Mercedes Benz dealership again and my father had been complaining bitterly about the Jew. My grandmother told him, 'The Jew was the more experienced businessman.' Her remark made my father furious. My mother told me after the war, 'It was undercapitalised, times were bad, and he lacked experience.'

My maternal grandmother taught me to pray and took me to church. I liked going to church because when everyone said 'Amen!' it sounded like my name! Grandmother was tucking me into bed one night. I said my prayers and she asked me what I had prayed for. Christmas was coming and I told her that I had prayed for presents. She scolded me and said I should not pray for myself, but for others. God, she said, nurtured us and allowed us to grow so that we could fulfil our own ambitions without relying on him. It was a lesson I've tried to remember all my life.

Things were hard after they lost the car dealership. Father became a car salesman again. In those days it was the salesman who delivered the car to the customer. So Father was away a lot. But I didn't mind his long absences.

Father was responsible for another traumatic memory. One morning I woke up and my deer was gone. I looked everywhere and couldn't find it. Eventually we found it killed in the forest. A poacher had killed it for its antlers. I went into shock. It had wire slits around his neck. Its antlers had been cut off. The poacher had also removed the gilded collar and bell. When I took my father to the carcass, I couldn't help the tears that filled my eyes. But Father made me help him drag it back to the house, grabbing two legs each. The next day it was hanging on a butcher's hook in our cellar, cut open with the intestines removed. Father decided to teach me how to skin it and then cut it up. I was queasy and almost threw up. He called me a weakling and told me how it was manly to butcher animals. To teach me a lesson he said he was going to give me the job of chopping off one of our chickens' heads.

I dreaded the prospect but he gave me a meat cleaver and told me to get on with it. Of course I botched the job. With barely enough strength to hold the wings tight with my left hand, while putting the chicken's head on the chopping block to cut it off, I became so scared I closed my eyes at the moment of decapitation. Strong muscle spasms jolted the wings with such a jerk I let go of the chicken. It flew against my body without a head, spewing blood all over me, then dropped to the ground. Horrified, I ran away. My father scolded me for my awkwardness and belittled me for acting like a girl.

This lesson in manliness took place in 1934, the year after Adolf Hitler had become the Führer.

At school there was a child with a hunched back called Rudi. Two other classmates and I used to make fun of him and bully him. He had no friends. Once we started a fight with him, not expecting him to defend himself. But he did and he managed to get the better of the three of us. We were all scratched and bruised. My nose was bleeding and there was blood all over my shirt. Our teacher was a mild-mannered man. That was not what was expected of teachers in those times. All German teachers were expected to be authoritarian. On this occasion though he handed a bamboo spanking rod to Rudi and told the three of us to bend over.

'Each one deserves 12 on the behind!' he told the hunchback.

'I can't do it!' said Rudi. 'They would only get me again.' He handed the rod back to the teacher.

I felt abashed and never forgot what he said. The teacher sent me home. When I told my mother what had happened she cycled over to Rudi's house to apologise for my behaviour. When my father heard he scolded me severely for taking part in a fight of three against one. He called me a coward and ordered me to bed early.

Rudi and I became friends. He loved animals too and his bedroom was like a zoo. There were canaries, tropical fish, white mice and a golden hamster. He also had a glass terrarium with snakes. His dream was to become a vet. But oddly to me at the time, his parents resisted the idea, even though they had bought and shared in caring for his many pets. I still remember how vehemently Rudi's father objected. He was in the *Sturm Abteilung* (SA) – one of Hitler's Brownshirts.

By then in Germany there were half a million Brownshirts. The SA was one of several paramilitary forces that developed in Germany after the humiliation of the First World War. Led by Captain Ernst Röhm and under the umbrella of the National Socialist movement, it was violently anti-Semitic and dedicated to continuing the 'German revolution'. Hitler tried to integrate Brownshirts fully into the Nazi Party but began to see that Röhm's organisation posed a threat to his own supremacy. He therefore engineered for Himmler's SS, originally subordinate to the SA, to supplant it in the notorious Night of the Long Knives. The black-shirted SS was originally Hitler's personal bodyguard of just 200 men. Under Himmler's leadership it was to become a vast empire within the Nazi state, charged with 'safeguarding the embodiment of the National Socialist idea' and translating the crude racist taunts of the regime into positive action.

Rudi's father told him: 'For you it will be best to stay at elementary school and learn a befitting trade.' It was strange because most blue-collar workers would want their children to aspire to higher education, especially since one of the constantly propagated aims of the National Socialists was to eliminate class barriers. But in retrospect I was able to see what was going on. Rudi's father might have known already that those considered unfit, the handicapped and mentally retarded, would be excluded from opportunities to advance. Or, perhaps even worse, they might be institutionalised. Unknown to us children, the Law to Protect Hereditary Health of 1935 had just gone into effect. As an SA man Rudi's father must have known about it and concluded his son had a better chance of survival as a manual labourer. Ironically, everyone knew that Hitler's Propaganda Minister Joseph Goebbels had a club-foot. A misshapen spine wasn't a crippling hereditary disease. But it was more noticeable.

Both of my parents joined a movement called Wandervögel (Birds of Passage). It was a 'back to nature' movement, a hiking companionship, cultivated by patriotic groups as a way of reuniting 'German' people across the continent. It revived all sorts of old folk-dancing rituals and festivals, and celebrated the summer and winter solstices. It grew into a powerful, romantic youth movement in the Germany of the 1920s and attracted followers such as Albert Speer, the future Armaments Minister and Hitler's favourite architect. Long before the Hitler salute had become commonplace in Germany, the members of this movement greeted each other with 'Heil!', meaning, 'Hail', a shout of welcome.

They hiked at first within Germany, but later in other parts of Europe where Germans had settled. They were among the many young Germans during the 1920s who made it their mission to contact ethnic Germans outside the Fatherland to renew cultural ties and to practise nationalism. Such German settlements could be found not only in territories that had formerly belonged to Germany, but also in Russia, Poland and the Baltic and Balkan countries because of migrations of many centuries ago. My parents visited the Saxons and Swabians of Rumania. Their settlements in Transylvania and in the Banat dated back to the twelfth century. Although these ethnic Germans had clung to their language, culture and customs, their devotion to the Fatherland and sense of nationalism was not as pronounced as had been anticipated. Later, many of these ethnic Germans supported Hitler's efforts to strengthen their German links as a matter of pride and commitment to their heritage. It seemed a noble cause.

In fact the Wandervögel movement was just one of the many German organisations that Himmler dissolved and channelled into the more overtly Nazi groups of the 1930s, notably the Hitler Youth. Himmler was gradually becoming one of the most powerful Nazis. The turning point in his career had been the purge of 1934 in which he smashed the power of Röhm's SA and paved the way for the SS to become the dominant military group within the Third Reich to enforce Nazi doctrine. In 1936 he was to become head of the Gestapo, the state police, giving him unrivalled power over internal law-enforcement.

Himmler's unique contribution to the history of the Third Reich was to make it the task of the SS to turn Nazi race theory into positive action, namely to rid Germany of Jews, Gypsies and Slavs, and to create a master race of blue-eyed, blond Aryans. He had introduced racial and hereditary laws that were intended to ensure the procreation of this superior race and the extermination of all inferior ones. Since 1933, when Himmler had set up the first concentration camp at Dachau, he had extended the range of people who could be interned in them. He boasted that the concentration camps, which contained 'deformed' and 'inferior' people, were living proof that the Nazis' hereditary and racial laws were valid.

I dreaded my father. He could be the most entertaining person when people came to visit us. But with me he was cold and distant. He always expected me to obey him without question. He imbued in me the importance of honesty. But I began to discover that he would, at times, slant the truth to serve his purposes.

My father was a bad salesman but he quickly discovered the advantages of following political trends. He joined the SS in the run-up to the war. To qualify for membership of the SS proof was required of a 'pure' heritage, in accordance with the Nazi regime's new racial doctrines. Racialism was now widely accepted in Germany. It became identified with nationalism. The Nuremberg Laws on citizenship and race limited German citizenship to Germans or kindred blood, and specifically excluded Jews. One of the aims during the Third Reich was to encourage *Blut und Boden* (Blood and Soil) awareness. It became vital for everyone to be able to identify where they had come from. Everyone was required to have an *Ahnenpass* (a genealogical record book). One compiled one's Ahnenpass from all the available church and municipal records. It had to be countersigned by an official and rubberstamped with a swastika. But it was a system that was open to much abuse and depended upon whom one knew in the Party as much as who one's ancestors were.

My father did his research into our bloodline. Unfortunately, Father seemed to have overlooked the slightly inconvenient fact that his maternal bloodline was not quite as 'pure' as he wanted it to be. Everyone in the family knew that Grandmother was of Slavic stock. (Although oddly, my maternal grandfather was the most Nordic-looking member of the family.) There was doubt too about my father's lineage. He did not look at all Nordic. His features were distinctly Slavic, with Asiatic cheekbones and not much of a beard either: just some growth above his upper lip and on his lower chin. The National Socialists considered all members of the Slavic race to be inferior. As my father saw it, it would have been a disgrace to our family to have been burdened with such dubious ancestral bloodlines. In fact, our family was a mixture of all sorts of blood. There was English and French, and we even had a Lord Mayor of Dublin somewhere in our background (Daniel Weybrandt, who was born in Ireland in 1599, and died in Amsterdam in 1657 after being driven from office by papal forces). Somehow or other, Father managed to persuade the authorities that we were 'pure' Aryan.

My father wasn't academically intelligent, but he had a sharp, 'street smart' intelligence. He knew how to spot trends and how to take advantage of the system and people. Shortly after he joined the SS Father asked me what I wanted to be when I grew up. I said: 'A forester,' and after some hesitation, 'or a poet.'

'A poet?' he asked with utter contempt. He gave me such a withering look that it made me feel as if I were the most lowly individual in existence.

A few days later a thick, registered letter arrived. My father told me he had new plans for my future. Success would depend on how well I could be conditioned mentally and physically. Without ever mentioning anything to me, he had entered my name for the admission exams to a *Nationalpolitische Erziehungsanstalt* (National Political Training Establishment or NAPOLA). NAPOLAs were newly created boarding schools to train future Nazi leaders. They were modelled on the traditional Prussian officers' academies. The principal aim was to select and train the future leadership of Hitler's new nation. They were considered a passport to the top of the Nazi hierarchy. The nearest one to us was located in Naumburg an der Saale, near Halle in Saxony. The all-important letter stated that I would be considered and explained the provisions for the admission exam, which would take an entire week. Every applicant had to undergo rigorous physical, mental and scholastic testing. The fact that my father was in the SS gave me a head start.

Father coached me intensely for my exams. At night we sang the German national anthem and the Horst Wessel song. (Horst Wessel was one of Hitler's stormtroopers killed in Berlin street-fighting with the Communists. The song was a glowing tribute to his bravery and became a rousing call for the Nazis.) It was laughable in retrospect but at the time he struck the fear of God into me. If I got one word wrong I'd be shouted at. He set some test papers. One was: 'Why I am Proud to be a German'. I wrote a long essay about the beauty of the woods and the land we lived on. Father was furious. He tore it up and dictated the correct response for me word for word. I was proud to be German because I had the privilege of growing up under Hitler's great leadership, which assured our nation would soon achieve world dominance. I was proud to be German because I belonged to the Nordic race and cherished my Aryan purity. So much for his much-vaunted honesty, I thought to myself. Wasn't this cheating?

The next day he took me to the station. On the journey in the car he gave me a few words of advice.

'Always pay attention!'

'I will.'

'Be sure to concentrate on what is asked of you!'

'I will.'

'Remember, you are my son and I expect you to succeed.'

'Yes.'

'It's the chance of a lifetime.'

'Yes, I know.'

He admonished me to keep in mind that the Führer had established the NAPOLAs. Without him there would be no opportunity. He told me to keep this in mind and to express it as well. At the train station he said, 'Goodbye.'

'Goodbye,' I replied.

We shook hands. Then he reached in his coat pocket and handed me a little case. '*Machs gut!*' ('Good luck!') he said to me. He slapped me on the back, turned, went back to his car, and drove off.

I opened the little box. To say I was astounded would be an understatement. It was a brand new watch, the most precious gift I had ever received during all of my young life – not from my mother, not from any of my grandparents, but from my father; my father who had always seemed disappointed in me. Gratified and perplexed at the same time, I wondered if I had reached a turning point and if my feelings towards my father were about to change.

I put it on and looked at it constantly. On the train everyone in the compartment noticed it. 'My father gave it to me,' I explained. It was the very first instance I felt proud to be my father's son.

I spent a week of intensive exams and indoctrination at the NAPOLA. I thought I had done all right.

Waiting for the letter seemed like an eternity. When it finally came in the post we all held our breath. Father ripped it open furiously and inspected the contents. From the look on his face I did not need to ask him if I had succeeded or failed. He was devastated. After much indecision he called the headmaster and addressed him as '*Herr Obersturmführer*' (First Lieutenant SS). I waited at the open doorway, quaking, as my father listened, silently, to the headmaster on the other end of the line. The headmaster seemed to be doing all the talking. Father was quiet but visibly upset. Then he uttered obediently, 'Heil Hitler', and put down the telephone. He didn't say a word to me, but went into the next room where my mother had also been waiting in silence. He said to her in a tone of absolute despondence: 'Our son is a *Waschlappen*' (flannel). The bottom had dropped out of his world.

Crushed, I wanted to know in what subjects or activities I had not succeeded. I asked my father what the headmaster had said. Apparently, I lacked mental and physical stamina. (My mother later told me that what the headmaster had actually said was that I appeared too delicate and prone to illness. I might not be able to withstand the intense physical and mental pressure that Nazi leadership required. Ironic indeed, given what was to come.) As a condolence, the headmaster said I might just be ready for one of the new Adolf Hitler Schools that accepted children when they were 12 years old. Father did not whip me this time, but he grabbed my arm and pulled off the precious timepiece he had given me. He didn't utter a word. His expression clearly showed I was not worthy of his expensive wristwatch.

∾ CHAPTER TWO ∾

War

PRESENTLY IT WAS ANNOUNCED THAT WE were moving to Breslau, where Father was to work in the Reich Radio station. It was part of Joseph Goebbels' propaganda network and a highly prestigious job. Father never admitted it, but in all probability he got the job because of his membership of the Nazi Party. He certainly had no previous training or qualifications to work in a radio station. His function was to be a watchdog, to keep an eye on what the radio station was broadcasting, making sure it always toed the Party line; looking out for subversives and so on.

It was the first time I had ever lived in a city. Breslau at the time was the capital of the province of Lower Silesia and straddled both banks of the River Oder. The old town had retained a charming medieval character with narrow streets and old churches. The streets of the inner city converged on the market square where the city hall, a splendid Gothic building dating from the sxteenth century, was located and where the diets of Silesia had been held in medieval times. At Christmas the streets were full of snow. It was a beautiful town. But we had to leave my dogs behind and I missed them. I soon tired of living in the confines of a second-floor apartment with only a communal patch of yard to play in.

The best thing was that I no longer saw much of Father, who was at work most of the time. He was now earning twice as much as before but didn't give Mother any more money. He spent most of it on his smart clothes and taking his new Nazi friends out to dinner or to hunting parties at the weekend. What annoyed my mother most was that he would bring his friends home to have dinner occasionally. Mother would get a call an hour or so beforehand and she was expected to have the dinner on the table by the time he and his guests arrived. She would tell him she had no money to buy any food but it made no difference.

One of the people who came to dinner was Fritz Naujocks, who would one day become infamous for providing the bogus excuse for invading Poland. (Naujocks dressed a group of concentration camp inmates in Polish army uniforms and staged an 'attack' on the Gleiwitz radio station. It gave Hitler the excuse to say that Poland had started hostilities.) Father also came into contact with Karl Hanke, an ardent Nazi and Party chief of Silesia who had had an affair with Magda Goebbels, the Propaganda Minister's beautiful wife. He never spoke about this to me, but I often overheard him talking about all the latest Nazi gossip with his cronies in the living-room.

My father was very full of himself in his new post and liked marching off to work once or twice a week in his new black uniform and shiny black boots. But the superintendent of our apartment complex thought he was an ass. She was a sinewy woman in her 40s. Once, dressed up in his black SS attire to impress her, he had complained to her about something. After he was out of sight, but I was still in the hall, she remarked: 'Dashing uniform but no medals.' Medals were a very important status symbol in Nazi Germany. In war there were medals for all sorts of physical achievement. There were even medals for getting wounded. The more wounds one acquired, the greater the distinction. In fact Father didn't even have the most elementary 'sport achievement' badge that a ten-year-old kid would have, because he had never learnt to swim! It was then that I began to realise how pathetic was the façade that my father presented to the world. But the superintendent didn't have much to boast about either. Her husband was the building's *Blockwart* (the official Party informer for the area). His job was to keep an eye out for insurrection and misbehaviour within the building precincts and they got extra rations for the honour. But he was an alcoholic and often ended up causing drunken brawls. The irony was that as a Blockwart he could not be reported – even by the SS!

The year of 1938 was a momentous one for me. It was then that I saw Hitler for the first time. The occasion was at the *Jahrhunderthalle* (Century Hall). There wasn't room inside for all those who wanted to be admitted and there were queues lined up around the block outside. I can't remember how I got in to see him, but it must have been something to do with my father's job at the Reich Radio station – I suppose the event must have been recorded. I can't describe the emotional wave of enthusiasm that Hitler generated. Even at a great distance, Hitler had a mesmerising effect on me. I was jubilant.

This was at a time when the majority of the population was uplifted by Hitler's accomplishments. He had established himself as a benevolent dictator with the abilities of a genius. The economy flourished. Unemployment had been eliminated. There seemed to be work for all. The network of new *Autobahnen* (motorways) kept expanding. The low-priced *Volkswagen* (people's car) had been introduced. Everything that Hitler had promised was coming to fruition.

And in 1938 I was initiated into the Jungvolk, the junior branch of the Hitler Youth. Every German child was invited to join the junior branches of the Hitler Youth when they were ten. The ceremony was on 20 April, Hitler's birthday. It was a great source of pride to me that I now had a recognised role in working for the community. My squad was a unit with 48 members and we met at the local school every Wednesday night. Sometimes, for special events, we met at the weekends as well. We went to camps outside the city. One of the tenets of the Hitler Youth was that youth was to be led by youth and that we were all committed to a close-knit comradeship. Field games, outings with campfires and sports activities I greatly enjoyed. But even drills to develop soldierly skills and historical indoctrination I absorbed enthusiastically. I knew no different. In the Jungvolk we were made to play soldiers and at a very young age told to obey orders unquestioningly.

All of Germany's youth at the time were, from birth, instructed at home, in school and in the Jungvolk to be loyal, honest, considerate and helpful. It was nothing short of a mission to be dedicated to *Führer, Volk und Vaterland* (leader, people and Fatherland). We were one *Volksgemeinschaft* (people's community) in which people cared for each other in terms of *Alle für Einen, Einer für Alle!* (All for one, one for all!)

I had been called by my Führer to participate to make my country great. And I was a member of the Jungvolk, among my peers, who were all enthusiastic about the designated activities. What was there for a ten- or eleven-year-old to question?

I do remember that concentration camps were discussed during our long evenings of indoctrination in the Jungvolk camp. We were told they were labour camps for political dissidents. Mainly, it was pointed out how important it was to develop strong characters, strength of will and self-control. It was also emphasised that although we were raised by our parents, we belonged to the nation. It was impressed upon us that Germany had never had such a great leader as Adolf Hitler.

We as Nordic people constituted the earth's supreme race. It was our responsibility to rid ourselves of all the bad habits that had been perpetuated by inferior races. The Jews and the Communists were out to destroy Germany. Since at the time I didn't know any Jews or Communists these were anonymous, non-personal enemies. It was not until Crystal Night that I realised those nice people in the candy store I frequented were Jewish.

It was around about this time that my father took two volumes from the bookshelves and said the time had come for me to read these two important books. One was *Mein Kampf* (My Struggle) by Adolf Hitler and the other was *Der Mythus des 20 Jahrhunderts* (The Myth of the 20th Century) by Alfred Rosenberg. It was my father's habit to question me closely on the contents of books, but in these instances I skipped through both of them. In Hitler's book I must have skipped the parts where he spelled out his political aims in such shocking detail, because the part of the narration where he dealt with his time as a struggling artist in Vienna and his experiences in the First World War were interesting. That's all I remembered. My young mind did not pick up on how dangerous were his non-scientific views of racial theory, or his dictatorial *Führerprinzip* (leader principle). The Rosenberg book seemed completely beyond my range of interest and understanding. Fortunately Father never questioned me about either book.

In 1938 I also became a high-school student. The Elisabet Gymnasium was one of the most renowned classical college preparatory schools in the city. The school's prevailing domain remained one of academic excellence in a humanistic tradition. It taught right and wrong on a moral basis although its standards had to change to conform to the new Nazi ideology, which it did only reluctantly. My first German teacher was my favourite for one simple reason. He discovered I wrote poetry and encouraged me to continue. He told my mother I was gifted. His name was Poppe and he did have some more zealous traits about him. He insisted on Germanising all words, ridding our language of any foreign words, and he treated us like a troop of soldiers. We had to jump to attention whenever he came into the classroom.

On my tenth birthday, 23 May, my brother Friedrich Wulf was born. My mother commented that if he had been born exactly ten years earlier I would have had a twin. But before that, in March 1938, Germany annexed Austria. It's difficult to describe the emotional wave that swept the country. On 1 October the Sudetenland was occupied. Many of these events were relayed by the official German newsreel, *Deutsche Wochenschau*, controlled by the Propaganda Ministry headed by Joseph Goebbels, effectively my father's ultimate boss. Goebbels was a genius but a man with a black soul.

Goebbels had emerged as the intellectual driving force and demagogue of the Nazi Party. It was he who had created the slogans, images and myths of National Socialism that transformed it from a small party into the most powerful political organisation in Germany. He was educated at a Roman Catholic school and studied history and literature at the

University of Heidelberg. He was rejected for military service in the First World War because of his crippled foot, the result of contracting polio as a child. He was a small man and had an unusual, grinning mask of a face that caricaturists found easy to mimic, and thick black hair.

But Goebbels had a great verbal dexterity and ranging intellect that made him a natural communicator. A tireless, tenacious agitator, he had the gift of paralysing his opponents with a guileful combination of venom, slander and insinuation. A cold, calculating and cynical man, Goebbels had a deep, powerful voice and a gift for rhetoric that appealed to the baser instincts of the unemployed masses. He could whip a crowd up into a frenzy of hatred with just a few select aphorisms. He designed posters, organised meetings and orchestrated street fights with the Nazis' Communist and Socialist opponents. One of his earliest followers was Artur Axmann, who as a teenager fought with Goebbels on the streets of Berlin against the Communists in the late 1920s and early 1930s. Axmann would become Leader of the Hitler Youth and would appoint me as his courier in the last days of Hitler's regime. It was Goebbels who created the myth of the Führer as the Messiah of the German people, a demi-god above all other human beings.

The occupation of the Sudetenland and the annexation of Austria should, theoretically, have led to war. The fact that neither of these aggressive actions did earned Hitler even more fame and glory. He was a genius! I remember watching the newsreel in the cinema. I remember seeing his black Mercedes accompanied by roaring motorcycles. Germans shall never be divided! The applause that we saw on the flickering newsreel before us was taken up by the audience in the theatre and went on and on. People were ecstatic.

In the early morning of 10 November 1938, Father was at home and the telephone rang. It was somebody from his unit. Father appeared jubilant. Then he put the phone down. His eyes were wild with joy. 'Tonight, for once, we really made it hot for the Jews!' It was Crystal Night. I cannot think of a more appropriate name. At the corner where I changed trams on my way to school, a basement shoe store owned by Jews had been one of the targets. Glass from the broken shop windows was still scattered along the pavement. The display windows were already covered with boards. I, as did others, looked through the cracks and watched two men, in black caftans with long beards and wearing black hats, taking inventory. The younger one was counting; the older one, who might have been his father, wrote down the information calculating the damage.

A few days later, I also walked by the candy shop where I had occasionally bought bonbons or a chocolate. It had either been spared or the plate-glass windows had already been replaced. I saw no damage. But the store was empty. It had been closed. I also remember driving in a tram by the burned-out synagogue. The ruins were still smouldering. The entire site of the fire had been roped off. There was no one on the pavement.

How many people were ashamed of what had happened? We will never know. They kept it to themselves. Both of my grandmothers were, as I found out much later. But when Crystal Night took place, my mind did not react humanely. I should have remembered the words of my first teacher, who always told me to put myself in other people's shoes. Such thoughts didn't even cross my mind.

In 1939, during the summer holidays, my grandfather took me to Munich. We went to Prinzregentenplatz, where Hitler had once lived, and ate at an Italian artists' tavern where he had eaten. Such was the hero-worship of Hitler in Germany at the time. In August it was announced ration cards would be coming. 'That means war for certain,' said my mother. My father only saw the advantage of having another ration card. On 31 August my second brother, Ulrich Georg, was born. Next day the war broke out. It was 1 September 1939. In Breslau I saw motorised troops all day. I waved and they waved back. After Hitler launched the *Blitzkrieg* I was glued to the radio all day long. We all thought revenge was sweet.

The news started with the daily report issued by the OKW (OberKommando der Wehrmacht), the German Armed Forces High Command. In addition, there were Sondermeldungen, special bulletins important enough to warrant the interruption of the regular programme. Fanfares were interjected, followed by the announcements of significant victories, such as the one broadcast on 4 September 1939, proclaiming that German troops had crossed the entire Polish Corridor and set foot in Eastern Prussia. This province, severed from the Reich after the First World War, had been reunited with the Fatherland.

On 6 September, our troops had conquered Krakow as well as Bromberg, a city in which Poles, supposedly, had murdered many Germans prior to the outbreak of the war. A victory bulletin, late in the evening of 8 September, proclaimed our forces had advanced into Warsaw, the Polish capital. Fanfares upon fanfares! Victories upon victories! Jubilation upon jubilation!

There was only one person who made me stop and think whether what we were doing was right. Schuster Stefan was the neighbourhood cobbler. He was a real Hans Sachs type (Hans Sachs was a fifteenth-century cobbler who was also an important dramatist and poet). Stefan used to let me sit at his little three-legged stool as he was fixing our shoes and my father's black shiny leather boots. His homespun philosophy was a great comfort to me. He brought to my attention how much of a racial melting pot Poland had become during its turbulent history. He expressed concerns most Germans didn't realise. Besides the *Volksdeutschen* (ethnic Germans), there were many Poles with a lot of German blood in their veins, he said. The population surrounding the city of Lodz was mostly of German stock although their names sounded Slavic.

In a subtle way, just as the last battles were being fought, he made me realise that many racial mixtures were to be found within the Polish population, pointing out that in reverse many Silesians had Polish family names but were considered pure Germans. There was Polish blood in many Silesians. He named people in the neighbourhood whose names I no longer recall. Then I also thought of Rudi, my friend in first and second grade. He had a Polish-sounding name, but his father was tall and, like Rudi, had Nordic-looking facial features.

Schuster Stefan, who for over a year now had been putting new heels and soles on my father's black boots, knew he was a member of the SS. I have a hunch, but no proof, that he didn't approve. He might not have liked that I belonged to the Jungvolk or the great enthusiasm with which other boys and I followed the rapid military advances or how we belittled the Polish army after its devastating defeats.

It was then Schuster Stefan quizzed me by asking questions about Nicolaus Copernicus, the Polish astronomer who developed the Copernican system that proved that the earth revolves around the sun. He asked me if I knew of Marie Sklodowska (Curie), the chemist, although of course she was French but chose to marry a Pole. Or Frédéric Chopin, the composer and pianist. He even asked me about Marshall Pulaski, the Polish folk hero who participated in the American Revolution.

Perhaps he wanted me to realise that the derogatory term 'Polacks', commonly used to refer to the Polish people, was inappropriate in view of all these notable Poles. I didn't entertain such thoughts. I believed what I was expected to believe. The Poles were our enemies, they hated and massacred Germans and they were now, deservedly, being defeated by our brave soldiers.

On 16 October the news came that German and Russian troops had met at the agreed upon German–Russian *Interessengrenze* (sphere-of-influence border). The war was apparently over and the occupation had been concluded. This military bulletin proclaimed itself as the last from the Eastern Front.

I got my first war injury at the age of 12, in 1940. One of my mother's uncles was assigned to be an administrator in occupied Poland and we went to stay with him at his farmhouse. In the night we were attacked by some starving Polish troops who had been hiding in the woods. We retreated to the cellar and I fired a shot through the window with my revolver. It shattered through the pane, of course, and my face was covered in shards of glass. My uncle was furious. Not only had I injured myself, but I had given our position away. The Poles attacked once more the next day. We held out for a day before a nearby military unit came to our rescue.

At about that time I started filling a scrapbook with newspaper clippings depicting the glorious exploits of our heroic U-boat commanders and Luftwaffe aces. We were fed an endless diet of propaganda about our glorious armed forces' amazing achievements. There was the story of Captain Prien, the 28-year-old commander of *U-47*. In October 1939, Prien penetrated the submarine defences of the British naval base at Scapa Flow and sank the British battleship *Royal Oak*. It was one of the most audacious naval attacks in history. It was so audacious that it was regarded as heroic by the British as much as the Germans. We read about the exploits of the Luftwaffe aces Werner Mölders, who was the first to down 20 enemy planes and who would eventually bag 115 before his death in 1941, and Adolf Galland, who, at 31 years of age, became the youngest general serving in the German armed forces.

At first I too wanted to be a fighter pilot, then a U-boat commander. Later, my love of animals encouraged me to want to be a cavalry officer. It was only when I realised that most cavalry regiments were now equipped with tanks and not horses that I was put off the idea. I had heard that tank crews fried to death if their tank was hit by a shell. The idea of burning to death seemed the worst way to die to me.

At the beginning of the war, Hitler was victorious, according to the news presented to us, with no major setbacks. For the most part, this was true. Although all news was controlled and propaganda shrewdly created, the military bulletins, from what I can determine after having read numerous historical accounts of the Second World War, reflected the facts. They were partial to the German cause, of course, and contained exaggerations to embellish victories and omissions to minimise defeats.

We had no access to any but the government-controlled press. We were forbidden to listen to foreign broadcasts and threatened with penalties for treason – which included death. Our sphere of information was a very isolated one. We were bombarded by Joseph Goebbels' propaganda. Words such as heroic, fearless, steadfast, unwavering, courageous, valiant, glorious, majestic, noble, distinguished and lustrous were used as abundantly as possible, and increasingly in conjunction with death and dying. Death, even for the very young, was something to be embraced since it would leave behind memories of bravery and glory.

I don't think I nourished a death wish, but I had convinced myself I had to be willing and prepared to die. My main concern was that I be given the opportunity to prove I was capable of bravery, perhaps even of becoming a hero. If the war lasted long enough, as I hoped it would, I, too, envisioned my name on the honour roll of the heroes who had fought so valiantly in great battles. I was immovably certain of a supreme German victory.

The war continued. We were told that the first part of the conflict had been to disengage us from the Treaty of Versailles. The second part was to free Europe from British imperialism, the third part to free Germany from the threat of Bolshevism. Denmark and Norway were occupied. Belgium and the Netherlands were occupied. On my 12th birthday, 23 May 1940, we heard on the radio of Dunkirk. It was not recorded to us Germans as a great British triumph in getting 300,000 of their troops back across the Channel. It was recorded as a triumphant rout in which the British imperialists cowardly abandoned their French so-called Allies. (I would later realise that Dunkirk was also the beginning of the souring of relations between Hitler and Hermann Göring. Hitler held back the army's Panzer divisions only because the air Reich Marshal had promised Hitler his Luftwaffe would contain the fleeing British. It didn't, and 300,000 Tommies were left to fight another day.) My father claimed he was involved in aspects of the planning of operation Sea Lion – the invasion plan of England. He said he would have had a similar role in the BBC, the British state broadcasting system after the invasion, as he had in Breslau. How much truth there was in this boast, I will never know.

In 1940 my father was hoping I would become an Adolf Hitler *Schüler* (student of an Adolf Hitler School). These were not quite as prestigious as NAPOLAs but they were 'the next best thing'. In the Jungvolk I had already become one of the youngest *Jungzugführer* (leader of 30 to 40) in our *Fähnlein* (unit of more than 100). As a Jungzugführer I was able to give orders and even make speeches. My father had always insisted we must control our minds, and he was not the only one to do so. Discipline was one virtue by which we were judged at home, in school and in the Jungvolk. Moreover, having just reached the qualifying age of 12, I had completed in rapid succession all of the requirements for obtaining the *DJ-Leistungsabzeichen*, the Jungvolk proficiency badge. I felt that I was at last living up to my father's expectations.

But I was to disappoint him once more. I wasn't even selected to be given the entrance examination for the Adolf Hitler School. Yet again my father's endless tutoring and conditioning had been in vain. I was, once again, a failure. I remained '*ein schwacher Kerl*' ('a feeble fellow'). My schoolboy friend Dieter Heinrich did get a place in the Adolf Hitler School. In my despondency I took great interest and succour in the accomplishments of Germany's heroes, who emerged in rapidly increasing numbers.

On the battlefields, wherever our forces fought, they won. That was the ongoing news. If there were minor setbacks somewhere, immediate counter-attacks took place. Defeats on land were never mentioned. Were there none? When losses of aircraft and navy vessels were announced, they were usually compared with those suffered by the enemy. Ours appeared to be few, theirs sizeable.

On 14 June 1941 German troops marched into Paris. The wave of euphoria was unbelievable. Then on 22 June German troops invaded Russia. That was the beginning of the end. I didn't know it at the time but Hitler's Thousand-Year Reich was about to crack. (It lasted twelve years, four months and eight days to be exact.)

In 1941, for the first and only time during the Nazi era, I came into personal contact with a Jewish person. Occasionally, I had observed this blind or near-blind woman with a 'seeing-eye dog' crossing a street. She was an old lady who reminded me of my own grandmother. My grandmother had lost only one eye and wore a black patch over it. She could still see well with the other eye. The old lady was led by a beautiful German shepherd dog and was apparently blind in both eyes. This was before it was mandatory for Jews to wear a yellow star. Perhaps it was the dog that triggered my attention, but I noted that the woman wore a yellow armlet with three big dots, indicating that she was blind.

On the last occasion that I saw this sightless woman, I also saw the yellow star. This time she was without her dog and seemed insecure, almost lost, traversing with her cane to where she wanted to go. When she had to cross the street, I went to assist her and asked: 'Where is your dog?' I still remember clearly her reply because she used the German word '*eingezogen*' which means 'drafted'. She explained that the army had claimed her loyal companion, on whom she depended so much. Seeing-eye dogs were (apparently) needed for soldiers who had lost their sight. She also mentioned that she hoped to get another through the Association for the Blind, an older seeing-eye dog no longer suitable for service in the military.

She shed tears and asked, 'Can I cross now?' With our arms linked, I guided her across the street. A stranger, probably two or three years older than me, jumped off his bicycle and punched me in the face. He shouted, 'Don't give help to the Jew-pig!' I tried to fight back. A small crowd had assembled, although the old woman wisely disappeared and the cyclist, apparently with my blood on his shirt, took off. It was most likely my nose that had been bleeding. Although I was wearing my hiking knife, the official blade sidearm of the Jungvolk, it had been strictly a fist-fight and, as I recall, I was the only one bleeding.

I felt nothing of the harshness and cold-bloodedness that this totalitarian regime applied towards those in opposition, or to those oppressed. I didn't know. I didn't have any suspicions. None of my teachers ever talked about *Konzentrationslager* (concentration camps), or what their function was. I knew concentration camps existed, but my mother had explained to me that ordinary offenders were put into prisons, dangerous criminals were put into state penitentiaries and enemies of the state were put into concentration camps. She believed they were similar to labour camps, and so I did too. At the time detention in concentration camps was called protective custody. Those detained, I remember, were described as reactionary Communists and other terrorists – opponents of the Reich who had to be re-educated. My understanding was that on being converted to National Socialist ideology the inmates regained their freedom.

My life was not solely occupied with the war. I became ever more exposed to written art, especially drama and poetry. My love for language must have gone back to my very early childhood. My mother told me that, before I could read, I would take a big book as a prop, open it up and put it on the rim of the balcony and make short speeches. I would raise my voice and repeat some phrases over and over again, trying to imitate the oratory style of those who had spoken to us over the radio – Hitler and Goebbels most of all. Declarations such as 'I will be your leader!' or 'Follow me, follow me!' or even 'Sieg Heil, Sieg Heil!'. I had no audience. Mostly, I spoke to the trees.

As far back as 10 May 1933, when I was five years old, the Nazis had burnt books publicly. So all the greatest literary works had been turned to ashes. I no longer had access to great literature. I read the writing of the officially recognised authors who had the blessings of the regime, authors who, for example, celebrated the 'back to the soil' movement. I didn't read books like *All Quiet on the Western Front* until after the war when once-forbidden books were again published in Germany. It was the first time I read a book that described war realistically rather than glorified it. Pacifist novels were considered not suitable to be read by Germany's youth, as were many important works by writers such as Albert Einstein, Thomas Mann, Sigmund Freud, Romain Rolland, Arnold Zweig, Leon Feuchtwanger and Heinrich Heine, to name but a few. All these books were consigned to the incinerators in 1933.

Since I wrote poetry and some short stories, my interest in the written word increased. I pored over literature more and more, mostly at night in bed using a flashlight. After 10 p.m., my room light had to be turned off. I remember reading sometimes until 2 a.m. and having to get up four hours later.

Germany's greatest poet was, of course, Johann Wolfgang von Goethe, universally acknowledged as a genius. One of his first dramas, based on the memoirs of Götz von Berlichingen, became a favourite on the stages of German theatres during the time of the Third Reich. His plays *Egmont*, *Iphigenie in Tauris* and of course *Faust*, his masterpiece, were produced continually. But no dramatist performed in Germany at the time of my youth made as deep and stirring an impression on me as Friedrich von Schiller. In Schiller we had a literary giant second only to Goethe and known for his idealism and hatred of tyranny.

In *Die Räuber* (The Robbers), Schiller, confronted in his youth with the hardships and injustices caused by the use and abuse of power, had written a play in protest. The play is a scathing indictment of a society that drove someone, fundamentally noble in character, to crime before he realised wrongdoing does not restore right conditions. What a play to have seen at a young age when idealism filled one's mind! And how uplifting it was. It mirrored despicable conditions of the past, similar to those that – as we had been taught – Hitler had changed.

Shortly after I had seen *Die Räuber* I had written an 'Ode to Schiller'. A year or so later, I wrote an 'Ode to Gerhart Hauptmann', the prolific dramatist and novelist, upon seeing his play *The Weavers*. It also dramatised an uprising of the spirit. A strike of workers in Silesia's textile industry ended up being squelched by military force. This drama projected human misery and the misfortunes of the less privileged.

The former leader of the Hitler Youth movement, Baldur von Schirach, was a published poet and songwriter. He wrote three of the songs of the *Bewegung* (movement). One was '*Vorwärts! Vorwärts!*' ('Move on! Move on!'). The second was '*Stellt Euch um die Standarte Rund*' ('Assemble all Around the Banner'). The third one was '*Unsere Fahne flatter uns voran*' ('Our Flag Leads Us On'), which became the banner song of the Hitler Youth. Von Schirach had written the lyrics while contemporary musicians, Borgmann and Blumensaat, had composed the melodies. Unknown to me my headmaster, impressed by my poetry, sent him some of my poems to see what he thought of them, never really expecting to get a reply.

But while I was on special assignment at a Jungvolk camp in Bavaria, I received a letter from Baldur von Schirach. My hands were shaking as I opened the envelope. He had singled out four of my poems he thought quite good, encouraging me to keep on writing. He remarked that he regretted having no more time to write poetry. His many duties no longer allowed time to write. I wondered if I should write to my father and tell him about it. I decided against it, and I no longer know why. Perhaps it would have been seen as a confrontation. He was against my writing poetry and didn't think my poems amounted to anything, while one of the nation's recognised leaders, a published poet, encouraged me to keep on writing!

I no longer have any of the poems I wrote during this time but I have recreated some of them. I was fascinated with the interrelations of nature and man. I wrote about the river, the waves, the reflection of the clouds and my perception of natural phenomena.

∽ CHAPTER THREE ∽

First Blood

SINCE THE GERMAN INVASION OF RUSSIA, Germany's fortunes, at first in the ascendant, had very quickly began to ebb. By 1943, Germany was in dire straights. The full might of the Allies was being turned on the Third Reich. On 18 February 1943 Dr Joseph Goebbels broadcast his 'total war' proclamation. At a massive gathering of Nazi faithful in Berlin, he demanded: 'Do you want total war?' The audience was full of celebrities, Party members, wounded and highly decorated soldiers. 'Yes!' they roared back. I was almost 15 years old at the time of that speech. To me it seemed the entire population was prepared to sacrifice themselves for the Führer. Less than a year after the total war proclamation the situation had deteriorated to such an extent that Bormann, Himmler and Goebbels jointly called for a *Volksopfer* (a people's sacrifice, or a sacrificial offering).

In 1943 volunteers were sought from the Hitler Youth for a new fighting corps of the Waffen-SS. The new leader, Artur Axmann, who had taken over from Baldur von Schirach, had had the idea. Some of my fellow Jungvolk leaders who were born in the year 1926, and therefore a little older than me, were encouraged to join this new elite unit. The Hitler Jugend Panzer Division, as it was called, developed a high degree of *esprit de corps*.

They were considered *daredevils* (Draufgänger) and 15 of them won the Knight's Cross or Iron Cross before the end of the war. In Normandy the division fought with an unequalled ferocity. But even they could not stem the *Übermacht* (literally: over-might, or superior force) of the advancing Allies. The Allies were superior especially in air power. Some time after

Normandy even younger volunteers were called for – those born in 1927. The division was ordered to recapture Budapest. It was an impossible task and they were swept back into Austria.

I longed to join this elite Hitler Youth division. But at first I was too young. By the time those born in 1928 were accepted, I had already committed myself to joining the mountain troops. To qualify for mountain training required proof that I had mountain-climbing experience and that I was an accomplished skier. It also required a medical. As it turned out it wasn't much of one. I was marched forward completely naked to a doctor. He asked some questions and listened to my lungs before signing my papers 'kv' – *Kriegsverwendungsfähig* (suitable for combat). I was elated. I asked my mother for my father's address in order to send him a note. I was destined to become a wartime soldier and fight for his country and his Führer.

My premilitary training was due to begin in January 1945. Meanwhile I had gained enough seniority in the Jungvolk to become a *Lagermannsehaftsführer* (camp counsellor) at one of the schools outside urban environments where city children were evacuated to avoid the bombing raids. KLV camp counsellors were in charge of organising the children's free-time activity. The one I chose was close to Waldgut Horka, where I had grown up. It was called Schloss Ullersdorf. I hoped to be reunited with my schoolboy friend Rudi. Ever since I had joined the Jungvolk I had wondered how Rudi was getting along.

When I arrived at Schloss Ullersdorf it was nine long years since I had seen Rudi. I would soon be a soldier. But what about him? I located the house he used to live in, but something looked strange about the place. The front door was locked. There was no response to my knocks. There was not a living creature in sight. I knocked on a neighbour's door.

'Rudi?' she looked at me almost disdainfully. 'Rudi the cripple? He went to an *Anstalt* (institution) years ago.'

I asked her if she knew where. She shook her head. Did she know where Rudi's parents were? 'Rudi's father is dead. Fallen in Russia.'

'His mother?'

'Wasn't she a Red Cross nurse?'

'Where can I find Rudi?'

'I have no idea . . . he might be in heaven with his pets.'

I was devastated.

I cycled to the old wooded estate where we had lived. The road had decayed. When I approached the house a dog growled. When I lived there dogs would have come out barking with excitement and friendliness to greet a new arrival. I felt forsaken. I remembered the remark of my teacher who had said of Rudi, '*Was für ein Kerl!*' (What a guy!) The teacher had explained that it was God's doing that Rudi was a hunchback. 'How would you feel if you were him?' I hadn't known how to answer. I never found out what happened to Rudi. Perhaps he had gone to heaven with his pets after all.

As the war progressed my father had become a war correspondent filing radio reports from the battlefront. The one and only report that I listened to during the two years that my father was working there was one dispatched from the Italian front. Entitled *Das Kreuz am Monte Acuto* (The Cross on Acuto Mountain) it told the story of a hero's death during the battle for Italy. My father described an attack aimed at the battalion headquarters in a farmhouse to which he was assigned. He and the first lieutenant were looking through their field binoculars when the former was killed instantly in a direct hit. The battalion commander ordered that the farmhouse be defended as long as it took to bury the fallen officer in the yard behind the building. My father used wood from shelving in the house to put together a cross that was thrust into the grave with the officer's helmet on top. This report made quite an impression on me and I was proud of my father.

It seemed as if a miracle had happened. For Christmas 1944, our entire family celebrated the holidays together. I came home from Ullersdorf in good spirits. Holidays in our house were always very festive and, even in the fifth year of the war, my parents, especially my mother, managed to make it a memorable event. I knew that right after the holidays I would be leaving for the Bavarian Alps to attend the pre-military training camp for prospective mountain troops. It gave me an additional sense of purpose and a feeling of importance.

Living at home were my youngest sister, Dörte, who was nine, my brothers Wulf and Ulrich, six and five, together with my mother and our corpulent maid, Hanna. My oldest sisters, Anje (14) and Ute (11), arrived from Strehlen, a small town southeast of Breslau to which they, as students of the Augusta High School, had been evacuated. Both of the oldest girls played the flute and practised. They would play for us on Christmas Eve before we all sang some German Christmas songs. Moreover, during the Christmas holidays, they would report to their *Rundfunkspielschar* (radio performance group) and entertain wounded soldiers in local military hospitals.

Right up to Christmas Eve, my mother, helped by our maid, seemed to be baking non-stop – an assortment of cookies, gingerbread, several almond varieties, and also *Stollen* (a Christmas bread with candied fruit). My father, who had come home from the Mediterranean, had supplied the almonds, oranges and lemons.

On Christmas Day I decided to show him the letter I had received from Baldur von Schirach, encouraging me to continue writing poetry. By now, my father had agreed to my becoming a professional Hitler Youth leader. I figured he couldn't object if I continued to write as long as my future livelihood would not depend on it. I wanted to show my mother the letter, since she would be pleased by it, but felt that I had to show it to my father first.

He was visibly surprised. The letter was short. I think he read it twice. He looked me in the eyes. 'Make sure to keep it.' That was all he said.

It was more than I had expected. Suddenly, I felt like I was wearing a laurel and it had not been taken from me.

That was the last occasion our family would be together before the end of the war. I went off to begin my pre-military mountain training in the Bavarian Alps. As I boarded the train to leave the city I had no way of knowing that Breslau was on the verge of complete encirclement by the Red Army, so woefully deceitful had been the Nazi propaganda. I would soon be getting a taste for the war that I had longed for. And so would my family.

The holidays over, I arrived in Bavaria on New Year's Eve. My mountain training course would take three weeks in some of the most spectacular alpine settings I have ever encountered. We were taught to ski, and the basics of mountain climbing. We were also given training in how to operate small-calibre rifles. But it was hardly an exhaustive introduction to mountain warfare. The three weeks passed very quickly, and as the end of the course approached, news of the Russian advance was filtering through. I couldn't believe that Breslau was about to fall into enemy hands and I desperately wanted to get back there to be with my family. I made the decision to leave the training course three days before it was officially due to end. I escaped through a window just before dawn and found a train destined for Breslau. On the journey back I saw for the first time the chaos wrought by the war. There were refugees everywhere. It took me two train journeys to eventually get to Breslau. Most of the trains were being diverted to the west. When I finally arrived in the city there was chaos everywhere. People were running about the streets in a frenzy of fear and panic. Loud speakers blared announcements. I eventually got to our apartment. But it was completely empty. There was an eerie silence. Everything was tidy and in order, but there was no sign of my brothers and sisters, mother or father. I washed and changed my underwear, but kept my uniform on. I turned on the radio and heard the announcer say: 'This hour demands total *Einsatzbereitschaft* (commitment) to save the Fatherland.' The announcer said Breslau had been declared a fortress. Karl Hanke was the Gaulieter of Breslau. He was a fanatical Nazi and he was determined that every man – and boy – would defend the city against the Red horde. I had a lump in my throat.

I lay down on the bed, still in my uniform, and tried to sort out my many thoughts. I felt overwhelmed. Overcome by tiredness I fell asleep. But not for long. I awoke with a start at a dream so frightening I can still remember it. I was about to be executed by my own classmates, the classmates whom at that very moment were so valiantly defending the city while I lay there asleep. For a few seconds I didn't realise that I was at home. My heart raced. I was drenched in cold sweat. The radio was still on. The announcer proclaimed that all deserters would face firing squads. Women, children and men over 60 years old were to proceed to designated assembly points. All others had to report to the nearest *Volkssturm* registration unit. Nervousness, inner doubts and at times fear stirred my thoughts as I pondered what to do.

I did report to my nearest registration unit but was told I must go somewhere else. I don't know what was going through my mind but I felt I needed to talk to a friend before I did so. I began wandering around Breslau looking for various friends. None were anywhere to be found. I still wonder to this day why I never went to the radio station to find my father. Announcements were blaring wherever I turned. '*Bis zum letzen kaempfen und zum Opfertod bereit sein!*' (Fight to the end and be willing to sacrifice one's life!) The hour had come. Soon I would have to face death. I became aware of the severity of the situation.

I didn't want to be a coward. But was I ready to die? Suddenly a thought came into my head. I had not qualified to serve as a *Flakhelfer* (Flak helper) in the air defence force because of health reasons. That is why I had been designated a KLV camp counsellor instead. Although I had been accepted as a volunteer in the mountain troops, I had not yet been required to pass a real physical. I had experienced dizziness during the training. I decided to ignore the orders given on the radio. I would present myself at the KLV office instead. Perhaps they would return me to the evacuated school at Ullersdorf where I had been a camp counsellor. Who would I find to talk to? They were setting up *Panzersperren* (tank barricades) in the streets by now. I returned home once more and left a note for my mother. Then I set off for the KLV office. Had I made the right decision?

My question was answered when my superior at the KLV office, Karl Gutschke, spotted me outside his door. He was now dressed in the uniform of an *Oberleutnant* (First Lieutenant). 'Armin, I am glad that you made it. We are putting together an elite unit.'

I saluted. But instantly I was filled with doubts. Gutschke was a disabled veteran. He had lost a lung. Now with two disabled *Unteroffiziere* (NCOs), he had been given orders to lead into battle the very young who were able to bear arms. Soon we would have to fire, with our guns and with our souls. Now we would be tested.

Gutschke, together with the non-commissioned officers straight out of a military hospital, assembled our elite unit called *Kampfgruppe Gutschke*.

Kampfgruppe translated literally means fighting group. Thus we would become a special Volkssturm task force, comprised of KLV staff members and camp counsellors, of students of the Adolf Hitler School in Wartha and of members of a WE-Lager, a pre-military training camp.

We were all, to different degrees, conditioned by the Third Reich's educational system. My newly issued field-grey Volkssturm outfit, actually an army uniform without insignia, did not fit. It was too wide around the shoulders and around the waist. The boots were too big, but I was used to wearing two pairs of socks.

The training had been minimal. Even those of us who had been instructed in pre-military training camps had only practised with small-bore (sub-calibre) rifles. Now we would be assigned military carbines, even machine guns, no longer the practice hand-grenades but live ones, and *Panzerfaust* (bazookas).

We were to be part of the Hitler Youth-Fortress Regiment Breslau and we were to go into action straight away. Gutschke had received orders to advance. Our task was to meet the Russian forces southeast of the capital at a village which the Russians had taken. I was glad that the fighting would be in open country instead of being sealed up inside a fortress. Subconsciously, I hoped for survival. There can be no doubt of that. My senses stretched time. Yesterday seemed a year ago. Tomorrow, the unknown future still appeared far, far away. I felt compelled to write. Powerful life-affirming thoughts filled my mind. Those of a soldier to be. In retrospect, I can see the conflict inside my mind when I wrote the following poem:

> Although war
> Is a struggle
> For liberty
> The road
> To victory
> Is a row
> Of graves
> Thus I strive
> To be brave
> But to survive
> To be alive
> To come home
> Free
> To Live.

This poem I tucked away in my breast pocket. Looking at it now, I see it's not even a poem. It is a hastily crafted plea for survival. While I wanted to live, we followed orders to kill. And so did the Russians. The gifted writer, Ilya Ehrenburg, implored the Russian fighting men to drench the soil with German blood. 'There is no one who is innocent in Germany, neither in the living nor in the unborn. Follow Stalin's command, smash the Fascist beast in his cave, strip the German women of their pride and take them as your lawful prey. Kill, kill, you brave soldiers, advance death as you conquer!'

Hitler, of course, was as ruthless and brutal a despot as Stalin. Dr Goebbels, although slightly more subtle than Ilya Ehrenburg, proclaimed hate as our duty and revenge as our virtue. He challenged us to kill and to bury the Soviet hordes in mass graves. In the circumstances my desire to live was not a wish to be expressed openly. If I had been a real Nazi I should have proclaimed my fervour to fight, my willingness to kill, my readiness to die!

Gutschke took me under his wing and wanted me to be his courier. 'I need you as my courier,' he reassured me. 'You will remain with me.'

It was on 29 January that we were picked up by trucks and taken to the front. We were under orders to recapture a village taken by the Russians. The attack was scheduled for 5 a.m. Despite troubled sleep, the next morning we were all up ahead of time. Our column assembled in a barn. Gutschke spoke, with a low voice and matter of factly. We had to fulfil our duty. We had a job to do. Silesia had to be saved for Germany to survive.

He spoke of us as soldiers. He expected us to bring honour to the Fatherland and reminded us to be brave, yet not to be careless. 'There are the Russians,' he said, pointing in the direction of the village we had to capture. 'They are after our lives and we are after theirs. They are well-trained soldiers and they can be very tough. We have to show them that we will be even better fighters, indomitable, unfaltering, resolute.' Gutschke explained that we would be supported by three Tiger Panzers (tanks) on each flank. Two companies of older, seasoned Volksgrenadiere would follow the tanks. We would not be alone.

We had not been trained for infantry attacks. We belonged to a *Panzernahkampfbrigade* (close-range tank-attack brigade), a crack unit armed with bazookas. The bazookas were portable, hand-held, anti-tank, armour-piercing rockets called Panzerfaust (literally: tank fist) because they could knock out tanks at close range. We had been instructed, ever so briefly, in how to use them. This morning, however, our objective was to storm the village, in a surprise attack if possible. We had to take it and hold it. If they came with tanks, we would 'crack' them with our 'tank fists'.

My stomach started to grumble. I suddenly realised that we had not had breakfast. I remembered reading that soldiers in the First World War had a saying: 'A good breakfast keeps body and soul together!' My stomach was empty but I carried an iron ration with me. It made me think of the survival exercise of a couple of years earlier and how proud I was when my group came in first.

My earliest understanding of what approaching battle would be like was of a horseman, riding through day and night, as told in *The Tale of the Life and Death of Cornet Christoph Rilke* by Rainer Maria von Rilke. It is a wistful, rhythmical narration of a warrior in love who charges, holding up his flag, into the sabres of the enemy. This type of warfare had taken place almost 200 years ago. But Rilke's sorrowful poetic tale had romanticised and glorified in my mind the death of his hero and of all heroes who sacrificed their lives in battle.

Just two nights previously, someone had mentioned how wars had changed. Now, sabres were only worn on dress uniforms and no longer used in battle. But we had bayonets that could be mounted on our carbines should enemy soldiers be encountered within stabbing distance.

It was the crack of dawn. The Russians couldn't possibly see us, unless they had a *Spähtrupp* (a small reconnaissance unit) in the field. There were no noticeable movements ahead of us. The tanks were held back at first to keep our attack as silent as possible for as long as practicable. Then they were to advance at both flanks. Under the thin snow-blanket the ground was frozen and stone-hard. But there were drifts. We advanced slowly over the rugged winter soil in a triangular formation with Gutschke and me at the apex. Gutschke jumped forwards in short intervals. He kept advancing and I followed close behind.

Nothing happened at our flanks at first. The early light of dawn heightened. The first shot that sounded came from behind us, not from the Russians in the village ahead. Gutschke cursed. 'Idiot!'

Soon, I heard tanks rolling. But only on the southeastern flank.

What had happened to those supposed to be on the other side of us?

Suddenly there were shots everywhere. Machine-gun fire.

Everything happened so fast.

The earth, with its icy snow-crust, shook, quivered and trembled. Gutschke was down on his belly. I was down on mine. We both were in the midst of a barrage of shelling, fierce detonations, blasts, grenades bursting into pieces, bullets whizzing by.

Instinctively, I crawled up next to Gutschke. He shouted as loud as he could: 'We will wait here a short while and let them squander ammunition. When our tanks come, we'll move on.'

Our tanks did not come and the fire increased. The Russians had sharpshooters up in the church tower. Right next to me a heavy shell exploded. My head banged against the icy snow on the ground. My left leg jumped. A sharp, burning pain seared through me. I put my hand on the wound. When I lifted it, it was full of blood.

'Damn! I'm hit!'

Gutschke crawled back and pulled me behind a snowdrift. 'Stay here!' He went ahead alone.

It seemed like an eternity. The hail of fire kept increasing. I tried to dig deeper into the snow. It was too icy. I lifted my face and it burned. There was no halt to the downpour of bursting shells. Sharp, whining bullets cut through the air over my head. It made no sense for me to shoot. The enemy wasn't in sight.

Our corporals, who had first-aid kits, were nowhere near. Amid the deafening clamour of battle, there were cries of pain. I saw badly wounded comrades. Although Gutschke had ordered me to remain where I was, I could not stay. I had to pull some of the wounded into the more protective ravine. I knew enough about first aid to grasp that bleeding limbs had to be tied up.

I always carried a pocket knife. I cut up some cloth. One of the wounded looked OK; I couldn't even tell where he was hit. Then blood came out of his mouth. Another had no hand. I placed a tourniquet on his upper arm as tight as I could to arrest the bleeding.

I pulled more wounded into the small gully. By the time I lacked the strength to get up again, there were four or five of us there. One made the sign of the cross and closed his eyes. His last gesture prompted me to think of God. God could not be watching over all of us individually, I thought. God most certainly would not control the path of every bullet shot, of all the shrapnel from every exploding grenade or bomb.

When I lifted my head I could see the silhouette of an enemy soldier through the embrasure of the bell tower, the barrel of his rifle up on a sill, aiming at us. This sharpshooter became my very first human target. I aimed my gun and missed. Fortunately, he failed to hit us too. I kept bleeding and ceased shooting to keep my hand on the gash. It felt like a fist-sized hole in my left buttock. The snow around me had turned red.

Another close hit. My head, again, thumped on the ice. Shrieks. Groans.

Even though I was wounded, I couldn't just remain inactive. I decided to move forward. I checked my hurting thigh again. My torn trousers were increasingly soaked with blood. In front of us more and more smoke was rising. Houses in the village were burning.

Soon a light-headed feeling overcame me. I lost my balance. Pain pierced through and throbbed in my thigh. It shot up as far up as my heart and as far down as my toe. I could still crawl very short stretches, resting in between.

Finally the artillery fire seemed to let up. Some dull 'plub-plubs' from mortars could still be heard as could machine-gun fire at both ends of the flanks. My pain increased but, peculiar as it may seem, with the increase of pain I regained some strength. Pressing my right hand at my wound, I limped forward.

Now the village appeared to be much closer. At least six houses were burning. Flames, bright red and yellow, created clouds of smoke. The battle sounds, even the machine-gun fire and rifle shots, lessened. Just a while ago, with detonations and fire all around me, I had remained unruffled. Now every shot startled me.

The Russians had retreated. There were comrades behind me. Fallen ones and wounded ones. I approached a dead Russian soldier. His skull was shattered and bloody, and his brain spattered the area. Why hadn't he worn a helmet? It was a physically painful sight and made me feel sick to my stomach. I swallowed back the acid that came up my throat. I closed my eyes and commanded myself not to collapse.

I passed out anyway and only regained consciousness when the surviving NCO arrived with a horse-drawn cart, apparently one that a local farmer had used for transporting coal. Small pieces of *steinkohle* (anthracite) and a layer of black dust had remained. Two of the *Volksgrenadiere* (older soldiers of the Home Defence Force), not even medics, picked up the wounded and the dead, placing them on the coal cart, tightly, like sardines. My thoughts wandered through pain and grey dreams. To blend in with the winter landscapes, we had worn snow-capes over our uniforms. My poetic mind called them 'soul capes'. A row of fallen soldiers entering heaven?

The next one loaded into the cart jolted me out of my daydream. '*Um Gottes willen!*' ('Oh, my God!') It was the handsome, straw-blond youngster. I recognised him at once – Dieter Eberhard Heinrich, my boyhood buddy. I didn't see any signs of injury. But he was gone. Dead.

'Dieter!' My voice cracked. I felt the impulse to cry and had to bite my lips. A *Hitlerjunge* doesn't cry! I had just turned into a soldier.

I still can't describe the depth of my despair.

The next body put on the cart had a faceless head, consisting of blood, raw flesh and bone fragments from the torn-off nose. His eyes had been smashed and seeped out of the sockets. The sick feeling increased. It became so acute that I had to throw up, right on the cart, soiling two of my comrades, one dead, but the other still alive.

Although conditions were horrendously sickening, I was appalled at myself for not being able to control what I viewed as war-sickness. We had been conditioned in so many ways, but I was totally unprepared for warfare's abominable, ghastly cruelties. I was unprepared for the helplessness I felt at not being able to master the situation. Not capable of control seemed bad enough, but being the only one on the cart who couldn't stomach the unnerving sights of the mutilated bodies devastated me.

There were no blankets, nothing to cover the gory head facing down into the coal dust on the cart. I kept on choking and vomiting. At final count, there must have been ten to twelve bodies on this horse cart, at least five of them dead. Along with Dieter Eberhard Heinrich, another two showed hardly any sign of a hit, no blood, no mutilation, just frozen facial expressions.

By now my stomach must have been empty. My nausea finally subsided, but I did not regain control over my nerves. My body quivered. The sound of every shot, no matter how far, made me jerk. The wounded were taken to the local tavern, set up as an emergency dressing-station. The fallen were declared dead and taken to the cemetery for burial.

I kept on mumbling '*Auf wiedersehen*' to Dieter.

See you again?

Where?

If there was a comforting thought about Dieter's death, it was that he had not been mutilated. In heaven, will all the bodies be restored?

The repulsive, unnerving image of our faceless comrade was by far the most gruesome sight I had had to view in my young life. We were told he had activated a hand grenade but then froze, not throwing it, and it exploded in his face. Someone even commented, 'That's what happens to cowards!' This I did not believe.

I learned later that the Russians had been shooting with *Knallerbsen*, bullets that exploded on impact. I am convinced that this comrade was hit in the face by such an explosive and that it tore his countenance to shreds.

Feeling sick and frightened brought death so very close and in a much more heinous way than I had ever imagined. My thoughts drowned in an abyss of horror. One of my comrades stated later that I seemed lifeless. But then he saw my arm twitch. And I was breathing. Did I have a chance to survive, he wondered?

I was lying on the floor. I don't remember sighing or complaining, but I was in pain and surrounded by others, moaning and groaning. I shivered uncontrollably. The floor was cold. At first there were no blankets, nothing to provide warmth to comfort those of us who were suffering. There were no drugs to numb our pain. Only cups filled with water were being handed out. There were desperate cries for help.

We were told that a doctor would arrive and see us soon. It didn't happen.

We were transferred in a truck filled with straw from the *Gasthaus* (local pub) to a *Hauptverbandsplatz* (main dressing-station). By then my leg was stiff and had turned blue. Someone predicted that it would have to be amputated. Where we were now, there were medics but still no physician. The medics had some drugs, but were out of anaesthetics already. I remember that my wound had to be cleansed, that it was very painful, and in order not to scream, the serviceman who performed the medical work put his belt in my mouth with the words: 'Bite into the leather!'

A pal lit a cigarette for me and I started smoking to find relief from the pain. With bleeding lips lacerated from biting the leather belt, I lit cigarette after cigarette, using the end of one to light the next. I kept on smoking until finally I passed out. Hours later, I was told that a medic had taken the last cigarette from me. Had I dropped it into the straw mattress, I could have burned to death. He had counted the butts. I had smoked 17 in a row.

My pal, only slightly wounded on the upper arm, was clever at *Organisieren* (an expression used for getting things by nifty means, short of stealing). He helped even more in easing my suffering. He brought me some *Schnapps* (home-made spirits of high alcoholic content). I drank straight out of the bottle. It burned my throat, but I gulped down several swallows. I inhaled even more deeply. The combination of alcohol and nicotine continued to take the edge off my increasing, gnawing pain.

For the first time in many days, we received a copy of a newspaper. It was the *Silesian Daily* or the *Daily Observer* of Schweidnitz. I clearly remember reading a bold-printed notice that the death penalty now applied not only to deserters but also in the case of those who refused to follow orders.

Published excerpts from a Führer speech again emphasised his belief that *Vorsehung* (Providence) had saved him from the assassination attempt on 20 July of the previous year. Thus he would lead Germany to victory. He challenged all Germans to harden their spirit of resistance and to fulfil their duties.

The Führer, once more, brought to the fore that everyone able to fight had to fight so that the great German nation would emerge victorious. Having just faced my baptism of fire and lying here among the wounded, I felt that I, indeed, was doing my duty. In his speech, he had mentioned how much Germany had shrunk already. Although I realised that the Russians were less than 200 kilometres away from the Reich capital, I didn't comprehend in any way how hopeless the overall situation had become.

Another news item caught my attention. I was familiar with Klettendorf, a village near where we had lived, where there was a plant that produced syrup from sugar beet. My parents knew the plant manager and the party officials there, including the *Ortsgruppenleiter* (district leader), Paul Glückel. I was shocked to read a notice that Glückel had been executed. Instead of mobilising the men in his village to form a home-defence unit, the newspaper article stated, he had left Klettendorf. Upon being located, he was shot on the spot. Someone I knew had been executed! I trembled.

An entire series of *Todesurteile* (death sentences) were published, no doubt as a deterrent for anyone thinking of retreat. I didn't recognise any names besides Glückel's, but I noticed that among those executed, Glückel had not been the only one who held a high Party office. How deplorable that some of Hitler's followers would desert him now, at this critical stage of the war, when everyone's total commitment was needed to turn the tide. That was the way I thought at the time and the so-called *Abschreckungsmassnahmen* (deterrence measures) reinforced my thinking.

A few days later, a train arrived for us to be taken to Dresden, by then known as a hospital town. Dresden was considered to be relatively secure from air raids. We were reassured that it would be a safe place for us to recover. The nuns stayed behind. So did my pal, the organiser. His wound didn't require an operation, just dressing and healing. In a week or so, he would be well enough to be returned to the Front.

Fewer than 30 of us could be transported. A *Feldunterarzt* (junior field doctor) and three or four older medics came along. We left behind some who had died and some others who were close to death. There was hope for those of us who departed. My only memory of Dresden, which was once known as 'Germany's Florence', was as a boy, when I had travelled by train through this beautiful city two or three times. Once I had spent a weekend in Dresden. It was a lovely place.

Schools and other public buildings were used as emergency medical facilities in Dresden. Thousands of refugees flocked there. But on the successive nights of 13 and 14 February waves of Allied bombers created a firestorm that enveloped the entire city and killed an estimated 30,000 innocent civilians. The Allied bombing of Dresden has gone down in history as an act of terrible vengeance.

For the Lehmann family, however, the dates of 13 and 14 February proved to be days of great deliverance. We all could have died in the carnage of Dresden. It was only by luck that all of us survived it. I was in Dresden just before the bombing began, waiting in the Hauptbahnhof (the main train station) to be transferred from the military hospital train to a makeshift medical facility in a school. But little did I know that my mother and my brothers and sisters were also in Dresden and were at one stage in the same station, possibly at the same time as me. They had joined the tidal wave of refugees that had headed towards the city. And by another coincidence my father was in Dresden too. He was on a secret mission (which he never elaborated on) to the radio station. He was caught in the firestorm, but survived it.

I knew nothing of their presence so near to me when the military hospital train reached Dresden's main train station on 12 February 1945. We expected to be unloaded and taken to a school building designated to become an emergency military hospital, a common practice then. It was announced that the school we were meant to occupy had, in a desperate move by the officials, already been assigned to a refugee group from the East. Many of these people were very old and too sick to be moved again. Other quarters had to be found for us. Until then, our train could not be unloaded. We had to wait for orders. Where they would come from, nobody seemed to know. Our medics became frustrated. The supplies were depleted. We were hungry, but there were no meals. The mood on the train became one of increasing despair. Most of us were in pain and the carriage was full of the sounds of moaning and agony.

To make matters even more uncomfortable, some refugees from other treks, apparently hardship cases, were admitted to our train, which was already overcrowded. Among them were two boys who had lost their mother and one young, pregnant woman in great pain, probably already in labour. The *Sanitätsfeldwebel* (medic sergeant-major) was at a loss to know what to do. Every sentence he uttered seemed to start with '*schrecklich*' (awful).

'Awful, we are out of water.'

'Awful, we used up all of our food.'

'My God, these boys. How awful, they lost their mother.'

'How awful, this woman is ready to give birth.'

Awful! Awful! Awful! I can still hear his gruff, throaty words today. When would our doctor return? Supposedly, he was still in the city, assisting Party or military officials in the search to find a place where yet another emergency military hospital could be established, one to house us. We had already spent too much time packed in the train. Most of us were in great pain and downcast because we felt so miserable. Our water was depleted. The kitchen remained closed. In dire need of medical supplies, our medic kept on repeating this one expression that summed it all up: 'Awful.'

He wanted to take better care of us and help the young boys, who were starving. The pregnant woman he put in another carriage, in the cot of a soldier who had died and been removed. He had died of gangrene, we were told. Some boys from a fire-fighting unit had come to pick up his body.

Finally, one of the medics decided that he would take things into his own hands. He left the train and reassured us that he would be back soon. I felt uneasy from the moment he was gone, abandoned. This feeling of having been deserted increased as time went on. Late at night he returned. Water and food would arrive soon, he reassured us. This was a sure sign we wouldn't be unloaded soon. Very early the next morning, 13 February, before daybreak, we were awakened by our carriage knocking and banging us around painfully.

The medic explained that the carriages of another hospital train were being added to ours. Apparently the locomotive had broken down or been destroyed by fire from an enemy plane, stranding all the carriages filled with injured and sick soldiers. While these hospital wagons were added to our train, a lot of moving forward and backward, tugging and yanking took place, affecting the seriously wounded most of all. The jars and jolts increased the sounds of agony.

When, finally, all these carriages had been added to our train and the doctor had returned, we were moved from the main train station to an *Abstellgleis* (railway yard) outside Dresden, perhaps 15 to 20 kilometres away from town. We were told in which direction we were travelling. We were all a bit uneasy about that because that would take us towards Chemnitz, an industrial city that had by then become a constant target of air raids. In fact we were about to be delivered from a firestorm that would undoubtedly have claimed all our lives.

I was wide awake in the hospital train, probably about 20 kilometres south of the city, and could clearly hear the undulating sound of air-raid sirens warning the citizens of approaching enemy aircraft.

'That cannot be!' remarked one of the wounded. 'They won't bomb Dresden!'

'It could be Russians! Coming from the East,' someone remarked.

But I pointed out: 'They would destroy Breslau before hitting Dresden.'

'Breslau might already be in rubble.'

'I hope not, most of my classmates are there!'

I listened anxiously, every muscle straining to hear. Far away, a humming of heavy engines in unison soon escalated into a vibrating, droning sound. I envisioned, high in the sky, the approach of a mighty phalanx of metal birds. There were also some sounds of faster planes criss-crossing. We thought that German fighters had taken off and were up in the skies to attack the approaching enemy. But none of us could see any planes or hear any shots being fired. I noticed flares, some in the shape of small Christmas trees, falling from heaven and illuminating spheres of the firmament. Most fizzled out before hitting ground. Then there were some flaming flashes. Firebombs?

Suddenly I could hear 'plub-plub' sounds. But instead of increasing, these bursts decreased. Why was there no anti-aircraft fire? Bombs were falling in jam-packed succession. It felt as if we were closer now than 20 kilometres from the sites of the impacts. Much closer. How many planes could there be up in the sky? From several directions, hissing sounds cut into the roar of the bombers' engines.

On the ground, strangely enough, there seemed to be few explosions on impact. I didn't know then that firebombs don't explode like demolition bombs, but, like flame-throwers, ignite upon impact. One of the other wounded soldiers in our carriage also had a view through a window. He yelled 'incendiary bombs!' over and over.

By now, it must have been close to 11 p.m. Through the dirty, opaque glass of the railway carriage, the sky in front of me was totally ablaze. In the confines of our train, we weren't aware of the firestorms, the whirling heat twisters. But, through my small window, huge glowing tongues were spitting up spirals of smoke. Without a doubt, a beautiful city, thought to be safe, crowded with people, was being scourged before my eyes and blown into fragments. I was overcome by the sight of the sea of fire. It had always been my greatest fear, death in flames. Fire, I was convinced, caused the highest degree of excruciating pain. A whole city was being turned into a blasting furnace, scorching living people, frying them, reducing them to ashes. Had I known that my father was in the inferno I would have been mortified.

The explosions made the ground tremble. In my cot, I could feel the earth shake. An ocean of flames expanded and approached our location, increasing my fears. Why wasn't our train being moved? Didn't the enemy suffer any losses? Only once did I observe what looked like a flaming comet crashing down to earth. Had one of their planes been downed, a single plane out of what must be hundreds?

While I kept watching, overtaken by fright, others in the carriage wanted to get out. Some who could walk got up, opened the door and left the train. Nobody stopped them. They ran to the field and threw themselves into the dirt. Several scraped out enough soil, with their hands to find some protection. Hours went by. Only after the second attack did my comrades return. Fortunately, the firestorms had not reached us and our train had not been bombed.

CHAPTER FOUR

First Love

IT MUST HAVE BEEN TWO DAYS later when we reached Hof, located on the River Saale. There the most serious cases were to be discharged from the train. We were told that an emergency military hospital had been set up downtown in an elementary school and we would be taken there for emergency care. A classroom had been vacated when we arrived. Old men had moved the school benches into the hallways where we had been waiting. Along with the shrieks of pain now came curses and complaints about the cold draught coming through the hall. We shuddered and shivered. First we had to be deloused, an embarrassing procedure, especially in front of young nurses. I was taken straight from the hallway to a makeshift operating-room. I don't recall anything about the surgery. Obviously, drugs and anaesthesia had arrived, together with a surgical team.

When I regained consciousness, the first thing I checked was to see if they had amputated my leg. It was still there; they had only removed the shrapnel. A young Red Cross nurse in a blue-striped dress covered with a white apron introduced herself: 'Good morning, I am *Schwester* (Sister) Anne-Maria.' She carried a pot of coffee and a tray with slices of bread spread with jam. She went from cot to cot.

When she reached me, I only took the cup. My hands were shaking.

'No bread?' she asked.

After the surgery, I still felt nauseous. 'No thanks,' I replied and spilled some coffee.

She looked deep into my eyes. 'How old are you?'

'Sixteen.'

She stroked my head. I felt suffused with warmth and gentleness. I was falling in love.

The ward was a converted classroom and 16 cots had been crammed into the room. The NCO in charge of the ward had a crush on Anne-Maria. Almost everyone in our room seemed to love Sister Anne-Maria. She was a 19-year-old beauty, thoughtful and caring, despite the enormous hardships she and her fellow nurses encountered.

Most of the nurses were good-looking, one of them even a 'femme fatale' type – leggy and flirty. Another one, when off duty, wore a very tight sweater. She had voluptuous breasts and stirred my young mind with her flaunting seductiveness. But such incitements did not divert my heart from longing for Anne-Maria. From the first moment I had seen her, I had fallen in love with her. Increasingly, she seemed to respond, giving me more attention, an extra touch, a devoted look, sometimes a whisper, a few words meant only for me to hear. It made me happy, but at times I also felt awkward or embarrassed.

The first week after my operation, I had to observe strict bed-rest, even having to use a bedpan. I managed not to ask for it while Anne-Maria was on duty. Then the day came when I was permitted to use the toilet located down the hallway. That evening I put on my trousers and borrowed a uniform jacket (my own had probably been left on the train) from a room-mate who also had a walking stick. Painful as it was to walk, I left the room and went into the schoolyard to get some fresh air.

The next morning, I told Anne-Maria that I had taken my first walk.

First she thought that I was pushing my luck, but I convinced her to meet me that evening, after her shift was over, for a walk. I had no pass. Anne-Maria and I walked to the Saale, which became 'our' river and the topic for a couple of poems. I had the desire to write again. Our excursions became a nightly occurrence. I returned later and later until, one morning, the NCO openly scolded Anne-Maria: 'Sister, how can you get involved with a child?'

She turned red and didn't reply. I felt angry and ashamed but also kept quiet.

Most of the others in the room also disapproved of the apparent romance going on between the *Junge* (kid) and this vivacious young woman. All in our room felt attracted to her. The NCO must have reported her to her superior because I was ordered not to leave the hospital without permission. Anne-Maria was reprimanded severely. When she told me about it, she cried.

Outraged, I confronted the NCO, with everyone in the room witnessing my outburst. 'I am not too young to die.'

'But you are too young to marry!' he replied.

Was he right? Although only 16 years old, as a *Volkssturmmann*, I was a soldier. I had been wounded in battle and then wounded again on the way to this hospital. I smoked. I had proven, several times by now, that I was able to hold my liquor. What else could make me an adult? How could anyone, no matter how superior in rank, be able to restrain me from associating with a nurse, especially one who was also in the service of the Fatherland? If I wanted to marry Anne-Maria, and she was willing to become my wife, why would we have to wait until I turned 18? What were the odds I would be alive then?

Soon I would return to the Front. My chances of survival were ever so slim. I was suddenly consumed by the thought that I should have an heir, that I should exemplify my manhood not only by being a soldier, but also by being a progenitor of ongoing life. Anne-Maria wanted my child. Hers was a vision of love and patriotism.

Should I soon be among the battle dead, my blood would continue in the veins of our child. I wrote with flaming idealism about my wish to secure my place in the eternal river of life. I described the river as filled with the blood of the fallen soldiers, to which my own blood might be added. Anne-Maria was impressed by what I had written. We both were willing to forego our lives, as a sacrifice for Führer and Fatherland. In the great scheme of things, we had been taught, our individual lives belonged to the nation. Not for us to live on, but for the nation to survive.

One day a high-ranking officer turned up at the hospital. We were told to be prepared to be presented to him. When he came in he addressed us as '*Kameraden*' (comrades) and I was impressed. He mentioned that we were deserving of the nation's gratitude and that, in the name of the Führer, it was his honour to award some of us with decorations. I was among the ones to be decorated. Gutschke had found out where I was and ordered that, in addition to the Black Wounded Badge, I was to be awarded the Iron Cross II (Second Class). I was elated. I was a *Junger Held* (a young hero).

It seemed that, thereafter, all of my room-mates treated me with some respect. I remained the Junge, but now was often referred to as '*der mutige Junge*' (the brave kid), the one with the Iron Cross.

By now, full recovery for me seemed to be assured. I would return to the Front. This was important to me, for, at that time I was still committed to the Führer and the Fatherland. Moreover, having fallen in love with Anne-Maria, I longed to be recognised as a brave soldier, as a man.

As time progressed and new patients arrived, the doctor remained devotedly committed to his patients but, increasingly, he openly decried the '*verdammte Krieg*' (damn war) for the sufferings he encountered and the miseries near and far.

'He'd better be careful. If Party officials hear him make such comments, he could end up in Flossenbürg!'

'What's in Flossenbürg?' I wanted to know.

'It's a concentration camp. Where they put *Meuterer* (mutineers), *Miesmacher* (defeatists) and other *Volksfeinde* (enemies of the people).'

I belonged to the Volkssturm and never received any pay. Anne-Maria would buy magazines and newspapers for me. Once in a while, she got hold of an old paper she knew would interest me. It included news about the fighting in and around Fortress Breslau. I longed desperately for information about my home town where classmates and friends were putting up a valiant fight. The Russians had still not been able to capture this city. The nurses received one day off per week. I applied for a day-pass on Anne-Maria's free day, which would have allowed me to leave the hospital. It was denied. My facial cuts had healed; the wound on my arm was still open, but I could bend my elbow again. Only my upper thigh still caused concern. Most of the shrapnel had been removed. However, I still had a fever in the low 39s (Celsius) and required strong pain medication.

That I had been able to leave the hospital several evenings in a row was due to the fact that there was no security. There were no guards. Only my room-mate and the night nurse knew, until the NCO decided that he had to report me. We had made plans on Anne-Maria's day off to make a trip to Marktredwitz, my paternal grandmother's home town.

My leave denied, I considered leaving without a pass. One of the older room-mates, who liked both of us and thought that we should get as much enjoyment out of life as we possibly could, nevertheless discouraged me from just taking off on Anne-Maria's free day. 'You could be stopped and without papers you would be a deserter and you could be shot!' He pointed out that we couldn't check into a room in a hotel or rent a *Fremdenzimmer* (room rented out in a private home) since whoever rented it to us would commit a crime known as *Kuppelei* (pro-curing/pandering). The NCO had also hinted that I might be taken to Flossenbürg. Deserters ended up there to be shot. Did he know for sure or just surmise that this could be the case?

For Anna-Maria and me, the seriousness of the situation began to sink in.

We didn't leave town, but escaped within the school complex. During air raids, those who could walk had to leave our building and assemble in the cellar of a nearby high-school building that served as a shelter and as an underground storage for turnips. In this school building, the upper classrooms, when not occupied, were left open. In such a classroom, in the early evening, we found privacy.

'We love each other,' she said, 'and I want your child. You will be leaving soon to return to the Front.'

The intensity of our relationship escalated because we knew we had so little time. While my condition improved, Anne-Maria's heavy workload increased even more.

My own recent experiences on the battlefield caused phantasmagorias. Nightmares invaded my head. Again and again, the horrible sight of the faceless head appeared, without nose and eyes, flesh mixed with blood and bone fragments and slimy fluids.

When I was given my orders to return to the Front it was a wrench for both of us. Anne-Maria burst into tears. I felt the same but I held mine inside me. Anne-Maria saw that I had my mother's ring on my hand. She ripped off her own ring, a small gold one with a coral and put it on my little finger. We pledged undying allegiance to one another and we promised that we would find one another as soon as the war was over. Her last words to me were: 'You can't leave me!' But I had no choice in the matter.

Anne-Maria did succeed in changing her schedule so that she could accompany me to the train station. Baggage was no problem. I had none. All I possessed was the uniform I wore, a small bag of toiletries, two notebooks which contained some of my writings I wanted to save, and a pillbox with the medication I still had to take. Anne-Maria had also made me some sandwiches. I carried everything in a shopping bag made out of netting.

There we were. A Red Cross nurse arm-in-arm with a young soldier still limping slightly, both downcast. Intermittently, Anne-Maria said, 'You will be back!'

'Yes, in just a week,' I replied, knowing already that it might be for just a few hours. We reached the station; Anne-Maria wiped her eyes with her handkerchief.

I wanted to say one more time how much I loved her, but I had this fear that I might be overcome by emotions. I was in public. I was in uniform. I had to control my feelings. 'Can't we part smiling?' I asked, pressing her hand. She tried to smile and so did I.

'I miss you already,' she said, 'and you are not even gone.'

One last hug.

'*Tapfer sein!*' (Let's be brave!) were her last words. She swung around and left, not turning her head back but still waving.

I elbowed myself into the overcrowded train and remained at the door, waiting for her to look back just once more. She didn't. Still I kept waving and didn't stop until she was completely out of sight. As I watched her retreating form I recalled a Latin phrase we had learnt in school. '*Fata viam inverient*': fate will find a way.

The old rickety train shuttled through the town and picked up speed when we reached the country. I thought of Anne-Maria constantly. The intensity and radiance of her personality, the brightness of her eyes, her wavy, often wind-blown brown hair, the sensuality not only of her body but of her face. For the first time in my life, I thought about the various types of love and how they expressed themselves in different types of feelings.

From as far back as I could remember, at home, in school and in the Jungvolk, it had been ingrained in me to love our Führer, and I thought that I did. I did not realise how much of a make-believe emotion it was, a child's adoration of an inspiring leader to be worshipped.

While growing up, I didn't think of boys loving each other. Our perception was that, as youngsters, we created bonds of comradeship. We believed that they were much stronger than the bonds of love. To have a comrade is to have found someone to rely on. Combat fellowships were comradeships of the highest order. I never thought of (or had the feeling of) loving my father. He was an authority figure and I looked up to him. I had been fearful of him, but I can't remember ever having had feelings of affection for him. I knew he liked it that way. According to Hitler's vision, the next generation of Germany's soldiers was to 'maintain sentiments as hard as steel'.

I considered my love for my mother as a dominant, strong and everlasting devotion.

Now, passionate love had entered my life, a new force that had ignited my soul, my mind and my body. Was the love between a young soldier and a Red Cross nurse a bond of comradeship interwoven with a bond of love?

I was finally reunited with my unit. There were celebrations because I had returned. Gutschke confessed he had not thought I'd make it. That's why he'd instructed the military commander in Hof to award me the Iron Cross. Now he wanted to read, in front of all, the citation: 'After being wounded, he pulled other wounded into a snow ravine for protection and, despite heavy loss of blood, he was among the first and the bravest who captured the village.'

There was applause and cheering and I was expected to make a speech. I remembered having pulled the wounded on the field into the snow ravine. However, I made it only to the edge of the village before I collapsed and later was thrown on the horse-drawn carriage together with wounded comrades and others who had fallen. What was I supposed to say?

Of our original unit of 120, less than 40 were present. Yet we hadn't retreated or given ground. The last Soviet attempt to take Breslau had been repelled with 64 enemy tanks taken out by hand-held bazookas. That was some achievement – bazookas had to be held at a very close distance. It was not a weapon for the faint-hearted.

On Easter Sunday I wrote to Anne-Maria. The only paper that was available was the official stationery with the Hitler Youth national emblem of an eagle holding the HJ-diamond with the swastika, not the type of writing paper usually used for intimate letters. Never mind. It was a long, heart-felt letter in which I tried to be poetic. She never got it. I later found that none of my letters to Anne-Maria or my mother or my sisters was received. And I never received any of theirs. It was said that the Allies' fighter bombers were attacking the mail trains. But I wonder?

Presently we learned that we were going to be thrown back into battle in Frankfurt an der Oder. Artur Axmann, the leader of the Hitler Youth, himself had dictated that we should be diverted there as battle-hardened veterans to give hope and encouragement to our younger comrades who were still a little wet behind the ears. But then came even more remarkable news.

Artur Axmann was one of the youngest Nazis among high Party officials but he was rapidly becoming one of the closest to Hitler. Axmann had been responsible for turning it from what was little more than a boy scout movement into a fanatical political and military organisation. Axmann's much repeated mantra was, 'There is nothing but victory or annihilation.' His model was *Sparta*, which he invoked at every opportunity. Like Hitler, Axmann believed the sacrifice of blood was good; that the strong should survive the weak. Like Hitler, he was himself a decorated war hero. He had fought valiantly on the Eastern Front and had had his hand blown off. In its place was a wooden hand. And in these, the last bloody days of the war, Axmann was determined that the Hitler Youth would fight to the death for the Führer and the Fatherland. When so many erstwhile allies of the Führer were abandoning him, Axmann's own extraordinary loyalty and fealty was earning him Hitler's admiration. He soon became one of the few Nazis who retained Hitler's ear amid a tight circle that included Joseph Goebbels and Martin Bormann. Others, who suggested to Hitler that it was probably not a good thing to send boys into battle, were being excluded from his circle or accused of cowardice.

We were told that we were all to be inducted into the Waffen-SS. I couldn't believe it. My father would be so proud of me. We were asked to turn in our Voksssturm pay-books for new Waffen-SS ones. But I wanted to hang on to mine as it contained official entries of my decorations: the Iron Cross II and the Black Wound Badge. I think it also listed the dates, places and types of the war injuries I had suffered on the Front and in the hospital train. They agreed and said the certifications would be transferred by the physician who would administer our physicals. I was permitted to keep both until that time. We never received a physical and, thus, we were never tattooed. (Every member of the Waffen-SS had his blood type tattooed under his armpit.)

We received some basic instruction into the ways of the Waffen-SS. We were told that the Waffen-SS attracted idealistic, intelligent and, above all, brave men. Surprising, at least to me, was the large number of those who were not from Germany but were nationals from other European countries. A long list of Waffen-SS units was reviewed in which foreigners who served voluntarily were listed, including French and English contingents. This gave us a sense of belonging to a multi-national brotherhood, sharing a common world view where we jointly opposed Communism. We were also shown photographs and one of the instructors read eyewitness reports about cruelties committed by the invading Russians on German civilians, especially women. Thus we were incited to fight with extreme determination against the approaching enemy.

Last but not least, we were by now convinced that Adolf Hitler's greatness was unmatched in German history, that a sacred trust existed between him and those of us who were chosen to serve in the elite Waffen-SS. Our commander-in-chief had the right to continually demand from us the utmost fighting spirit. Victory was assured if we followed our sacred oath to our Führer to obey him and, if necessary, to die for him. There were no question-and-answer periods and the only explanation offered for the retreat of the German forces was that all of our allies, except Japan, had failed in decisive battles and didn't match up to our troops militarily. The tide would turn soon, we were assured. The Führer had learned that he could depend only on his own troops: tough, battle-tried and courageous – with the Waffen-SS leading the way. And now we belonged to the Waffen-SS!

Then, another stroke of fate. Unexpectedly, our unit was visited by Axmann. My Iron Cross ribbon caught Axmann's attention. Then with his right, wooden hand, he pointed to my wounded badge. 'So you are back for action?'

'Yes indeed,' I blurted out enthusiastically.

Axmann lingered a while. He was obviously toying with an idea in his mind. He asked me about my combat experience. When I told him I had been a runner his eyebrows raised sharply. 'The Führer was a runner in the Great War!'

'Yes, I know,' I replied.

Without any further hesitation he said: 'I want you and two of your comrades to come to Berlin, the day after tomorrow, to join a delegation to be presented to the Führer on the occasion of his birthday.'

I was speechless. I couldn't believe it. Me? Being ordered to go to Berlin to be introduced to Adolf Hitler? The man I was in awe of and had been for as long as I could think back? At this crucial time, when he was just about to turn things around, to lead us to final victory? Here I was, a 16-year-old who had been taught that Adolf Hitler was the supreme human being on this earth, and I had been invited to his birthday! Before I knew it an official correspondent of the Party's news agency was interviewing me and the others who had been selected for the privilege. Anne-Maria would read about me.

So would my mother, sisters, and brothers. So would my friends and classmates, those who were still alive. But most of all so would my father. As Axmann had reminded me, Hitler, in the First World War, had been a regimental staff runner. Now I, a runner in the Second World War, would meet the once unknown soldier who had become Germany's leader.

Thanks to Axmann I was heading in the opposite direction, and glad of it. But the journey into Berlin was not to be a reassuring one. We were sent on our way in an army bus, and we quickly ran into the sea of refugees and retreating soldiers trying to get as far away from the Russian line as possible. When we eventually entered the capital through the suburbs the full catastrophe of what had befallen Germany was soon apparent to even our young, blinkered eyes. Bomb craters pockmarked the roads and whole avenues of houses lay in ruins. Clouds of pale smoke drifted across the sky. Some indefatigable souls had daubed heroic slogans on the sides of their homes: 'Our walls may break but never our hearts.' But the flow of retreating soldiers and civilian refugees told a different story. I had never seen such misery etched on so many faces, their features covered in dirt and grime, many with blood-soiled bandages wrapped around their heads or limbs. It was like a diabolical parody of a carnival procession with people slogging their way though the mud, many of them pulling handcarts and prams loaded with the pathetic remnants of their ruined lives. Kettles, pans, battered old suitcases: anything they could rescue from the ruins of their homes. What should have been a two-hour journey was turning into one that would take up most of the day.

Closer into the centre of town, the streets were strewn with trolley cars, trucks and automobiles that had been hit by bombs and shells. Some Volkssturm units were putting them to use as makeshift *Panzersperren* (tank barricades), which forced our driver to make long detours around back streets. But rubble covered every thoroughfare, all of which were pitted with deep craters, so much so that occasionally the driver could continue no further and we had to turn back and try and find another route. Burst water mains and sewage pipes spewed a lethal mixture of clean water and putrid filth, turning the potholes into cesspools. Women and children carrying buckets, pails and pitchers formed lengthy queues at the few points where clean water could be obtained. The chaos became worse towards the centre as we approached. Not one building seemed to have escaped the relentless Allied bombing campaign.

Street after street of apartment buildings had been reduced to rubble. Those that had managed to at least stay standing rose above us like ghostly spectres, their windows punched out and the sky clearly visible through their roofs. Other windows were boarded up with wooden planks. The mood inside the bus was gloomy as we sat in silence watching this forlorn picture unfold before our eyes. Finally, we arrived at the Reichsjugendführung (the headquarters of the Hitler Youth) on Kaiserdamm. Our military bus driver looked relieved to be able to wave us a friendly goodbye. 'Remember,' he shouted, 'tell the Führer that we need those miracle weapons *soon!*' There was persistent talk of all sorts of *Wunderwaffen* (miracle weapons) that Nazi scientists were supposedly working on. The nature of these devices was never discussed. But the implication was that Germany was only days away from unleashing a terrifying new force that would change the course of the war.

The day after my arrival in Berlin, Axmann took me and others of the Hitler Youth delegation to a large gathering of Hitler Youth in the city's Reichssportsfeld. Axmann had created the Hitler Youth Division and was training them at the nearby Reichssportsfeld in the use of Panzerfaust. I had come to see groups of ten-year-old boys and girls being inducted in the lower echelons of the organisation, the Jungvolk and Jungmädel. It reminded me of my own induction in Breslau six years ago. The sight of them brought back happy memories. It made me feel like a veteran. Axmann rose to speak. He told the gathering that they were Germany's future. 'There is only victory or annihilation!' he said with great emphasis as if a commander addressing his troops. His voice carried very well. He wanted them to show boundless love for their Fatherland and intense, limitless hate for the enemy. He urged them to resist the enemy's advance fanatically, thereby demonstrating unshakeable loyalty to and love for the Führer. It was a very moving speech, to me at least, and in the past it would have produced uproarious applause. But when Axmann finished, there was only a faint ripple. Afterwards the Hitler Youth's own chamber orchestra performed. Axmann and his staff left us. We went back to our lodgings. Later, I went to the Reich Radio station.

It was traditional on Hitler's birthday for Nazi Party chiefs to congratulate their Führer the moment midnight struck. It was a great competition to see who could get there first. Usually Hitler's closest entourage lined up outside his door. And senior Party officials like Goebbels issued radio addresses. On that particular occasion the Propaganda Minister's birthday address was a typical product of his black heart.

It should go down in infamy as a testimony to the deluded fanaticism that was the hallmark of the Third Reich's mythmaker-in-chief and his fantasist of a Führer. Exhorting Berliners to fight until the very end and put their faith in Hitler's 'lucky star', Goebbels railed against the enemy 'foaming at the mouth, international Jewry, which does not want peace because their diabolical aim is to see the world destroyed'. Goebbels urged the German people not to 'give a gleefully watching world the satisfaction of witnessing the spectacle of belly-crawling submission, but proudly to unfurl the swastika in the face of the enemy'.

∽ CHAPTER FIVE ∽

Happy Birthday, Führer

FRIDAY, 20 APRIL 1945. ADOLF HITLER'S birthday. Birthdays are treated as an important milestone in Germany. The German people have always celebrated them in an extravagant way. Hitler was no exception. The Nazi Party had turned his birthday into a day of national celebration, a day to give thanks and praise to the man who was destined to make Germany great again. On this, his 56th birthday, we had been told to be ready to greet Hitler at noon. That morning we had breakfasted on fried herring from a can and freshly boiled potatoes, a rare treat in ration-starved Germany. We were all excited about our meeting with the Führer. But the time was put back repeatedly and it was almost evening before we were taken to the Chancellery. I later discovered that he had been up all night receiving dispatches that were bringing the full catastrophic collapse of the military situation home to him.

At about 5 p.m. we were taken to the Old Reich Chancellery and passed through the Foreign Ministry to the garden behind. The garden had obviously once been a grand affair. But today whatever green lawns there may have been once had disappeared under hundreds of craters made by British and American bombs. The day was cloudy and overcast. There was none of the thick, black and yellow smoke in the skies that would very soon become a permanent feature of the city, although one could smell the burnt ash all around before the Führer arrived with his entourage. I remember distinctly some civilians at work, cleaning up rubble from the latest bombing raid that morning. They were definitely *Fremdarbeiter* (foreign workers), which I thought odd because they must surely have posed a danger to the Führer. I later discovered that there was very little security and anyone with a rifle and a telescopic lens could have killed him from one of the buildings in the neighbourhood.

We were one of three delegations of highly decorated Hitler Youth, SS and Volkssturm who had been hand-picked to be presented to the Führer. There were nine of us Hitler Youth. To the right of us there was the Frundsberg delegation of Waffen-SS. The Frundsberg group had been chosen for their commander's refusal to give in to the Red Army advance to the south-east of Berlin. To the left were around 12 representatives from the Kurland army group, which was holding out on the eastern shore of the Baltic Sea entirely encircled by the Russians. Hitler had invited representatives of the group to be there that day because of Kurland's heroic refusal to surrender. I was told that Hitler had also wanted a delegation from Fortress Breslau but it had not been possible to fly anyone out of my city.

There were about 25 of us in all. There were lots of Nazi Party officials milling around, SS officers and some Wehrmacht. I scanned their faces, hoping to recognise some of them, but none were familiar. A Party official was preparing to record the whole affair with a newsreel camera.

In these somewhat depressing circumstances, there was no trace of the pomp and grandeur with which Hitler had celebrated his birthdays in the past. But there was an air of surreal calmness among the Nazi Party officials who had brought us to the garden and who were now making preparations for the Führer's arrival. None of those present seemed to acknowledge the catastrophic military situation Germany faced. The event had the air of a visit to a terminally ill patient where the victim and the well-wishers skirt delicately around the sad reason for their presence. There was more talk of Wunderwaffen and of a huge counter-attack that would throw the Russians all the way back to Moscow. I could hear others talk about rumours that the British and Americans were falling out with the Russians and would form with us an anti-Bolshevik alliance.

Eventually Hitler appeared surrounded by his most senior aides. He was instantly recognisable in his short army jacket and black trousers. On his left breast pocket were pinned his Iron Cross and Nazi Party gold badge. Accompanying him were Heinrich Himmler, the Reichsführer of the SS and the second most powerful man in Germany, and Joseph Goebbels. The Propaganda Minister was probably the most visible of all the Nazi leaders after Hitler. As *Gauleiter* (governor) of Berlin he visited the sites of bomb destruction almost every day. In contrast, Hitler rarely strayed out of the Chancellery and Berliners were probably unaware of the fact that Hitler was in their city at this stage of the war. I was curious to have a close look at Goebbels, whose voice I had heard so many times on the wireless, and who was my father's ultimate boss. As the mythmaker-in-chief of the Nazi Party, Goebbels had orchestrated the cult of Hitler as the saviour of Germany through skilful stage management and manipulation. His oratory was brilliant and he was constantly making speeches exhorting the German people in their struggle against Bolshevism and international Jewry. But by the end of my days in Berlin, I would have seen through the empty words of Joseph Goebbels and they would no longer exert any power over my young mind.

In the crowd around Hitler there were some of the most prominent military commanders, including Field Marshal Wilhelm Keitel and General Alfred Jodl. Present also were General Hans Krebs, the Army Chief of Staff, and General Wilhelm Burgdorf, although I did not know what any of them looked like then. I was not familiar with many of these faces at that moment, though all of them would play a key role in the drama that was to unfold. In the last days of his Reich Hitler had come to rely on those of his generals who would give him the answers he wanted. Closest to him was Field Marshal Keitel, who would be at his side until, almost, the very end. Keitel had had a favourite spot in the Führer's affections ever since the assassination plot of the previous year. In the mayhem and confusion that was to follow the explosion, Hitler had stumbled into the arms of Keitel. From then onwards the Führer regarded the Field Marshal as some sort of lucky totem. That Keitel was regarded as an obsequious fool by many other army generals had not tarnished Hitler's judgement. Keitel told the Führer what he wanted to hear.

Hitler's two adjutants were by his side. They both impressed me as being proficient military figures. Julius Schaub was an SS *Obergruppenführer* (Lieutenant General), the senior adjutant and an old guard servant of the Führer. Otto Günsche was a *Sturmbannführer* (Major) and the junior adjutant. I would come to have more contact with the latter in the future. Günsche was taller than any of the others and had a distinct military bearing. I remember he had many medals on his chest, including one of the Hitler Youth. Later, in the bunker, he would recognise me as one of the boys who had been introduced to the Führer on his birthday, and always give me words of encouragement.

This was quite the opposite to Reichsleiter Martin Bormann, who was also hovering by the Führer's side. Bormann was head of the Party Chancellery, Hitler's private secretary and Chief of Protocol. He was one of the most important people in the government. As the keeper of Hitler's appointments diary, he was essentially the gatekeeper of the Führer's office. As I was to find out, Bormann used his control of Hitler's private office to gain unprecedented influence over the Führer. Even the most senior Party officials and military commanders discovered that they could not get to Hitler without first going through Bormann.

The son of a Prussian sergeant-major, he had dropped out of school and as a member of a notorious rightist group in Mecklenburg was linked to several murders. In 1924 he had been sentenced to one year's imprisonment as the accomplice in the brutal vengeance murder of his former elementary school teacher, who had allegedly betrayed a proto-Nazi activist to the French occupation authorities in the Ruhr.

After his release he joined the Nazi Party and began his imperceptible rise to the centre of power. Through a succession of anodyne posts he rose eventually to become Party Reichsleiter and the right-hand man to Rudolf Hess when he became Deputy Führer. After Hess flew to Britain on his ill-conceived mission in 1941, Bormann stepped into his shoes as head of the Party Chancellery. But he not only controlled the Party. He even controlled Hitler's personal finances, buying the Berghof at Berchtesgaden, and running the complex of properties occupied there by senior Nazis such as the Speer family, the Himmlers and the Goebbels. Bormann was responsible for the construction and running of the vast underground Alpine Redoubt there. In these, the dying days of the Hitler regime, Bormann would rise to become second only in importance to Adolf Hitler himself.

Bormann came across as a crude and vulgar man who lacked any sort of grace or appreciation of culture. There was nothing romantic or heroic about him. Short and squat, he had the banal features of the anonymous bureaucrat that he was. He was thought of as little more than a glorified secretary by Hitler's more elevated generals and Party apparatchiks. But it was his apparent insignificance and coarseness that made his enemies underestimate him. Whatever else he was, he was diligent and efficient and he used these skills to make himself indispensable to his master.

I might have been unusual in Germany at that time for knowing who Bormann was. He was not a well-known figure to the public at large. But my grandfather was friends with his wife's side of the family and so there had been a great deal of talk about the Bormanns amongst the Lehmann family. My grandfather had always told me that Bormann was something of a 'grey eminence' at the heart of Hitler's Nazi machine. That was meant as an insult. Had he said 'brown eminence' that would have been high praise indeed. But 'grey' had Machiavellian insinuations. He was the Rasputin of the Reich Chancellery. Another term people used for the likes of Bormann was '*Goldfasan*' (golden pheasant). These were the senior Nazis who dealt in death but were too cowardly to face it themselves. Bormann had Hitler's absolute confidence. It was extraordinary the degree of influence he had and I would learn over the next few weeks how Bormann would use it ruthlessly.

It was a sensational experience for me, a 16-year-old Hitler Youth, getting glimpses of these figures that had played such an important role in the creation of the new Germany. I could not believe that I was being granted such a grandstand on history. I believed I was privileged to be in these people's presence and that I too was part of the next act in the glorious history of the Third Reich. I was indeed part of the next act – but it was not a glorious one. And in retrospect, on that April day in 1945 in the garden of the Chancellery, I was witnessing probably the last gathering of some of the most notorious murderers, psychopaths and plain fantasists who had done so much to bring Germany to her knees.

Hitler was slowly working his way along the line towards me. We had strict instructions to look directly ahead of us and so I stood motionless with my head held high and chest jutted out. But as Hitler approached I swivelled my eyes as much as I dared to see what I could. And what I saw gave me a jolt. He looked like an old man. Both my grandfathers were in better shape than he was and they were in their 70s. When I had seen him in Breslau, seven years earlier, he had radiated power, strength and energy. When he had spoken then, he had mesmerised the entire audience with his hypnotic charisma. Now, he appeared to have shrunk, his head set deeper between his shoulders. His voice was a whisper. The pallor of his skin was a deathly white. His steps appeared uncoordinated as if he were drunk and might trip himself up. His entire body trembled, even his head. But most obvious was the shaking of his arm and hand, which he tried to control by holding on to his coat-flap in the back.

He was wearing a field-grey uniform jacket with his golden party emblem, the Iron Cross and below it the Black Wounded Badge which, of course, he won when he was a courier in the First World War. He was looking rather dapper despite his obvious poor health.

Out of the corner of my eye I could see his hands shaking. Then he reached me. Once more I could not believe my eyes that this withered old man in front of me was the visionary leader who had led our nation to greatness. As he looked me in the eye I was praying that my own eyes were not registering their profound shock. If Axmann was in the least bit disconcerted by the Führer's appearance he did not show it. Raising his left arm in the Nazi salute, and looking Hitler straight in the eyes, he spoke with great intensity, staccato-style: 'My Führer! In the name of Germany's youth I congratulate you on your birthday. I am proud once again to introduce you to the young fighters whose courage and valour is typical of the readiness for action of the Hitler Youth. They stand the test on the home front with an iron will to achieve the final victory.'

And he meant it. The leader of the Hitler Youth would promise Hitler time and time again that 'his boys' would fight to the bitter end. But it would not be just boys who died in the bitter battle for Berlin and Germany. Many teenage girls were killed in the battle too, sacrificing their young lives while the wretched golden pheasants who were responsible for their plight ran as fast as they could from the heat of conflict – the bloodthirsty conflict that they had done so much to bring about. No wonder the Führer was grateful to Axmann. Over the next few days my new mentor would become part of the Führer's inner circle which remained utterly loyal to the end, while those who questioned whether boys should be sent into battle were actually threatened with execution for cowardice. It is a source of amazement to me now to think that I willingly colluded with this madness. But on that April day it was a source of brimming pride.

'Thanks, thanks, Axmann,' Hitler replied. 'If in battle only all were as brave as these boys.' By now Axmann had lowered his arm. Hitler came towards me. I thought that Axmann would introduce me but he said nothing, which was a little disappointing. Hitler grabbed my upper left arm with his right hand and held on to the sleeve a second or two. We had each been told to tell him our name, what Hitler Youth unit we belonged to and where we participated in combat.

The moment had come. I trembled. Hitler quivered involuntarily. It affected his entire body. I could feel it when he let go of my arm to shake my hand, actually enclosing my outstretched right hand in both of his. He came very close. Suddenly, his eyes seemed to shine with a lambent, captivating brilliance.

Despite the temporary brightness of his eyes, they were also surrounded by moisture as if through tears. Black bags under them added to the effect caused by his wrinkled, ashen face. I stammered my name. Before I could continue, he started to query me using the familiar 'Du' ('you') instead of the formal 'Sie'. I was flattered.

'Where did you fight?' was his first question, spoken rather softly.

'In Silesia, southeast of Breslau, my Führer,' I replied.

He wanted to know the exact location. As I described it, my nervousness subsided. 'And you were brave and earned the Iron Cross?'

'I was wounded, pulled other wounded into a snow-ravine and kept on fighting.'

Before I could finish, he asked the next question. 'What was your injury?'

I was not prepared for this question. Nor was I sure what words to use to answer it. In the hospital my room-mates had often remarked that I had been shot in the arse and for a split second it crossed my mind that the Führer might appreciate this teasing remark. I thought better of it.

'I was shot through my upper thigh, my Führer!'

He patted me once more on my upper left arm, but looked at Axmann who was still standing next to me and said: 'Moreover, a brave boy!' I would rather have heard him say 'soldier' instead of 'boy'. But it was clear that in Hitler's eyes, I, too, was looked upon as one of Axmann's boys.

Hitler was 56 years old and his Third Reich was just 12. Little did I realise that overcast morning nearly 60 years ago that neither of these formidable creations that had dominated my life would survive to celebrate another anniversary. As I looked at Hitler I reflected how proud my father would have been at the sight of his 16-year-old son being presented to the Führer.

After Hitler had finished shaking hands with the delegations, he stepped forward to address us. Now his voice was strong and his words were short and poignant. Each of us was captivated and listened intently to every single word he uttered.

> On all fronts heavy fighting is taking place. Here in Berlin we are facing the great, decisive battle. Germany's destiny will be decided by the performance of the German soldier: his exemplary steadfastness and his unbending will to fight. You are witnesses to the fact that with dogged resistance even an enemy that outnumbers us can be repelled.
>
> Our belief that we will win the battle for Berlin has to remain unbroken. The situation can be compared with that of a patient believed to have reached the end. Yet, he does not have to die. He can be saved with a new medication, discovered just in time to save him, which is now being produced. We just have to be determined to hold out until this medication can be applied, to achieve final victory. That is what counts, to keep on fighting with an iron will!

With that, he attempted a salute, but the effect was more like a dolphin's waggling of its damaged flipper. 'Heil Euch!'

What happened next was extraordinary. The Führer's salutation remained unanswered. There was no response: absolutely none. Although we had been briefed beforehand to respond to Hitler's parting salute with 'Heil, mein Führer!' no one replied: no one from our delegation; no one from the Frundsberg delegation; no one from the Kurland delegation; no one from his entourage; no one at all.

What had shocked us? Hitler's appearance, no doubt. His condition appeared to be that of a dying man. Perhaps some of us were puzzled by his reference to the miracle weapons and the dying patient. But if any of those in attendance felt deceived by what he said, I was not among them. For me, he had just reinforced what I believed and wanted to believe.

After the war I talked to Axmann at great length about those dark days. He claimed to me that he had presented us to Hitler to show just how weary and beaten we were, to convince him that the struggle was over and it would be futile to sacrifice our young lives. That was not the impression I had at the time. Then it was crystal clear to me that Axmann wanted to ingratiate himself with the Führer by demonstrating how loyal and brave the Hitler Youth were.

Whether or not Hitler was pleased to see us, I couldn't tell. Watching him, it appeared that the whole reception was a painful experience for him. Axmann seemed to be taken in by Hitler just as much as we were. Later, as Berlin was crashing around us, Axmann would maintain, ridiculously, that the miracle weapons existed but couldn't be used in Berlin since they would kill soldiers on both sides. As it turned out, the casualties on both sides were enormous with just the conventional weapons. The Russian superiority, in numbers alone, caused catastrophic death statistics as the battle went on.

Armageddon was upon us. That *we* were the forces of evil was a thought that never entered my mind. It was only later that I realised how the nation's so-called 'first soldier' (Hitler) had lied flagrantly to his very 'last soldiers' that the scale of the deception dawned upon me. The miracle medication and the miracle weapons did not exist. But Hitler was trapped in his own lie. Before I realised that, though, I was determined to contribute all I could, physically and mentally, to defend the leader and the Fatherland.

At that moment Hitler was still able to impose his will on those under his command, particularly the very young. His carefully crafted image of almost divine 'greatness' had permeated every facet of every medium of our lives. My mind had not been exposed to any other channel of communication. There were no others I had access to. None! This idol, who would turn out to be a monumental liar and mass-murderer, was still, on 20 April 1945, able to produce within me a great sense of hope and renewed dedication to fight on.

After Adolf Hitler had finished shaking hands and spoken to all of us, Heinrich Himmler came up to greet the Frundsberg delegation. I overheard some of the words spoken between him and the delegate next to me. Himmler told him how he had assured the Führer that the Waffen-SS would always fight heroically and be prepared to make the necessary sacrifices.

'*Jawohl, Reichsführer!*' he replied.

Then Himmler stepped in front of our delegation. He stretched out his hand and used the formal 'Sie' in addressing me. He told me that I would become a member of the Waffen-SS soon. When I told him I already was a member of the Waffen-SS, he seemed surprised. '*Was? Sind Sie nicht ein Hitlerjunge im Volkssturm?*' ('What? Aren't you a Hitler Youth in the Volkssturm?')

I told him I had been when I was awarded the Iron Cross, but in Fürstenwalde we became part of the Waffen-SS.

'Why then did you not appear here in a Waffen-SS uniform?'

Because, I told him, we were only issued with Hitler Youth uniforms at the Reich Youth headquarters.

'This I will take up with Axmann,' he said.

There was some internecine rivalry between the two. But by that stage in the war, Axmann's star was on the rise and Himmler's was on the wane. The latter had failed miserably as a military commander. Hitler had replaced him as commander of the army group Vistula, with Colonel-General Gothard Henrici. What Hitler didn't realise was that Henrici had little appetite for defending Berlin. Like many of Hitler's military commanders, Henrici was more concerned now with avoiding bloodshed among his own troops and civilians rather than achieving mythical military glory.

Himmler might have been the second most powerful man in the nation, but on this day he looked almost feminine with shiny, soft skin. His appearance was not soldierly or even athletic. And we boys couldn't help commenting later that neither he nor Bormann had any military medals, only Nazi Party badges. Had I not known who he was, I would have thought him effeminate, homosexual even. That's the impression he made. One of my comrades called him 'Reichsführer Nivea Face Cream'. But his countenance and demeanour on this day were diametrically opposite to Hitler's. His body language reflected health and buoyancy, arrogance even. Perhaps the fact that he was involved in secret peace negotiations with the Allies was the reason for his calmness and optimism.

By 20 April, Himmler had met twice with Count Folke Bernadotte, the representative of the Swedish Red Cross. Himmler's plan was to succeed Hitler as the Führer of a new Reich and open peace negotiations with the Western Allies. Bernadotte was the conduit. Had Hitler had the slightest inklings of these talks he would have had Himmler swinging from a noose without further ado. But Himmler was confident the Führer would no longer be around to stand in the way of his ambitions. Never one to make any major move without first consulting his astrologers, Himmler had been presented with remarkably prescient prophecies. The year before, his favourite astrologer had predicted that Hitler would survive a dangerous threat on 20 July. As surely as light follows dark, Hitler had survived the assassination plot. The astrologer had predicted that the Führer would be ill in November and he had been. Now the astrologer was telling Himmler that Hitler would not live beyond 8 May. Himmler was biding his time confidently. That evening he would drive the 60 kilometres north-east of Berlin to his castle at Ziethen and continue the negotiations with the Allies.

After a while Hitler's entire entourage melted into a concrete pillbox with a small tower that looked rather ungainly amid the imposing grandeur of the Chancellery buildings. I did not know then that it was the emergency entrance to Hitler's bunker. But as Axmann's influence over the Führer grew, both of us would find ourselves spending our last days in Berlin there. Axmann disappeared with Hitler into the bunker. Henceforth Axmann would attend all of Hitler's daily briefings in recognition of the role 'his boys' were playing in the war.

Far from presenting us boys to Hitler as a ploy to make the Führer realise how exhausted and wasted we were, Axmann was actively accelerating the involvement of Hitler Youth in a futile fight. Two days earlier he had paid an unsolicited visit to General Helmuth Weidling in the cellar of his headquarters to the east of Berlin. Weidling was commander of the 56th Panzer Corps attached to General Theodor Busse's Ninth Army which was desperately fighting to shore up the defences to the southeast of Berlin. Such was the rate of the Russian advance Weidling had already had to relocate his headquarters twice on the day that Axmann paid him an unsolicited visit.

It was obvious the war was nearing its end, but not to Artur Axmann. He told Weidling all 'his boys' were at the general's disposal. They would prove their loyalty to the Führer and the Fatherland by fighting to the death. He cited as an example the scores of boys armed with old rifles and hand grenades scavenged from the enemy that were reinforcing Volkssturm units on the outskirts of the capital. (In fact the one weapon this army of children did possess that struck fear into the Russians was the stockpiled Panzerfaust, which could be devastating against even the mighty T-34 tanks.)

Weidling was exasperated. It was utterly futile, he protested, to send 12-year-old boys into battle, Panzerfausts or no Panzerfausts. He told Axmann the fight was already over (a remark that could have secured Weidling's prompt execution – it was an offence to be defeatist in Nazi Germany). 'You cannot sacrifice these children for a cause that is already lost,' he said. 'I will not use them and I demand that the order sending these children into battle is rescinded.' Axmann, chastened, conceded that the boys had not received enough training and he left promising to reverse the order, but he failed to recall a single one of them from the battle.

Hitler was impressed by Axmann's efforts to extend the bloodbath to Germany's youth. Henceforth, all the orders given to Hitler Youth came directly from Axmann or Hitler and bypassed the military commanders.

As for us boys in the Chancellery Garden, we were dismissed, not yet to be led to the slaughter, as some 30,000 Hitler Youth were in the last four months of the battle. Instead we were taken back to our comfortable lodgings west of the city near the aerodrome at Gatow. I was elated. Elated because I had met my Führer face to face. Elated because I had made an appearance on the stage of world history, albeit in a brief and minor role. Elated because it sounded like the big counter-offensive was just about to begin. I don't think any of us present that day had any idea that our perspective of this memorable event would soon change drastically.

In the evening Axmann asked me for a private word. I wondered if I had done something wrong. But first he inquired about the impression the Führer had made on me. I was frank. I told him how surprised I had been at his looking so old.

'But isn't it amazing what strength of will he still radiates, how clearly he thinks, and how much on target his decisions are?' he responded. 'Every detail he takes into consideration. Nothing escapes him.'

To me it had seemed that the Führer had been in a world of his own. Perhaps his thoughts were on the new miracle weapons. I said nothing.

'Weren't you impressed by the Führer's speech?' continued Axmann.

'Yes, I was!' I replied obediently but I had really not been sure what to think.

'So was I,' he said enthusiastically.

Then Axmann wanted to know if I had an explanation why today no one responded to Hitler's parting salute.

'I froze. Perhaps the others did, too.'

Axmann said that at the presentation of Hitler Youth a month earlier, the boys had replied with a fervent: 'Heil, mein Führer!'

I asked what the Führer had said to them on that occasion.

'Basically the same as he said today,' said Axmann.

He shook his head and then changed the subject. Could I drive a motorcycle? (I could). Did I know my way around Berlin? (I didn't). Then he pointed an inquiring finger at my left hand and the two rings I was wearing.

'My mother's and my girlfriend's,' I explained.

I had not felt comfortable to elaborate further, but he was clearly curious to know who my girlfriend was.

'A Red Cross nurse at the military hospital in Hof where I recovered from my wounds.'

'In wartime, that's what happens,' he replied, vaguely.

At the end of the meeting Axmann told me I would be his courier, working as part of the fighting group, Kampfgruppe Axmann, that he had decided to establish. The job would entail running messages to some 20 Hitler Youth fighting groups that had been assigned to defend the city, mainly guarding bridges and key roads. I couldn't believe that I had been chosen for such an illustrious posting. Axmann, surrounded by so many members of his staff and by Hitler Youth Leaders with whom he was acquainted, had selected me to be one of his couriers. I was from Breslau and didn't know the city. Why had he not chosen someone who was from Berlin? I asked myself: why? It didn't even cross my mind at all that I might end up having to deliver some of the Führer's last dispatches. I wrote to Anne-Maria giving her the news. Before signing off I hesitated. Could I put on paper that I loved her? I decided I could, and when I added 'with love' at the end I experienced a rush of elation. Then I went to bed and fell asleep straight away.

CHAPTER SIX

Hitler and His Women

THAT FATEFUL FRIDAY HAD BEEN A day of comings and goings in the Reich Chancellery. But many of the Nazi Party officials and military commanders who had arrived in Berlin that morning had not come to wish the Führer happy birthday as much as to pay their last respects. Few of the Nazi leaders who had so exhorted the German people to fight to the death were prepared to sacrifice their own lives on the funeral pyre that Berlin was soon to become. As Hitler disappeared down into the depths of his bunker, there was a quiet communal gasp of relief among many of the inhabitants of the Reich Chancellery. Only minutes later, the Chancellery courtyard witnessed chaotic scenes of confusion as servants and orderlies loaded a fleet of cars and trucks with suitcases and crates ready to make the headlong rush out of Berlin and to safety. Berlin was almost completely encircled and there was only one road left open, to Bavaria in the south. It was only a matter of hours before the Russians took it.

Hitler had been urged to take this route that very morning. Or to fly south to the Berghof, his Alpine retreat in Berchtesgaden. The Berghof was at the centre of the Nazis' National Redoubt, a vast area of wooded mountains and lakeland south of Munich and stretching into Austria, some 30,000 square kilometres in size. It was criss-crossed with military bases, radar stations, arms, ammunition and oil dumps. Many of Hitler's senior advisers clung on to the hope that the National Redoubt would withstand the Allied onslaught and that they might find sanctuary there. (In fact, one reason the Western Allies did not launch a full-frontal attack on Berlin was that *their* military planners thought the last battle would be fought there too.) Bormann, Himmler, Göring and Speer all had homes in Berchtesgaden within the orbit of the Berghof. All were equipped with bunkers. On Hitler's orders Bormann had overseen the construction of a vast underground bunker complex under the Obersalzberg.

It had already been planned that Hitler would direct the war effort from this vast underground complex. His key staff had been transferred there ten days previously. But over the past few days Hitler had stubbornly refused to make a decision, at times claiming he would leave Berlin at the very last minute, at other times convincing himself that the Russians were about to be repelled eastwards by a masterful stroke of his own military genius.

Right until the very end, Hitler would display this curious schizophrenic state of mind. Simultaneously, he would wail that 'all is lost' and talk about how he would take his own life. Shortly afterwards he would take an aide aside and discuss his plans to build a spectacular new city at the Austrian town of Linz, or claim that the massive German counter-attack was about to come true. (Many of Hitler's allies blamed his sudden changes of mood on the bizarre and perhaps lethal cocktail of tranquillisers and booster pills prescribed for him by Dr Morell that seemed to rob the Führer of control over his behaviour.)

But in the last ten days the military situation had deteriorated so catastrophically that it was now obvious to Hitler that the war could not possibly be won. Germany was facing certain defeat. The only question that had been uppermost in his mind for the last few days was how he should end his life: whether he should run away and die in what Speer had memorably called 'the weekend bungalow', or stay in Berlin and die a death in the inferno that the Reich capital was about to become. He had made his decision. That morning he indicated that he would not be going to Bavaria. But if anyone else wanted to go, they were welcome to. Over the next few days several planes bearing Hitler's personal staff would leave Berlin for Berchtesgaden.

But on Hitler's birthday Hermann Göring was the first to flee Berlin. The air Reich Marshal had turned up that morning to see Hitler for once without his customary silver-grey uniform with gold epaulettes. Instead he wore the plain olive green uniform of a field commander (like an American field commander, as one of Hitler's aides sniffed). Göring had sent his wife Emmy and daughter Edda to the safety of Berchtesgaden months ago. And that morning he had finally bidden farewell to his country estate of Karinhall on the Schorfheide, north-east of Berlin. The many rooms of the palatial mansion were decorated with fabulous works of art, several of them looted from Jews and countries overrun by the Nazis. But that morning Göring had awoken to find the Russians had crossed the Oder, only 8 kilometres away. Awaiting this very moment, his art treasures had already been crated up, ready for evacuation. Now they were loaded onto a fleet of 24 lorries and dispatched to Bavaria.

As they left, Göring personally detonated the mansion to oblivion with thousands of kilograms of high explosives. 'It's the kind of thing a man has to do once in a lifetime,' the jocular Luftwaffe chief is said to have joked. He wasn't going to give Stalin the satisfaction of seeing his muddy Red Army desecrating Hermann Göring's beloved home. As Göring said happy birthday to Hitler in Berlin, the fleet of lorries with their precious treasures were waiting on the outskirts of the city for him to join them and make the journey south. Göring would never see Hitler again. The air Reich Marshal left behind him two of his senior officers to take the wrath of the Führer. From now on his chief of staff General Karl Koller, a bumbling, indecisive man, was to be the recipient of much of the Führer's invective aimed at the Luftwaffe. General Eckard Christian was a former Luftwaffe ace and husband of one of Hitler's secretaries, Gerda Christian.

Albert Speer, Hitler's favourite architect and Armaments Minister, had also visited Hitler on his birthday. The relationship between Speer and Hitler went back many years. Hitler was a father figure to Speer, and Speer had a special part in the heart of the Führer, who indulged him as if he were the son he had never had. Speer never lost his affection for the man who had been responsible for his remarkable rise. But in recent months he had come to believe his mentor's actions were taking Germany down into the depths of a damnation that was not necessary. Hitler had ordered a 'scorched earth' policy, dozens of bridges were to be destroyed and the last vestiges of German industry were to be obliterated rather than fall into enemy hands. Speer could not countenance such bloody-minded nihilism, which could only serve to hurt the German people who had suffered already. For the past few months, Speer had been touring Germany, begging district leaders not to execute the policy.

Speer had also already taken the precaution of secretly moving his family away from his own house at Berchtesgaden. He had six children and they were precious to him. He didn't want their lives sacrificed to a cause that had long lost any sense of sanity. They were now in the relative safety of the Baltic in the north, still under the firm control of German armies. That afternoon after seeing the Führer, Speer melted way. He did not say a proper goodbye, which was to weigh on his conscience. After he left the Chancellery he would drive to his own new quarters 80 miles north-west of Berlin at Bad Wilsnack. That too was a comfortable distance from Berlin, and comfortably closer to the American and British lines than the Russian ones.

Speer, like Heinrich Himmler, expected the Führer to die shortly. But unlike Himmler, he had mixed feelings. Speer, like Himmler, was actively betraying the Führer. But in Speer's case he was doing very little to keep it a secret. He knew the details of his visits to local district leaders would sooner or later find their way back to Hitler. And he was right. Martin Bormann was, very helpfully, keeping the Führer informed of them, and of the Speer family's removal from Berchtesgaden to the Baltic.

In Berlin the decision had already been taken to divide the German forces into two commands should the Allied advance split the country in two, which it appeared to be doing. The Grand Admiral of the Navy, Karl Dönitz, would be commander-in-chief of the northern part. Dönitz was a convinced Nazi and could be trusted to prosecute the war to the bitter end, as Hitler wished. The Northern Command was to be based at Plön in Schleswig-Holstein. Field Marshal Albert Kesselring was to take responsibility for the military command of the south. At the conference in the Führerbunker that morning of his birthday, Hitler confirmed Dönitz in his role, but not Kesselring. Perhaps the Führer was still entertaining thoughts of removing his headquarters to the south and assuming control himself. Or perhaps he suspected Kesselring was not to be trusted to continue the war to the bloody end. If so, he was right. At that very moment Kesselring's own thoughts were turning to the possibility of surrendering to the Allies.

That afternoon, as was his habit, Hitler entertained his secretaries to tea and cakes in his private sitting-room in the bunker. Hitler had always been fond of the company of women, and the younger and prettier the women the better. In this he was carrying on a family tradition. His father Alois had had a string of relationships with girls very much younger than himself. They were easy to impress and even easier to dominate. In Hitler's circles women were never treated as equals. He liked to flatter his women in a patronising, old Bavarian, kind of way. He would refer to them as 'my child' or 'my dear' and kiss them grandiloquently on their hands. He occasionally flirted with them, but not in anything other than a very superficial way. He had a mildly flirtatious relationship with Christa Schroeder, who was one of his longest-serving secretaries. Schroeder always called him 'AH' or '*der Chef*' (the boss). In 1938 when she was ill in hospital, he visited her with flowers. 'People are going to think that I am visiting a secret lover!' he said, and she admitted to a 'room's length' crush on the boss – but no more than that. At 30 years of age Schroeder was one of his older secretaries in the Führerbunker. The oldest was Johanna Wolf, who had worked for him since 1924. She was now in her mid-30s. Hitler particularly liked Wolf because his own nickname among his closest confidants was 'Wolf'. He would call her 'Wolfie' with a brotherly affection.

The youngest secretaries were Gertud (Traudl) Junge and Gerda

Christian. Junge was a slim blonde of 25. On that Friday afternoon she was shocked to hear the Führer admit for the first time that he didn't think victory was possible. She had up until then accepted everything he had said about miracle weapons and massive counter-attacks against the Soviets. Now he was talking as if it was all over and their lives were at an end. But her life was just beginning. As she sipped her tea that afternoon Junge silently vowed that she would survive whatever was to come.

Traudl Junge had become one of his secretaries in 1942 when she applied to join the Chancellery secretarial pool and was surprised to find herself short-listed to work in the Führer's office. She had served with Hitler in his East Prussian headquarters at Rastenburg. She had been married to his aide-de-camp Hans Junge, who had been killed in action against the 1944 Normandy landings. Hitler had liked Hans Junge and was so upset by his death that he broke the news to her personally. It was one of the rare occasions the Führer had been affected by the death of someone he knew.

Hitler would call Traudl 'child', and being the most junior of his secretaries, all the most menial tasks would be delegated to her. It was Junge who would write Hitler's last political will and testament in his dying days, sitting up until 4 a.m. while everyone else enjoyed cakes and champagne. He was, she later said, 'a captivating figure', who liked nothing better than playing with his dog Blondi. 'Hitler's greatest pleasure was when Blondi would jump a few centimetres higher than the last time, and he would say that going out with his dog was the most relaxing thing he could do,' she recalled after the war. Junge was later to confess that perhaps she had been a little too much in awe of the Führer. 'I was fascinated by Adolf Hitler,' she said. 'He was a pleasant boss and a fatherly friend. I deliberately ignored all the warning voices inside me and enjoyed the time by his side almost to the bitter end. It wasn't what he said, but the way he said things and how he did things.'

Gerda Christian was the other young secretary. Like Junge she was very pretty. Aged about 30, Christian was the centre of a curious love triangle within Hitler's inner circle. She had once been engaged to Hitler's Berlin chauffeur and transport manager the SS Colonel Erich Kempka. Kempka would also spend the last days of the war in the Chancellery complex attending to Hitler, and as the custodian of the fuel depot would play a key role in Hitler's final moments. But now Gerda was married to the Luftwaffe General Eckard Christian who, as Göring's liaison officer, would attend most of Hitler's conferences in the bunker. But the former fighter ace would abandon the Führer at the last moment, while his wife stayed by Hitler's side. 'He went his way and I went mine,' she said after the war, dismissing her husband as a 'lout'. 'I couldn't forgive that kind of desertion.' They were divorced in 1946. There was one curious thing about Hitler's secretaries. After the war, none of them would settle down with husbands. As Christian later commented: 'How could any of us have done so after having known a man like Hitler?'

Also present at the tea party was the Führer's dietician Constanze Manziarly, a small mousy woman from Innsbruck in Hitler's native Austria. Manziarly maintained the Führer's strict vegetarian diet in the small kitchens of the upper bunker. Manziarly often dined alone with the Führer. In fact, Hitler's youngest secretary Traudl Junge would later claim that his Austrian cook didn't think life was worth living without meat, and she would occasionally slip a bit of animal broth or fat into his meals. 'Mostly the Führer would notice the attempt at deception, would get very annoyed and then get tummy ache,' said Junge. 'At the end he would only let [her] cook him clear soup and mashed potato.'

The most intriguing woman present that day in Hitler's private quarters was an attractive blonde-haired young lady by the name of Eva Braun. Most Germans would have been astonished to know of her presence by Hitler's side at the time. Very few people outside the Führer's inner circle had heard of Eva Braun. A plain-speaking woman in her mid-thirties but with the demeanour of a much younger woman, Eva Braun spoke with a 'perky' Bavarian accent and could be remarkably naïve. She had first met the future Führer in 1929 when she was an assistant working for his photographer Heinrich Hoffmann. She became his mistress and *grand dame* of the Berghof two years later. But his lover had been firmly kept away from public view.

Hitler refused to allow her to be present at any diplomatic or other newsworthy occasions of all his years in office. Even at the Berghof, Hitler only allowed her out when his closest confidants were present: the Speers, the Goebbels, the Bormanns and the Himmlers. Her exclusion was partly orchestrated by Goebbels himself to perpetrate the myth of the untouchable Führer divinely destined to be Germany's saviour. But it was partly at the instigation of Hitler. It was a bizarre relationship. Perhaps he was embarrassed by her humble Bavarian roots. She was one of three sisters. He usually called her a 'friend'. He often humiliated Eva in front of others. Yet at the same time he was irritated by Magda Goebbels' open condescension of Eva Braun. Eva had tried to commit suicide twice, the first in November 1932, when she was found with a bullet in her neck. It was obviously a *cri de coeur* and possibly instigated by his apparent indifference to her. The only occasion when he ever really displayed any overt affection for her was in April 1945. They were in the bunker together and Eva Braun stated her intention to remain with Hitler and be at his side when the end came. He kissed her fully on the lips, much to the surprise and embarrassment of onlookers.

But it was the first and only time he had publicly shown his feelings for her. Heinrich Hoffmann once said that nothing about Hitler indicated he had ever had any deep feelings for Eva Braun. 'To him she was just an attractive little thing, in whom, in spite of her inconsequential and feather-brained outlook – or perhaps just because of it – he found the type of relaxation and repose he sought.' In 1943 Hitler told Speer that he would soon only have two real friends around him, Eva Braun and his pet Alsatian, Blondi.

In the early days of the Nazi Party Hitler liked nothing better than to hold forth with his cronies in his favourite Munich restaurants and beer cellars. Women were occasionally allowed along, but only as an adornment to what was essentially a male world. Hoffmann recalled that a woman guest would be allowed and, 'She could, occasionally, take a small part in the conversation, but never was she allowed to hold forth or contradict Hitler.'

Now, in the long afternoon of the Third Reich's endless defeats, the Führer rarely dined with his generals or even his closest Party officials. It was said that he had never once had a meal alone with Joseph Goebbels, the man who was responsible more than anyone else for creating the myth of the Führer. Instead he enjoyed being with his secretaries and cook (and possibly his mistress occasionally). Cynical observers have pointed out that there was one very good reason why. Hitler's table talk was so monotonous that only someone who was on his payroll would happily put up with it. His conversation usually amounted to nothing more than a dreary monologue that rarely extended beyond his pet subjects of the evils of international Jewry, the delights of fine architecture and the intricacies of racial theory. It was once commented that anyone with any intelligence could simply not put up with the Führer's conversation.

But Hitler did exert a fascination over many women in his lifetime. And the subject of his sexuality has been thoroughly exhausted. Some historians have claimed he was a repressed pedophile who channelled his homoerotic impulses into war. Many doubt that he ever had a sexual relationship with Eva Braun, or any other woman. That was disputed by the testimony of a maid at the Berchtesgaden who said that Eva Braun took medication to suppress her menstrual cycle when the Führer was going to be there. The truth is probably that nobody will ever get to the bottom of Adolf Hitler and his sexuality.

Much of the speculation was fuelled by the curious and still unexplained case of Hitler's niece, Geli Raubal. The daughter of his half-sister Angela Raubal, Geli had lived with her mother on the Obersalzberg. She was an attractive brunette with a vivacious character and a string of admirers. In 1929 Hitler summoned her to come and live with him at his Munich apartment in Prinzregentenplatz. She was 21, he was 40 and already a formidable political figure. Hitler was to have many relationships with women who were very much younger than himself, but Geli was special.

Geli was studying at a music academy in Munich but seemed to spend scant time on her studies and lots of time out on the town with her 'Uncle Alf', as she mischievously called him. He took her to the opera and the theatre; he went on drives out into the countryside with her. She was one of the few women ever allowed to take part in café discussions with him and his Nazi Party cronies. There was a great deal of speculation as to their exact relationship. One of her many admirers was one of Hitler's early bodyguards and chauffeur. One day Hitler caught Geli in a liaison with him. He flew into such a blind rage that the chauffeur was convinced his boss was going to shoot him. From then onwards Hitler insisted Geli should not go anywhere without a chaperone.

On 19 September 1931, Geli was found shot dead in his apartment, with his pistol. Hitler's political opponents had a field day. It was suggested either that he had killed her in a lover's tiff or he had arranged for her to be killed. Neither seems likely. Towards the end of her life it is true that Geli had complained that she was trying to escape his clutches: 'My uncle is a monster. No one can imagine what he demands of me.' But she did not make it clear what sort of demands he placed on her. Hitler certainly seemed obsessed by Geli, and there was talk about her body bearing the marks of beatings. But this has never been confirmed. It is unlikely Hitler killed her. He was on his way to Nuremberg when the body was found and was visibly shocked when told the news. If he had arranged for her to be killed, using his own gun in his own apartment was an odd way to go about things. The only explanation that his supporters could offer was that Geli might have been playing with his pistol and it went off accidentally. This too sounds unconvincing. After the war Geli's mother Angela said that her daughter had said she wanted to leave Hitler for a boyfriend in Linz and her uncle had forbidden her to do so. But there is no evidence that he took any actions to prevent her. The only conclusion can be that there will never be a satisfactory explanation of what really happened in the last hours of Geli Raubal's short life. The most likely theory is that she committed suicide, the only way to escape the attentions of her Uncle Alf. It would not be the first time one of Hitler's women had turned to suicide to escape his emotional dominance.

What is most interesting about the relationship is that it appears to be the one and only time Hitler was dependent on a woman. Whether it was a sexual dependence, again we will never know. But it was certainly an emotional one as illustrated by the deep depression Hitler fell into after she died. He turned her rooms in the Prinzregentenplatz apartment into a shrine. Neither before nor after did Hitler have such an emotional involvement with a woman (except possibly with his mother Klara). To his secretaries and cooks he was an indulgent employer who treated them like children and occasionally flirted with them but never in more than an entirely superficial way. To his ardent admirers, like Magda Goebbels, Hanna Reitsch and Winifred Wagner, he was a cold and distant icon who failed to return their attentions. But they were strong-willed, powerful women in their own right. They had minds of their own, and perhaps that didn't fit easily with a man who wanted his women to sit adoringly, and quietly, at his feet.

Winifred Wagner, the wife of the composer's (Richard Wagner's) son Siegfried, became entranced with Hitler. The couple became so close that the Führer seriously entertained thoughts of marrying her and creating a Hitler–Wagner dynasty. Leni Riefenstahl, the actress and film-maker, was bewitched by the Führer. The British aristocratic sisters Unity and Diana Mitford were unapologetic admirers. There was Hanna Reitsch, the leading German test pilot of the day and chief test pilot of the Luftwaffe (der Flugkapitän). Captain Reitsch loved Hitler and Nazism with an equal passion. Her heroic arrival in Berlin as the capital fell was going to be one of the more colourful episodes of the last days in the bunker.

But the woman who more than anyone else adored Adolf Hitler was the wife of his Propaganda Minister. In the typically coarse words of one of the bunker servants, the SS telephone operator Rochus Misch, one could hear Magda Goebbels' ovaries rattle whenever she was in the Führer's presence. But even if he was exaggerating and Magda Goebbels was not actually in love with Hitler, she certainly had been obsessed with him for years. But Magda's devotion to Hitler was not the blind awe of Eva Braun. She couldn't bear his conversation. 'It is always Hitler who talks,' she complained to a friend about the endless gatherings around the lunch-table at Berchtesgaden. 'He can be Führer as much as he likes but he always repeats himself and bores his guests.'

An attractive, vivacious and flirtatious woman, Magda Goebbels knew how to manipulate men. She had had a series of romantic entanglements, including one with a Jewish suitor while she was also sleeping with the Jew-baiting Joseph Goebbels. She loved the high life and adored luxury. Before she married Goebbels she caught the attention of a successful industrialist almost twice her age. She was at a Catholic boarding school when the impossibly wealthy Günther Quandt asked if he could take the teenager out with her girlfriends for tea and cakes. Soon Magda consented to marry him. She had one child by him, called Harald, of whom she was inordinately fond. In 1930, after eight years, she divorced Quandt and started dating Joseph Goebbels. It was an odd match. She was beautiful. Goebbels, with his club foot, one leg so much shorter than the other that he had to wear a built-up shoe, had a leering grinning countenance that political cartoonists found easy to mimic, turning it into something quite animal-like.

While Magda was dating Goebbels she was also romantically involved with a young Jew called Victor Arlosoroff. When Arlosoroff found out she was seeing another man he was disappointed. When he discovered the other man was the Nazi Party district leader for Berlin he was appalled. Goebbels married Magda in 1931. Hitler was a witness at their wedding. When the Nazis came to power two years later and anti-Semitism became public policy the climate very quickly became unbearable for Jews. Magda Goebbels had a stepfather called Richard Friedlander. He doted on her. He was also a Jew. When the violence against the Jews began to escalate Friedlander decided his only recourse was to appeal for help to his son-in-law at the Propaganda Ministry. When Friedlander turned up at Goebbels' office in Wilhelmplatz the minister is said to have told an aide: 'Ask this Jew Friedlander what he wants here?' In 1938 Friedlander was arrested by the Nazis. His stepdaughter did little to help him. He died in Buchenwald in 1939.

The Goebbels family became an important symbol of family life in the Third Reich. Since Hitler had no wife or offspring of his own, Magda and Joseph and their ever-growing brood were presented to the German public as the First Family of the Third Reich, Magda the unanointed First Lady. They eventually had six children, and if there was ever any doubt about where Magda's true affections lay, they were revealed in her choice of names for her offspring. Each of them was given a name with an 'H' in honour of Hitler.

In reality both the Goebbels were serial adulterers. At times they loathed one another. She famously had an affair with his deputy, Karl Hanke, who had a house near the Goebbels' own villa at Berchtesgaden. He had a string of liaisons with aspiring actresses, which were eased in his position as Propaganda Minister with overall responsibility for the arts and culture and Germany's thriving film industry. In 1936 Goebbels met the stunning 22-year-old Czechoslovakian actress Lida Baarova. They began an affair. She signed a lucrative contract with Germany's UFA film company, a deal no doubt oiled by her suitor's position. Hitler was at the Bayreuth home of Winifred Wagner, her guest for the summer festival, when he found out about the affair. He was appalled. What would the German people think of their Propaganda Minister sleeping with a Slav – when Nazi theory had Slavs firmly categorised as sub-human? The Munich Crisis was looming, which made the Führer's difficulties even more pressing. Besides, he could not tolerate the possible exposure of the Goebbels' marriage as being a sham far from the happy family of Third Reich myth.

Hitler was genuinely fond of the Goebbels children. When they visited him in Berchtesgaden they called him 'Uncle Adolf' or 'Uncle Führer'. Magda confessed to him that she too was having an affair, with Karl

Armin Dieter Lehmann as a child on horseback. The photograph was taken about 1941 or 1942.

Armin's father, Fritz Armin Lehmann, in 1941, Breslau.

The Lehmann Family together in 1942. (From left to right) Dorte, Anje, Wulf, Ute, Fritz Armin Lehmann, and Ulrich.

Armin with his mother and brothers and sisters in 1942 or 1943, taken in Breslau. (Left to right top) Mrs Lehmann and Armin. (Left to right bottom) Brother Ulrich, sister Dorte, and brother Wulf.

Armin's mother with her father.

Portrait of Armin Lehmann in 1945.

Armin's grandparents together.

Armin's beloved
grandfather.

Armin as a pupil at the Elisabet Gymnasium in Breslau.
Armin is fourth from the left, front row.

Armin in the uniform of the Hitler Youth, about 1943 or 1944.

Recruits at pre-military training in the Alps. Armin attended such a camp in January 1945 before Breslau was turned into a fortress.

Baldur von Schirach (far right) listens to Alfred Rosenberg, the leading proponent of Nazi ideology.

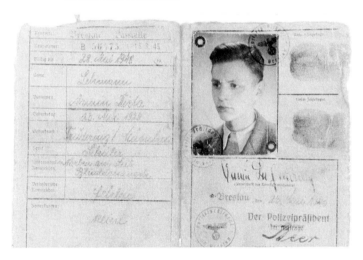

Two identity cards (*Ausweis*) of Armin issued in 1943 when he was 15 and in 1945, after his war experiences, when he was 17. Armin speculates that the change in his signature might have been caused by a personality change.

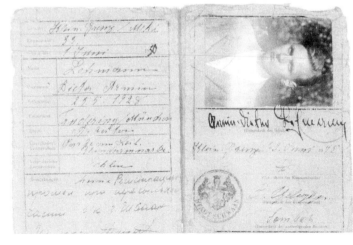

A newspaper report of the battle in which Armin was
wounded on the outskirts of Breslau.

The Zoo 'Bunker' to which Armin
completed a heroic mission in the face of
Red Army fire.

An aerial view of Berlin at the end of the
war. The Chancellery complex can be
seen at the bottom centre of the picture.

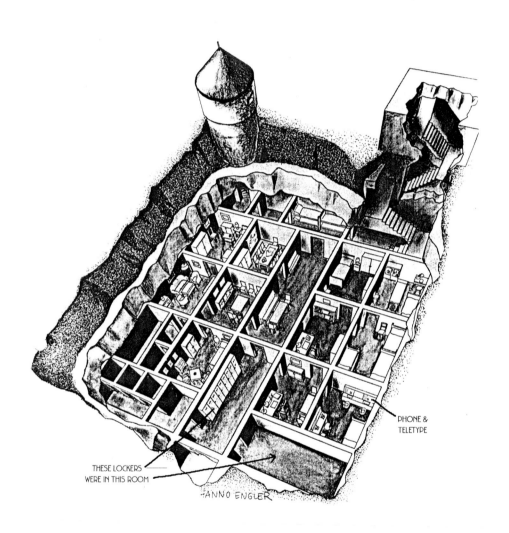

THESE LOCKERS
WERE IN THIS ROOM

PHONE &
TELETYPE

HANNO ENGLER

An artist's impression of the Führerbunker (from Soviet archives).

The Lehmann Family (except for Ute) reunited after the war.

Armin with his sisters Ute (on the left), Ange (on the right)
and Angela, who was born after the war.

Armin near his home on the
west coast of the United States.

Armin with his third wife Kim in Oregon.

Hanke. Hanke for his part wrote to the Führer asking for his permission to take Magda's hand in marriage. In the meantime Joseph Goebbels had become so obsessed with Baarova that he threatened to leave the country, at one stage pleading with Hitler to make him ambassador to Japan. Hitler refused to be moved. He told the Goebbels it was vital to keep up appearances. Baarova was sent back to Czechoslovakia. Her films were banned there and in Germany. The Goebbels' sixth and final child Heidi was always called their 'reconciliation child'. But it is unlikely they ever were fully reconciled. In May 1941 Magda Goebbels tried to escape with the children from Germany to Switzerland. She was caught on the Austro–Swiss border. Her attempt to get away coincided almost exactly with Rudolf Hess's flight to Scotland. It was only when Hitler was convinced that there were no political motivations involved that he pardoned Magda. She just wanted to escape her awful marriage.

Hitler's secretary Traudl Junge later said she was 'wracked with guilt' about working for Hitler. It is a source of fascination to many people as to how anyone could work for one of the greatest monsters of the twentieth century, the murderer of six million Jews. Junge, like many of his staff, insists she never heard him speak of the 'Final Solution' in front of them. One of Hitler's early adjutants, Richard Schulze-Kossens, an SS colonel, claimed that even in his most secret conclaves with Himmler the extermination of the Jews was never discussed. Technically it is true. Hitler was good at covering his tracks. But he railed all day long about the evils of 'international Jewry'. He specifically outlined his proposals for them in *Mein Kampf*. And in his last will and testament (the one Junge typed out) there would be a very clear hint about the Führer's involvement in the extermination of the Jews.

There was really no mystery as to why so many women fell under Hitler's spell. Since time immemorial, attractive and intelligent women have fallen for unattractive and powerful men. The women who fell for Hitler were probably attracted by the reflected glory of his powerful and 'hypnotic' presence. They conveniently forgot whatever scruples they may ever have had, just as thousands of other women were doing in Nazi Germany at the time. And when the war was over and they realised what a disastrously immoral choice they had made, their memories became fuzzier still.

That afternoon in his tea party with his secretaries Hitler said he would stay in Berlin come what may. Eva Braun had already expressed a desire to be by his side at the end, despite his protestations that she should seek the safety of the Berchtesgaden. It was an act of blind devotion that had won the approval of her erstwhile dismissive lover. Eva would be with him at the end. After they had finished tea, Hitler said he had a war to attend to but excused the secretaries for the afternoon. Eva Braun took them up to Hitler's old living-room in the Old Reich Chancellery building. A gramophone was turned on and champagne was served. They were joined by Martin Bormann, whose capacity for alcohol was rapidly increasing as his own personal demise approached. Hitler's physician, the dubious Dr Theodor Morell, also joined the secretaries for the music and dancing. As the Russian artillery boomed from the east, the women danced to a schmaltzy pre-war hit called, 'Red Roses Bring You Happiness'.

The Nazis never tired of twisting the truth that was self-evident to anyone with eyes. But I was one of the millions who fell for it time and time again. Hitler's birthday had begun with encouraging news. I woke up that morning to hear on the radio that attacks by the enemy were being repelled on all fronts. The front line was being pushed back remorselessly. At long last the massive German counter-offensive was beginning to have its effect. It was a relief to me after witnessing the devastation of the day before.

What I did not realise was that the occupation of Hof began five days earlier and was already complete by 20 April. All my comrades in the military hospital were POWs by then. Cologne was already in Allied hands, as was Frankfurt. All German troops in Italy had laid down their arms. The Russian Fifth Army was rapidly encircling Berlin. On 13 April Vienna had fallen into Russian hands. And on 17 April, 35,000 German troops, including 30 generals, had surrendered in the south. That morning of Hitler's last birthday the Red Army were barely 30 kilometres away from us in the south. They had taken Bernau, which was only 5 kilometres away to the north-east. They had broken through in the north and were at the Havel River with their field artillery. Russian shells had already pounded the far-flung north-eastern suburbs of Berlin. Now they had captured our own guns, which could fire half-tonne shells, and Red Army engineers were busily working to turn these mammoth guns on Berlin.

What I had no way of realising that day of Hitler's birthday was that the previous night had witnessed the first significant action of the German resistance movement, which had been so ruthlessly suppressed under Hitler for most of the war. That night it had re-emerged to express the German people's objection to the fate that awaited them and their capital. Dozens of members of the resistance movement had spent the night daubing the word '*Nein!*' (No!) all over the city. It was the biggest anti-Nazi demonstration since 1933. It was a very public rejection of Hitler's and Goebbels' appeals to defend the Reich capital to the death. Emboldened by the approach of the Allies from east and west, more and more people were finding the strength to protest. Leaflets were distributed describing Hitler as a 'lunatic' and Himmler as his 'bloodhound', treacherous insults that would have earned their propagators the noose only a few months earlier. Berliners were being urged to see sense and resist. But it was an appeal bound to fall on deaf ears among the Nazi hierarchy. Early that morning ten battalions of Volkssturm were sent westwards to bolster the flagging Ninth Army and help strengthen the crumbling new line. As news of their departure spread there arose a widespread assumption that Berlin was in effect disintegrating. It was in any case utterly futile.

The Ninth Army was falling apart, its depleted divisions smashed by Soviet armour and massive katyusha strikes, the multiple rockets launched from tubes on the backs of Russian lorries and capable of devastating an area the size of a soccer pitch with one terrifying blow. Columns of retreating soldiers were being strafed by low-level fighter-aircraft attacks. As the ragtag battalions of Volkssturm headed its way they encountered regular army troops exhausted and confused, fleeing the Front, each with exactly the same story to tell. 'Der Iwan kommt.' ('The Ivans are coming': we called the Russian troops 'Ivans' just as we called the British 'Tommies'.) The roads were clogged with horse-drawn carts and half-tracks carrying the wounded. Chaos reigned and there was panic etched on the troops' exhausted faces. Soldiers who had not seen their rations for days on end looted houses. Wehrmacht and Waffen-SS were indistinguishable from one another. Corpses lay by the side of the road. Civilians became accustomed to finding exhausted troops sleeping in their beds, too tired to go on. Others joined the tide of human misery heading for shelter in Berlin. Some officers attempted to restore order by cocking their pistols at the retreating soldiers. Other officers openly encouraged their men to go home and forget about the war. It was lost. All were in fear of the fanatical SS units who roamed around seeking out deserters for summary execution. Flying courts-martial were to become a common sight. The sight of soldiers hanging from trees by the side of the road became a familiar one. Soon though, the executioners themselves would be deserting in their hundreds. And they themselves would be facing imminent death at the hands of ferocious Red Army troops screaming: 'Die SS!'

That night Hitler ordered yet another of the 'counter-attacks' that he was convinced would repel the enemy. The goal this time was to 'hurl back' the massed ranks of artillery and tanks of the Red Army's rapidly advancing divisions. The Germans who were intended to pull off this remarkable military feat consisted of a division made up of boys rounded up from the Reich Labour Service. As the futile battle went on in the east, only kilometres away from where I was sleeping, the RAF flew its last air raid on Berlin, an onslaught I was only too well aware of when the sound of their bombs roused me from my slumber. That night, finally, on Hitler's birthday, Nuremburg fell. The city that had witnessed so many millions falling under the 'hypnotic personality' of the Führer was now in the hands of the Allies.

⤳ CHAPTER SEVEN ⤳

Hitler's Children

THE FOLLOWING MORNING AXMANN INTRODUCED ME to a woman who was going to mean a great deal to me over the next few days. Gertrud Huhn was a *Reichsärztin* (a Reich physician) based at the Hitler Youth headquarters on Kaiserdamm. She was in charge of the *Krankenrevier* (sick bay) in the underground cellar although in reality it was equipped no better than a very basic first-aid station. It was in the air-raid shelter one floor down and at that time was home to no more than ten, maybe twelve, patients. They were mostly fire-fighters who had suffered burning in trying to put out the fires. The sick bay had only a few beds. There was really very little medical equipment or supplies, just the basic bandages and medicines that were to be found in elementary Red Cross first-aid kits.

Dr Gertrud, as we all called her, illustrates how it was not just naïve young minds such as my own that were taken in by the Nazis. She was a kind and very gentle woman who was devoted to her patients. (And those patients would soon include a Russian soldier whom she cared for with as much dedication as she showed towards our own side.) Dr Gertrud was an enormously intelligent woman who was thoughtful and sensitive towards anyone she came into contact with. She too believed in Hitler with a passion. She was devoted to him and to the National Socialist movement. Dr Gertrud was prepared to sacrifice her life for Adolf Hitler.

Dr Gertrud had several young girls working for her in the Kaiserdamm sick bay. They were mainly members, as she was, of the BDM (Bund Deutscher Mädel), the girls' branch of the Hitler Youth. Some of them looked as young as 14 and frankly Dr Gertrud looked much younger when she was in her BDM uniform. Three girls in particular would play a role in my life in the last days of Hitler's Berlin.

Renate, who was only a child but behaved as if she were a fully-fledged physician, was a doctor's assistant and always at Dr Gertrud's side. She was a medical student aspiring to become a doctor. I remember her emotional bursts. 'What have the Russians done to you?' she would ask a new arrival and then bite her lips. Or, 'Isn't it horrible how they have hurt you?' Then she would shake her head. Those wounded severely, she would touch, putting her hand on a forehead or caressing a cheek. She would keep holding the hand of one who had just died.

Gudrun, from Bremen, was a no-nonsense type of person with great physical strength; and then there was Lotte, which was short for Charlotte. I shall never forget Lotte and I wonder to this day whatever became of her. There were several other girls working in that infirmary. They were barely out of their childhood and they had been sucked into the hellish cauldron of this devastating war. Had they been members of the victorious forces, history would probably now look upon them as heroines. But they happened to be Germans. Worse still, Hitler's Germans. They will be forever unsung.

Despite the catastrophe that was engulfing the city, Axmann remained a stickler for regulations. He had asked me the night before whether I could ride a motorcycle. I had said, 'Yes.' I was a very competent motorcycle rider. But he neglected to ask if I had a driving licence. The answer was, 'No.' I had never had a driving licence. When he discovered this on the Saturday morning he was plunged into despair. I couldn't possibly break the law. He announced he would assign me a driver. Given the massive shortage of manpower this sounded nothing short of madness to me. Did Axmann think I might be pulled over on Unter den Linden as I stormed back and forth dodging bullets and bombs? In the end I was pleased because the driver I was appointed became a great companion. I could never have performed alone what the two of us were able to accomplish together. In the short period of time we were together we became great friends. I remember him to this day, long after he disappeared into the morass that Berlin was about to become.

His name was Hannes and he had a dry sense of humour, typical of Berliners. He was also an idealistic member of the Hitler Youth. He had never seen combat but he was a skilful, courageous driver. We would spend the next week dodging shell-holes, barriers and other obstructions to deliver messages all over Berlin and beyond. And although this was to become a horrifyingly dangerous activity, I would always be overcome by a high sense of intoxication, a tingling rush of excitement, whenever we took off on Hannes' bike. I told him how when I was injured there had not been any anaesthetic available in the field and the young corpsman who extracted the shrapnel shoved his belt in my mouth and told me to 'Bite the leather!' From then onwards this became a mantra for Hannes and me whenever we had a difficult job to do. 'Bite the leather!' we'd shout in unison. It was our way of saying: 'Come on, let's just get through this shit.'

That morning I ran my first courier mission for Axmann. I was delighted to be told that I would be briefly reunited with my old fighting group. We were to find Karl Gutschke's unit, which was defending a strategically important road between Jacobsdorf and Petersdorf to the east of Berlin. It was under heavy attack by the Red Army. I was enthusiastic about the prospect of being reunited with Gutschke. And I was proud that once again his unit, battle-experienced and as heroic as ever, was being held up as an example to the other 19 Hitler Youth units defending Berlin. Axmann explained to me in no uncertain terms that Gutschke was not to retreat from his position under any circumstances. 'We will not disappoint the Führer,' Axmann declared.

I agreed. I had no idea, of course, how weak our forces were compared to the Russians'. Hitler's mania was such that his immediate reaction to any defeat was to blame the commanders in the field for cowardice or even treachery, while ignoring shortcomings in manpower, deficient weaponry and lack of ammunition. The only thing that would prove even more surprising was that Gutschke did manage to hold out against ridiculously overwhelming odds.

Hannes and I lost no time in getting out of Kaiserdamm. Hannes kicked the bike into life and with a roar of the throttle we were on the road for Petersdorf. Berlin was an even more ruinous sight than it was when I had arrived. Any building that had not been demolished by Russian artillery was now being pounded. As we sped out of town the ground was trembling beneath us. Every five seconds or so there was a massive crashing sound and an explosion of shrapnel as yet another shell hit its target.

I said to Hannes: 'If death catches us both, then we'll be reunited in Hell.'

Hannes replied: 'We have reached Hell already.'

We met our first obstacle within minutes. Thousands upon thousands of refugees, a human tidal wave of misery, dejection and agony, were heading down the autobahn. All of them had fear etched across their faces. They were freezing, hungry and many of them looked incapable of continuing. Even their horses were giving up. The side of the road was littered with lorries and horse-carts that had broken down. There were babies crying everywhere, their mothers desperately trying to shield them from the madness around them. They stopped us in our tracks. We just couldn't move.

While we were figuring a way around this impasse, I became aware of an old man by my side. He seemed to have picked himself up from the side of the road and was holding his hands out to me beseechingly. A look of weariness and agony was etched across the poor guy's features. He was at the end of his tether. He just couldn't take any more.

'Please, young man, please, finish me off. I cannot go on.'

He wanted me to deliver him a *coup de grace*.

'I can't cope any more,' he continued. 'Please, please, release me from my suffering.'

'Oh, my God,' I said to Hannes. 'I can't do this.' We both had pistols in our pockets. But the idea of what the old man wanted me to do repelled me.

Before we had time to think, the old man was approached by an NCO. 'Grandpa, I can't shoot you,' he said with a look of grim kindness on his face. 'But you can use my pistol.'

I was stupefied. Hannes and I stepped away, not wanting to witness what was about to happen. We heard the shot. Hannes made the sign of the cross. I turned back to see the officer reclaim his revolver. The old man's body lay slumped in the road. A young woman came running from behind the covered wagon, screamed and threw herself over the corpse as if to protect him. The woman's blouse was drenched with blood.

'It is kinder that way. Believe me,' the NCO said to me quietly as he sadly replaced the revolver in his holster. He too had a look of extreme exhaustion on his face. He too looked as if he might take the same option.

'We have got to go!' I shouted at Hannes, just wanting to get away from the horror of it all. Hannes kicked the motorbike into action and we were away. As often happens in war, there was suddenly a complete change in the situation. We were soon sailing down the autobahn without another person or vehicle in sight. It was an eerie feeling. We stopped for a smoke and to debate whether to remain on the autobahn or continue on a country road instead. We might be sitting ducks if we stayed on the autobahn.

Hannes retrieved the liquor flask that he was never without from his gear. He suggested we warm up our souls and offered me a swig of Schnapps. I took a swallow and handed the bottle back to him. I didn't like the taste.

He said a toast: 'To the poor grandfather.' Then he gulped down several swallows. I was more disturbed by the distress of the woman with the bloody blouse.

My thoughts were rudely interrupted by the rat-a-tat of machine-gun fire. A Russian fighter plane appeared from nowhere and swooped low over us. The cannon-fire drilled two lines of neat holes either side of us. That made up our minds pretty quickly and we looked for a muddy country road that would give us more cover. We encountered some old men manning a tank barricade but they didn't know where the Gutschke unit was. The Russians already seemed to be behind us. The risk of encirclement was very real. This was madness.

That morning of the Saturday, 21 April was to be an ominous one for Berlin. It began with a massive Russian artillery bombardment that Hannes and I experienced as we sped out of the city. It was the beginning of remorseless action that was calculated to demoralise Berliners as much as to destroy their city. It would continue almost unabated for the next 11 days. With hardly any respite, salvo after salvo of shells would be launched into the heart of the Reich capital. Some of the most devastating hits came from the German army's own railway guns that the Russians had captured and turned on Berlin. These mammoth beasts weighed 145 tonnes and could fire half-tonne shells that were as devastating over a range of 50 kilometres as a bomb.

From now on Berliners who ventured out into the open were at risk of being killed. Death and destruction were delivered at random. Some people, however, could not resist taking their lives into their own hands, particularly that Saturday morning. To celebrate Hitler's birthday extra rations had been authorised. Hundreds of shoppers took to Kurfurstendamm. But the Führer's munificence turned out to be a curse. They soon found themselves on the receiving end of something a little more than extra rations. The once-elegant boulevard was drenched in a hailstorm of steel and explosives for hours on end. It was the same in Unter den Linden, Wilhelmsstrasse and Kaiserdamm. Once attractive thoroughfares became targets for the deadly combination of the Red Army's artillery and lethal katyushas strikes. Berlin's gracious boulevards were soon little more than bomb-blasted avenues of masonry-ridden rubble. The thunder of artillery fire and the resulting explosions became a constant backdrop to everyday life, such as it was. Berliners called it '*Stalinorgeln*' (Stalin's Choir).

For the first time Russian artillery shells landed within the city limits. It took Hitler by such surprise that he emerged from his rooms bewildered. Surely the Russians could not be that close? The answer was yes, they surely could. The Luftwaffe was almost powerless to do anything. Its air bases across the country had been so systematically attacked that few could put planes into the air. It was yet another of Göring's perceived failures that prompted the Führer to rage that the whole of the air force's leadership should be strung up. General Koller took the full force of his invective in the Führerbunker. From the safe distance of Bavaria Göring responded by urging Hitler to leave Berlin.

Shortly after sunrise the Americans launched a deadly dawn chorus to match the Russian fusillade. Nearly 1,000 Flying Fortresses arrived over Berlin, their clean silver fuselages appearing like little avenging angels in the clear blue sky. It would be the last time the Western Allies bombed Berlin. From now on the Russians would take responsibility for air operations over the Reich capital.

This would prove a blessing of sorts to the population below because the Russian air force did not carry anywhere near the destructive power of the huge British and American bombing fleets. And indeed the first act of the Russian air force was no more harmful than dropping millions of leaflets urging Berliners to give up the struggle. Women were told they would not be raped. Their babies would be provided with much-needed food. They were implored to tell their men to stop fighting. The war was over and there was no point continuing the bloodshed. For once there was no Nazi response to Stalin's exhortations. That day Goebbels' once tireless propaganda machine finally began to give up. Berlin's Reich Radio station fell silent. Many Berliners began to openly listen to the BBC.

There was more bad news from the south that morning too. A large column of Russian T-34 tanks was spotted not far from the Zossen headquarters just 35 kilometres south of the city. The Red Army was just hours away from the nerve centre of the German war machine. Perhaps just minutes. The sudden appearance of the enemy tanks prompted a flurry of plaintive telephone calls from Zossen to the Führerbunker. General Hans Krebs, who was in command of the complex, was to receive no reassurance from the Führer. He was told to stand his ground. All he had to defend the headquarters with was a handful of light armoured vehicles.

The enormous military bunkers at Zossen were a marvel of German ingenuity and a symbol of the scale of Hitler's imperial ambitions. They consisted on the surface of two dozen concrete-reinforced buildings camouflaged from the air by netting and painted Zeltplanen, hidden from the nearby rural roads by trees and barbed-wire fences. Passers-by, or even enemy reconnaissance aircraft, would not guess that beneath the surface were two gigantic main bunkers equipped with the most up-to-date office equipment. There was also a huge communications centre 70 feet beneath the ground that had once linked the disparate parts of the German military machine.

The Zossen complex was the key to German war operations on both the Eastern and the Western Fronts. One of the bunkers housed the general staff of the OKH (the Oberkommando des Heeres). The OKH was the supreme headquarters of the German army, although in this latter part of the war it was mainly concerned with operations on the Russian Front. The other bunker was home to the OKW, the supreme headquarters of all the armed forces: the air force, the navy and the army. The OKW was responsible for all operations except the Eastern Front.

Zossen was the most obvious place from which the Führer could direct the war, and on many occasions he had been urged to go there. But since the previous year's assassination attempt he had not trusted any of the German military's regular officer corps. Instead Hitler had installed Krebs in the complex and he took his orders from the Führer's obsequious crony, Field Marshal Wilhelm Keitel, in the bunker. That morning Krebs did as best as he could and ordered the light armoured vehicles to attack the oncoming Russians. But in the meantime he began to prepare for the urgent evacuation of the general staff.

As the onslaught of their city escalated, Berliners sought whatever cover they could. The cellars of apartment buildings filled up. Those not lucky enough to have one headed for one of the city's many public air-raid shelters. All the main government buildings had them and there were several purpose-built structures, notably at the three vast flak towers overseeing the defence of the city, such as it was. Each had shelters with reinforced concrete some 2 metres thick. The largest refuge in the city was the bunker at the Zoo flak tower, which had four storeys above ground and two below and walls 4¹/₂ metres thick. But it was hardly big enough for the thousands of people to whom it became home. Conditions inside were atrocious, with no lavatories and no running water supply. Its inhabitants had to brave the street outside if they wanted any food and that took a great deal of nerve given that the station was a main target for the Red Army guns.

Thousands of other people sought refuge in the subway system despite rumours that the Russians planned to flood it. Meanwhile, above ground, intersections of the streets were now blocked by anti-tank barriers manned by the Feldgendarmerie, who were on the look out for deserters. Rumours of soldiers hanged from lamp-posts spread like wildfire. But more and more men were discarding their army uniforms and melting into the civilian population. There was a palpable sense of fear among the civilian population as stories of rape and pillage were passed on. The unspoken fear in the mind of every woman was rape at the hands of the Ivans.

Predictably, as many of the streets of Berlin became open sewers, the rats began to emerge and run for their lives. Goebbels (who was also the Reich Commissioner for Berlin) had ordained that no man capable of bearing arms should leave the city in her hour of need. The Führer, he pointed out, had no intention of fleeing to Bavaria, and those that did run away were cowards and traitors. There was only one department able to issue an exemption from this general rule. That was the headquarters of General Helmut Reymann on Hohenzollerndamm. Reymann was the military commander responsible for the defence of Berlin. Suddenly, on that Saturday morning, the building was besieged by scores of Nazi Party officials desperately demanding an exemption from officers. These were the very men who, throughout the past months and years of military failure, had endlessly accused the army of cowardice. The temptation for Reymann to withhold his permission to leave must have been great. But he was glad to see the back of them. They could hardly be any use in the battle that was to follow. That morning he issued 2,000 exemption certificates and the 'golden pheasants' began their flight from the capital.

Extraordinary as it may seem, as the golden pheasants deserted the city, fanatical Nazis from the foreign battalions of SS troops came pouring in. But not all the SS were being so loyal. That morning Himmler met Count Bernadotte once more in a further attempt to advance his peace negotiations with the Allies and his own ambition to replace the Führer.

At the headquarters of the general staff in Zossen the Russian army quickly decimated the German light armoury sent to stop it by General Krebs. So by lunchtime the supreme headquarters was virtually defenceless against the Russians. Miraculously, the Soviet tanks stopped short of Zossen for a while, but only because they had run out of fuel. They were attacked with some degree of success by a unit of Volkssturm and Hitler Youth with Panzerfausts. Only at 1 p.m. was Krebs finally given permission to evacuate the complex. The OKH moved to a Luftwaffe base at Eiche, near Potsdam on the western side of Berlin, and the OKW moved to a tank base at nearby Krampnitz. As the column of evacuees moved north-west it was strafed by the Luftwaffe seeking the Russian tanks. That afternoon Red Army troops marched into the Zossen compound. There was no resistance. Only four drunken soldiers were there to greet them. The Russians were astonished at what they found. As they were being shown around legend has it that one of the telephones rang. One of the Russian troops picked it up to find a German officer on the other end demanding to know what was happening at Zossen. 'Ivan is here,' said the Russian, offering a deliciously crude suggestion as to what the German could do with himself.

While the full scale of the military catastrophe was becoming apparent to the Führer in Berlin, Hannes and I were still riding out to the east of the city trying to find Gutschke. If we had gone on like this we would have run out of petrol. We spotted a silo in a field, so I told Hannes to hide there while I looked for Gutschke on foot. I set off alone and after what appeared an eternity found him. He was in Jakobsdorf, a village under heavy attack by Russian artillery. Gutschke was in a garden with a platoon of boys. The scene was mayhem. They were shooting through hedges at attacking Russian soldiers. Incoming fire was hitting the walls of the garden and the side of the farmhouse. Gutschke was hammering away with an MP-40 automatic weapon.

'What are you doing here?' he demanded, turning around briefly before reloading his weapon with another clip and letting off another round into the field beyond.

I yelled to him what my orders were. 'No surrender, no retreat. The line must be held to the last man.'

Gutschke looked at me grimly. 'We need reinforcements,' he said. 'Eat something and get some sleep,' Gutschke told me.

I didn't want to leave Hannes at the silo but orders were orders. The dead and wounded were collected. Several girls appeared with fresh milk and sandwiches made from freshly baked bread. I didn't know where the people who lived in this farmhouse were, or if they would come back. So rather than sleep in their living quarters I crumpled up on a bale of straw in their barn. I held on to the gun but took off my helmet. What I remember next resembles a dream.

Face down and sleeping on my stomach, I was awakened by boots kicking me in the back. A Russian soldier attempted to roll me over. Did he think I was dead? Instinctively, my body must have stiffened. I kept my eyes closed. He ripped the watch off my wrist and took my gun. I expected a shot. I thought death was only a moment away.

Although keeping my eyes closed and playing dead, my mind and my senses were wide awake now and razor-sharp. I felt heat and heard the crackling of fire and flames shooting off. I realised that the barn must be on fire. The Russian soldier will shoot me. I will burn to ashes. Nothing will be left of me! These thoughts raced through my mind. No one will be able to notify Hannes. Neither Gutschke nor Axmann will ever know of my death. Anne-Maria, my mother, my father, my sisters and brothers, my friends, my classmates, whoever survives and keeps waiting for me, will never learn of my fate. Forever unresolved, 'missing' will be the verdict. Unless my burned skeleton would be found with my dog tag not melted down. My thoughts were rushing, pleading! Pull the trigger! Stop my thoughts! Shoot! Shoot! Get it over with!

The scorching heat spread out. My skin burned. My throat seemed in flames. That's when my body snapped out of its rigidity. I turned my head around and opened my eyes. The Russian soldier had left. I choked. The smoke was suffocating and, with great speed, I fled from the heat, escaping the flames. Were Russians waiting outside to shoot me as soon as I ran through the door? A shot grazed my upper left arm, ripping off a shred from my uniform.

In front of me the smoke seemed to be filled with silhouettes and shadowy profiles. The first face turned out not to be a Russian soldier but a comrade of mine. The Russians had been repelled. In the very early morning hours, before dawn, Gutschke handed me my despatch. 'Enemy driven back. We are holding out. In urgent need of reinforcement!'

The last three words Gutschke spoke to me were: 'Reinforcement! Reinforcement! Reinforcement!' I never saw or heard from him again. He must have fallen, together with the thousands of the very young men/boys he led, palpably insufficient to repel the superior forces we were fighting against.

In Berlin the full magnitude of the disaster to come was creating mayhem in the Führerbunker. After Zossen had been taken the Russian commanders did not allow their troops to linger for long. Shortly afterwards the forward drive towards Berlin was continuing apace with the Russians heading for the southwest suburbs of Berlin and westwards to Potsdam. By the night of 21 April, when I was being nearly burnt to death in the barn, the Russians were infiltrating the outskirts of Berlin and had almost entirely encircled the city. In the east the Red Army was in control of the ring road from Wusterhausen in the south to Bernau in the north. Berlin was rapidly being crushed in a massive pincer movement.

The rapidly deteriorating military situation had produced a night of madness in the Führerbunker where Krebs had now joined Keitel. Ironically, just as the Russians were about to make the final push, the city no longer had an army officer in charge of its defence. Overnight Hitler had sacked General Reymann, convinced he was not up to the job. He appointed in his place a Nazi apparatchik only to unappoint him almost as quickly. In truth the defences of Berlin were so badly organised that it didn't really make a great deal of difference.

There was a growing row between Axmann and General Weidling. Weidling wanted to disband all of the Volkssturm Hitler Youth troops. He wanted to send the boys home and save their lives. Not so Axmann. He was intent on holding out until the bitter end. He was determined to prove to his Führer that the HJ would keep on fighting and remain loyal until victory or death. Axmann had expressed frequently in my presence that 'the Führer can depend on his Hitler Youth'. In Axmann's eyes our lives belonged to him and whatever he asked of us, we had to fulfil. Yet Axmann must have known by then that there was no new miracle weapon ready to be deployed. There was no future but death, disgrace or misery. Somehow or other Axmann won the day. It was he, not Weidling, who had won Hitler's ear.

In the Führerbunker, after his anger with the Luftwaffe and General Reymann had dissipated, Hitler was struck by a brilliant idea. In attempting to encircle Berlin from the north the Russians had dangerously exposed their right flank. Hitler saw this as yet another opportunity for a massive counter-attack while the Russian lines were so desperately stretched. In this instance the task would fall to the hopelessly depleted forces of Waffen-SS General Felix Steiner. Steiner was one of the best SS generals and held in high esteem by regular army chiefs. He commanded the Third SS Germanische Panzer Corps.

Theoretically the Panzer Corps was based northwest of the city near Eberswalde. But in fact Steiner himself was at Oranienburg in Berlin and it was a corps in name only. Thanks to Keitel's unwillingness to explain to Hitler the true military situation, the Führer was under the impression that Steiner's corps was performing well, heroically throwing back the attacking Russians. In fact most of his divisions had been diverted to help General Theodor Busse's Ninth Army in the east and those that remained had been decimated. Steiner's force by then consisted of no more than a few tanks and perhaps 1,000 starving and exhausted men, a mixture of Volkssturm and police as well as regular army, navy and air force troops.

But Hitler was not to know. Speaking grandly of Steiner's 'Army Detachment', he ordered the SS general to launch a counter-attack against the Russians southwards and link with Busse's army to present a German line in the southeast. When Steiner received his orders he couldn't believe what he was hearing. Hitler told him he was to requisition Göring's own Luftwaffe bodyguard based north of the city. Koller, Goring's chief of staff who was still in the bunker with Hitler, was also bewildered. Göring's bodyguard had left with Göring for Bavaria. Effectively, it no longer existed. In desperation Steiner telephoned Krebs in the Führerbunker to find out what was going on. But Krebs was standing by the Führer in the bunker when the call came through. Hitler took the handset off Krebs and spoke to Steiner. He assured him every available reinforcement would be made available for his action. Ominously, he ended the call by warning that any of his commanders who disobeyed would be executed within five hours.

✎ CHAPTER EIGHT ✎

Madness in the Führerbunker

TO THE EAST OF BERLIN I was running across a field desperately trying to find Hannes. By the time I got within sight of the silo I was panting furiously. In my hand was Gutschke's despatch demanding reinforcements. Suddenly I heard what every German dreaded.

'*Stoi!*'

We all knew what that meant in Russian. 'Stop!' What had seemed unimaginable until now happened. I lifted my arms. I had received absolutely no training for what to do or say in a situation like this. We were not to become POWs. We were expected to fight to the last and then die. Never to surrender. My comrades were in a battle. I was a courier. I had been careless, had not recognised a trap. I had no pistol. I was alone in a hopeless situation and overcome by sheer terror. Now death would come. I wondered how brutal it would be.

What sounded like commands were given in Russian. I did not understand Russian. What was I supposed to do? Remain standing? Walk with my raised hands toward the voice? I still couldn't see anyone, although more voices now shouted. Once again visions of horror tormented me: that death might not be swift but drawn out and torturous. We had been told over and over again the Russian soldiers were barbaric and never to expect to be treated humanely. Two enemy soldiers emerged from the woods. I couldn't believe what I saw. They looked almost as young as me. And they were not steady on their feet. Had I stumbled into an early victory celebration?

They must have bivouacked there all night. I noticed a campfire that had been put out, but light smoke was still rising. Had they caught Hannes and already killed him?

Now, one grabbed my collar and tore it as if he wanted to rip my uniform, yanking off several buttons. He yelled at me in Russian. He reeked of vodka. Then another one, also smelling of vodka, grabbed me, checked my wrists and then hit me. My arms were bare and that must have incensed him. The only visible thing of some value was my satchel: a leather pouch that contained, in a courier envelope, Gutschke's urgent request for reinforcements.

Two of the Russian soldiers began to quarrel over possession of my leather satchel. They had taken a prisoner, but they seemed disappointed. So little booty. In the breast pocket from which one of the soldiers had lifted my fountain pen, there were also the two rings belonging to my mother and Anne-Maria that I had taken off, but he didn't notice them.

After a few more pushes and kicks, a bottle made the rounds. To my utter surprise, I was offered a drink and I angered them even more when I refused. It was foolish to turn them down. I can't explain my reasoning. Perhaps I declined out of fear. In any case, it was a grave mistake and it almost cost me my life. I remember being thrown down and kicked in the ribs; they stepped on my face and one of the soldiers fired with a sub-machine gun into the ground so close that the dirt from the impact sprayed over my body and hit my head. They emptied the bottle and threw it at me. Surprisingly, they did not knock me out or kill me. They kept shouting and it sounded threatening, but unable to understand what I was being told, I just remained lying where I was. Less than an hour must have passed when the clamouring stopped.

One of them, probably an observer, must have spotted something alarming. Movements of approaching Germans? At the edge of the grove they had positioned a machine gun and camouflaged it. They started firing. Despite their inebriation, or perhaps because of it, they fired relentlessly. I couldn't see anything except this Russian machine-gun nest. Two of the soldiers were at the machine gun. The others fired in the same direction with sub-machine guns. No shots seemed to come our way. Then I seized the opportunity.

No one seemed to be watching me. I rose up and ran away as fast as I could. I expected to feel the thump, thump, thump of bullets in my back at any moment. But instead I reached a heap of straw and dived behind it. I almost fell over on Hannes and his motorcycle. Neither of us could believe our eyes. He had been waiting there all night. He had no idea a Russian encampment was just a few hundred yards away. Such is the confusion of war. We laughed at our good fortune. I slipped Anne-Maria's ring back on my finger.

'Let's get the hell out of here,' he said, kicking the motorcycle into gear.

We hit the same tide of human wretchedness on the way back. The sights of misery abounded with refugees, horse-drawn wagons, hand-pulled carts and prams, some with a child or even two children inside, others brimming with belongings. Sheep and goats tied to carts were dragged along, yammering. There were dogs, many running loose, yipping, yelping and barking. Scenes of sadness, distress and desolation.

I was in agony. I felt as if every rib in my body had been broken. I screamed and begged Hannes to take a break. We found a quiet farmhouse with a courtyard. An old woman was standing there. She inquired matter-of-factly: 'Are you looking for a hiding place?' Apparently there were several refugees hiding in the farm, waiting for the war to end.

'No,' Hannes replied emphatically. 'We have to get to Berlin.'

She shrugged, but insisted that we have something to eat and drink before going on. She brought a side of smoked pork, sliced some bread and heated up some milk for us. She also turned on the radio. The reception was poor and while eating I didn't pay much attention to the music until it was interrupted for an announcement. It was directed to those guarding the capital:

> Defenders of Berlin! The Bolshevists have assembled for the decisive attack on the German capital. Supported by every available means, they are now approaching the final goal of their mighty offensive: BERLIN!
>
> Towards Berlin! These words even resurrect the dead! With the promise 'just one more city to conquer and then the war is over and you can go home', the Jewish commissars of the Red Army incited their soldiers.
>
> The Reich capital is at stake.
>
> Countless German women and children are at stake. They look to Berlin's defenders. They look up to you! They expect you to fight with fanatical hatred to beat the Bolshevists. Make them bleed to death! Turn every house into a fortress! Turn every street into a mass grave! Bury the Red horde!
>
> Top their hatred with even greater hatred for them!
>
> Fight to the last!
>
> Seek bloody vengeance and thousand-fold revenge for the atrocities committed by the Bolshevists in our homeland!

Such rasping exhortations on the Reich Radio network were by now a familiar sound. We quickly set off for Berlin, eventually arriving in the shell-shocked city. I went straight to Axmann's command post in Kaiserdamm. He took one look at me and asked if we had been in an accident. I explained what had happened and he sent me to the sick bay to be treated. The woman physician who looked at me said I was so badly injured I needed to be in a military hospital. It would have been my salvation and I desperately needed a break. But I also desperately wanted to please Axmann. I told her he needed me. And he did: straightaway.

I was told to deliver orders to General Steiner at Oranienburg. The Führer was still depending upon Steiner to launch a counter-attack. I had no idea what the orders were. I was exhausted. I was in pain. But I had no choice. Hannes and I must have been two of dozens of couriers sent to find the elusive Steiner. Hannes set off at his usual breakneck speed. It was an impossible mission. We were looking for a battle 'division' that didn't exist. We had no idea where Steiner was. Nor did anyone else. At a village Gasthof we found a group of Reich Labour Force girls. The girls were packed and ready to go, but the vehicles to pick them up were long overdue. The result was bedlam. Some yelled at each other, a few were crying. For each of them was the unspoken horror of rape at the hands of the Russians. Hannes and I were mobbed with questions. Some of the girls gave us cigarettes and chocolate. Maybe they thought we could help them out of their predicament? We couldn't. Hannes and I got a few hours of sleep in the Gasthaus and took off again before dawn.

We didn't get far on our way to Oranienburg. Artillery thundered around us and suddenly we were in the midst of an enemy attack with bullets whizzing by, right and left. We tried to find cover. Another volley of shots. Suddenly, a sprinkle of pings as the bullets peppered the bike. And even more suddenly there was a piercing stab of pain in my hand. A bullet had hit my right hand, which was holding on to the back-seat handle. The little finger was practically shot off. Instinctively, I lifted it up to my eyes and saw that it was dangling on tendons and skin. Anne-Maria's ring was gone. I was bleeding profusely. Hannes stopped. I tied a cord around my wrist to stem the gush of blood.

We decided to head back to Berlin. We found ourselves amid a tide of soldiers and civilians retreating in the face of the enemy advance. There were groups of Feldgendarmerie everywhere rooting the soldiers out. Everyone was told to go back and make one last-ditch stand. The threat of immediate execution was in the air. Hannes and I were singled out along with another group of retreating soldiers. We told them we were couriers and eventually they let us continue. The others, I have no doubt, went to their deaths, either at the hands of Ivan or the noose of the Feldgendarmerie. When we arrived at the Hitler Youth headquarters in Kaiserdamm we were utterly exhausted.

I rushed right to Dr Gertrud's treatment room. She aligned the bone of my small finger on the hand, dressing it with a wooden splint as support. She gave me two injections. One was for pain; the other one was a tetanus shot. She thought that I needed a blood transfusion, but no blood was available. Axmann had made it known that he needed Hannes and me. Wanting to impress Axmann, I assured him that I did not want to be transferred to a military hospital. 'I am up to it!' I said.

He smiled back at me with a look of genuine gratitude and, I think, admiration. But Dr Gertrud insisted that, in my condition, I could not yet be released. There was a discussion about what I could do. Dr Gertrud insisted I was not capable of any serious physical effort. It was decided I would stay in her care but would be given a job to do as well. The Russians were getting perilously close to Kaiserdamm. Axmann had decided to switch his command post to the Party Chancellery on the Wilhelmsstrasse, across from the Old Reich Chancellery. Dr Gertrud and her clinic would have to come with us. It would be my job to see that the transfer went ahead smoothly. Although seemingly not the most dangerous job, it was a job that would win me the Iron Cross I (First Class) and let me see for myself the extraordinary bravery of Dr Gertrud's girls, not least Lotte.

While Hannes and I were on our wild-goose chase looking for Steiner's forces, the madness in the Führerbunker multiplied. It was to produce a rage of such cataclysmic proportions in Hitler that some of his officers believed they had witnessed him undergo a nervous breakdown. All that morning of 22 April Hitler kept demanding to know how Steiner's counter-attack was progressing. Keitel, Krebs and Jodl did not dare tell him that there was no counter-attack, that Steiner was, in all probability, sitting exhausted in a field with his depleted legions. Or might quite possibly be retreating in the face of overwhelming odds. Hitler turned his rage on whoever happened to be available.

A series of telephone calls from the Führerbunker produced ambiguous replies. Some of his generals assured him the attack was under way. Others said they had not heard a whisper from Steiner. The confusion lasted well into the afternoon, the Führer becoming more and more agitated as the hours passed. The afternoon conference of 3 p.m. was attended by Bormann, Burgdorf, Jodl, Keitel and Krebs. On the other side of the flimsy partition, their respective adjutants waited should they be required to join their superiors. They included Hermann Fegelein, Himmler's SS liaison officer in the bunker and husband of Eva Braun's sister Gretl. Fegelein would soon step on to centre stage of the underground drama.

The conference began with Krebs and Jodl outlining the military situation. It was not favourable. The Russians had broken into the northern suburbs of Berlin and Red Army artillery was now within the city limits of Berlin. Hitler could not believe what he was hearing. What about Steiner, he demanded to know. Amid much foot-shuffling between them, Krebs and Jodl admitted that there had been no counter-attack by Steiner. There had been no reports of any movements of any sort. Steiner had not ordered his men to do anything. The diversion of so many troops southwards to join the counter-attack, which never materialised, had allowed the Russians to make huge progress in the north.

Bewildered and angered at the apparent inaction of his troops, Hitler began to make connections in his mind. First he turned his rage on the sinister figure of his physician, Dr Theodor Morell. It is true, after all, what they say about Morell, the Führer decided. The doctor *was* slowly poisoning him for his own dastardly ends. Hitler convinced himself that Morell was part of some elaborate plot to render him senseless so that his body could be taken to Bavaria. Summoning Morell to his study, the Führer sacked him and ordered him out of the bunker. In his place in the treatment room came another doctor, the tall and gangly SS Colonel Ludwig Stumpfegger.

Then the focus of Hitler's rage turned on General Weidling, who by now had relocated his headquarters to the eastern suburbs of Berlin. Hitler ordered him to send his Panzer Corps back into the city. Weidling knew this was an insane idea. With all the tank traps that had been set up in Berlin, it would only result in the corps being destroyed. But Hitler warned him he would have him shot if he disobeyed orders. At the same time Weidling's commanding officer, General Busse, had ordered him to send his tanks to link up with the Ninth Army. Again, also on pain of death if he disobeyed him. Busse's orders made a great deal more sense but Weidling was in a quandary. There was no way of complying with Busse's orders. The Russians were pushing his corps backwards into Berlin. There was no way through to the Ninth Army. Weidling plumped for a compromise. He relocated his headquarters once more some 4 miles away from the city centre. When Hitler heard of Weidling's rank disobedience he raged at his cowardice and betrayal of the Third Reich. A senior officer was sent out to find and arrest him.

At one stage during this day of madness Hitler suddenly remembered the Prominenten. These were the several hundred prominent prisoners-of-war with high-level links to the Allied leadership. They were held in camps outside Berlin to be used as bargaining chips. But now Hitler had a better idea for them. Shoot them all, he ordered. Shoot every single last one of them! Even Keitel balked at this suggestion. The retribution from the Allies would be fearful. He cautioned against such a precipitous move. Hitler was pacified, but only for a few precious moments. His full rage was about to be ignited.

By the time the afternoon conference was convened in the bunker it was now obvious to Hitler that Steiner's troops had not moved an inch from their emplacements. It was quite obvious there had never been the slightest intention to stage a counter-attack. The explosion of rage that followed this revelation had even the adjutants on the other side of the partition quaking in disbelief. Hitler almost turned blue in the face as he screamed about the treachery of Steiner and the betrayal that was everywhere around him. The armed forces had been lying to him all along. Nobody was to be trusted. Nobody was telling him the truth. (Which, for once, was true.) The Luftwaffe could not be trusted. The army couldn't be trusted. And now even his trusty SS could no longer be believed. 'The war is lost! Everything is lost,' cried the Führer. It was the first time most of those present had heard him admit what had been obvious to them for months. Had anyone less than the Führer expressed such defeatism, it would have been a capital offence.

Hitler shrieked at the generals standing around the conference table. His hysterical screaming cut through the partition in the hallway and could be heard in the upper bunker beyond. At times the Führer's face became contorted with rage. Once he collapsed and began weeping like a child. Everything was lost, he kept repeating. Nobody was to be trusted. Slowly the hysterics ceased and the sobbing stopped. Hitler retired to his study with Keitel and Jodl.

What happened behind the closed doors of Hitler's study cannot be known for certain. But after the war both Keitel's and Jodl's testimony proved remarkably consistent. Sensing that the Führer had now realised beyond any shadow of a doubt that the war was lost, Keitel ventured that perhaps it was now time to consider suing for peace. In response to this erstwhile treacherous idea Hitler seems to have concurred, suggesting that Göring should be given the responsibility of leading Germany to peace. Both Keitel and Jodl told Hitler that not one soldier in Germany would serve under Göring. But Hitler pointed out that Göring was the only one of the senior Nazis who was capable of talking to the Allies on their terms.

Shortly after this exchange Hitler summoned Joseph Goebbels from the Propaganda Ministry and in the privacy of his office they discussed how each would approach the forthcoming end. For months the Goebbels had struggled with the thought of what they would do with their children if Germany were defeated. Like all the other top Nazis by now, they carried poison ampoules around with them and were determined to end their own lives. But what about the children?

Occasionally Goebbels had suggested that his wife take them to some western part of Germany where they might fall into the benevolent hands of the British. Goebbels was an admirer of the British and thought they would behave well towards his children. His worst fear was that they would fall into the hands of the Russians and be brainwashed into hating their father and everything he had stood for. The Americans he detested almost as much. But at other times he and Magda Goebbels realised the utter futility of their children's prospects. 'They are the children of Joseph Goebbels,' he would repeat quietly.

Goebbels told Hitler that he would die with him in the bunker, along with his wife and all his family. The Führer barely acknowledged this display of loyalty. Goebbels emerged from Hitler's study and returned to his office. From there he broadcast a short speech to the German nation to the effect that the Führer was in Berlin and he would die fighting with his troops defending the city. It was the first time the people had been told of their Führer's whereabouts for several weeks. Afterwards Goebbels presided over the destruction of his private papers, before joining his family at their opulent official residence not far from the Chancellery at 2 Hermann Göring Strasse.

In the meantime the Führer told Keitel and Jodl it was time for them to leave now for Bavaria where they should direct the war effort in the south. They in turn suggested he should accompany them and fly to Berchtesgaden while he still had the chance. But Hitler said he intended to stay in Berlin and die at his command post. He was too frail to fight. And he did not want to risk the humiliation of being captured by the Russians. He would kill himself at the very last moment. Those who wanted to stay with him in the bunker were welcome to do so. He would not stop those who wished to leave.

Then Hitler summoned his secretaries and his dietician Constanze Manziarly to his sitting-room to tell them of his decision to stay. Eva Braun was also present. 'It's all lost, hopelessly lost,' he told them. They should all go now and save themselves. Eva Braun had already said she would stay by his side. He ordered his oldest secretaries, Johanna Wolf and Christa Shroeder, to fly to Munich. They were to take care of his affairs there. He asked his two youngest secretaries if they wanted to go too. But Gerda Christian and Traudl Junge said they would stay by his side, as did Manziarly. The other woman to stay would be Martin Bormann's secretary, Else Krüger. 'If only my generals were as brave as my women,' lamented the Führer before turning his attention to tea and cakes. The small party sat quietly sipping their tea and not mentioning the war.

On Hermann Göring Strasse two official limousines were waiting for the Goebbels family. Eventually Magda and Joseph Goebbels emerged with their six children, each clutching one toy and what few possessions they would require over the remaining days, or possibly only hours, of their lives. The two cars drove the short distance to the bunker. As the six children filed into the upper bunker one by one their arrival had a curiously uplifting effect on the inhabitants of this subterranean world. To Hitler's secretaries it was something of a relief to have this sudden injection of humanity into their midst. The claustrophobia, mania and constant gloomy news of the last few days were relieved by the sound of innocent voices and the beaming smiles of happy faces ignorant of what fate lay ahead for them.

The upper dining corridor would henceforth be their playroom. Constanze Manziarly would take great delight in making the children sandwiches and cakes. Traudl Junge in a way took over the role of their governess in the absence of their mother. Magda retired to a room in the upper bunker as she was suffering from heart palpitations. For much of the following days she would be attended to by Dr Stumpfegger. Magda Goebbels' demonstration of loyalty to Hitler prompted him to present her with his gold Nazi Party badge. (Curiously, when I saw Hitler some days later, he was wearing his gold badge. After the war Otto Günsche, Hitler's junior adjutant in the bunker, told me that he was sure Hitler had duplicate badges and that he promptly replaced the one he gave Magda Goebbels with a new one, although not when she was present of course.)

As this melancholy scene was unfolding Christa Schroeder was rifling through Hitler's private papers. The Führer had given her the key to his safe and ordered her to hand the papers to his senior adjutant, Julius Schaub, and have them burned outside. Christa did as she was told. When she opened the safe she noticed Hitler's Walther pistol was sitting on top of the papers. And she did not throw away all the papers. She could not resist retrieving some mementoes for herself. Among them she salvaged some postcards that Hitler had drawn sketches on. One was a sketch of the Elbe Bridge at Hamburg; another was a head and shoulder portrait of a girl, possibly Geli Raubal. A third was a depiction of a Wandering Jew. And yet another was one of Hitler's favourite Hollywood stars, Charlie Chaplin, as 'The Tramp'. Schaub took the rest upstairs for burning. Shortly afterwards the adjutant disturbed the Führer in his study. Hitler was nursing the pistol in his hand. Schaub quickly withdrew, wondering whether the moment everyone had been waiting for had finally arrived. But there was no sound of a shot in the forthcoming minutes.

The Führer's concession in allowing those who wanted to leave to do so had produced, once more, a quiet communal gasp of relief. An exodus began. Between the evening of 22 April and the early hours of the following morning, scores of Chancellery staff left Berlin. Hitler spent much of the evening and early morning shaking hands with people and saying goodbye. The evacuation, code-named Operation Seraglio and organised by Hans Baur, Hitler's chief pilot, did not go faultlessly. Of the ten large transport planes that left from Gatow, the aerodrome on the western outskirts of Berlin, only nine made it to Bavaria. The one containing Hitler's most valuable documents crashed and was destroyed. The Führer was mortified that the transcripts of his 'table talks' went up in flames. Few who had actually listened to the endless monologues shared his concern. Those remaining in the bunker would be called 'living corpses' by those who left. But those who flew to Bavaria did not fly to freedom. Very soon the region was completely overtaken by the US Seventh Army.

The encirclement of Berlin was almost complete. Russian divisions were now just 10 kilometres away from Potsdam in the west and were closing the gap with enemy forces crushing into the city from the north, east and south-east. Further to the south-east of the city more Russians were already in the suburbs. The Sachsenhausen concentration camp to the north of Berlin at Oranienburg had been liberated and the appalling discoveries made there were soon to become common knowledge. The Red Army was now preparing for the most hazardous part of the operation, the street-to-street struggle that it anticipated as it fought its way to the centre of Berlin, block by block.

It was an evening of conflicting emotions and loyalties. After hearing of Hitler's breakdown in the bunker, Heinrich Himmler had offered to send his own honour guard to Berlin to defend the city. It was an offer the Führer gratefully accepted. Himmler stood by his words and sent the troops to Berlin. But soon Himmler would be meeting Count Bernadotte for the fourth and final time. Extraordinarily, Himmler was still under the delusion that the Allies might be prepared to come to some sort of accommodation with a new regime under his own leadership. It had not sunk in that they would not accept anything but unconditional surrender and total capitulation.

That evening in the Führerbunker, Field Marshal Keitel proposed a new plan to Hitler. He suggested to the Führer that he would try to find General Wenck and his Twelfth Army and tell him to march on Berlin from the south-west to liberate the city. Hitler agreed the idea had its merits. But before he let Keitel go on the mission, he insisted the Field Marshal be fortified with soup from the kitchen. Constanze Manziarly was ordered to cook up a bowl of pea soup and a couple of sandwiches for Keitel. As he left, the Führer presented him with a bottle of cognac and some chocolate. It was quite a sweet scene.

✺ CHAPTER NINE ✺

The Last Goodbyes

C✥BERLIN WAS ALIVE WITH COMINGS AND GOINGS that evening and well into the morning of 23 April. Keitel left with Jodl for the south-west to find Wenck. Jodl would separate from him and head for the new headquarters of the general staff at Krampnitz. 'Any man who wants may go!' Hitler had told anyone who cared to listen. And all night long buses and cars left the Reich Chancellery and the Party Chancellery for the aerodromes at Gatow and Rechlin 60 miles north-east of Berlin. Christa Schroeder and Johanna Wolf were ordered by the Führer to leave for Bavaria. His erstwhile doctor, Theodor Morell, would not be missed. 'I don't need drugs to see me through,' Hitler had said to him. General Christian was among those to leave – not only his Führer, but his wife Gerda too, who elected to stay by Hitler's side in the bunker rather than join her husband in flight.

At Rechlin, not everyone was leaving. When he arrived General Christian encountered Albert Speer who had made the decision to return, briefly, to Berlin. Speer had heard of the Führer's decision to die in Berlin. He still felt guilty about his meeting with Hitler on the previous Friday, the day of his birthday. Speer owed his entire career to Hitler. Yet in the past several months he had been openly treacherous towards the Führer, driving around Germany pleading with local district leaders not to implement Hitler's 'scorched earth' policy. The Führer knew. He had been helpfully kept abreast of Speer's progress by Martin Bormann. Speer probably knew he knew too.

His actions, for any other Nazi, would have resulted in immediate condemnation and the firing squad at best, a lingering death hanging from a meat hook at worst. But Speer resolved to return again to the lair of the Wolf at whatever cost to his own personal safety. He wanted to explain his actions to Hitler and, if he was allowed to, say his final farewell to the man to whom he owed so much.

That same evening Heinrich Himmler would have his fourth and final meeting with Count Bernadotte. Until 22 April, Himmler had dithered about his next step in his negotiations with the Swedish Red Cross representative. But he had been approaching a resolve not to take things any further out of loyalty to Hitler. Now, however, it was apparent that the Führer's life was approaching its end – just as Himmler's favourite clairvoyant had said it would. No time was to be lost. In a darkened room of the Swedish consulate in Lübeck, Himmler met Bernadotte one more time. The electricity had been knocked out and the proceedings were illuminated by candlelight. 'The Führer's great life is drawing to a close,' he told Bernadotte. He gave the Swedish aristocrat permission to forward his offer of surrender to the Western Allies. But he was not alone in his delusion that the victors would want to do business. His rival for power, Göring, also believed there was a role for him in post-war Germany. In a very short space of time, both men would be stripped of these illusions. Within an hour of the meeting in Lübeck Bernadotte was on a plane to Stockholm.

From Rechlin, Albert Speer flew with a Luftwaffe fighter escort to Gatow. At Gatow Speer found a pilot who was prepared to fly him in a Fieseler Storch trainer to the airstrip on the East–West Axis at the Brandenburg Gate. Having completed the precarious journey without injury to either man or machine, Speer drove the remainder of the short distance to the Chancellery and the Führerbunker. It was an act of great bravery. Speer knew he was Hitler's favourite protégé and he had been treated like a son by the Führer. But the reports he had heard of the madness in the bunker over the last 24 hours filled him with apprehension. On his arrival, however, he found that Hitler had regained his composure. (Several bunker inmates noticed that after the departure of Dr Morell, Hitler no longer displayed the frightening mood swings.)

The bunker now almost echoed to the sound of emptiness. The Goebbels' children's story books had yet to litter the upper dining corridor. They had arrived too late to settle in. The lights of the kitchen still shone as Constanze Manziarly kept up the flow of fresh sandwiches and soup from her pantry. But many of the staff officers and their secretaries, orderlies and valets had left the bunker for good. The only people who were left, besides Hitler and Eva Braun, were Manziarly and Hitler's two secretaries, Traudl Junge and Gerda Christian (General Christian's now estranged wife); Otto Günsche, his adjutant; Heinz

Linge, his valet; and Ludwig Stumpfegger, his personal physician. There was the Goebbels family too, he downstairs, wife and kids upstairs, and Joseph Goebbels' adjutant Hauptsturmführer Günther Schwägermann. Even those who would visit the bunker over the next few days had shrunk in number. They were mainly Hitler's Nazi Party stalwarts, Bormann and Axmann; his generals, Krebs, Burgdorf, Weidling and Mohnke; and his faithful chief pilot, Hans Baur.

One of the first people Speer met when he descended into the lower bunker was Martin Bormann. Bormann had not stayed by the Führer's side out of loyalty but because he had no choice. He derived all his power and prestige from Hitler, and without the Führer's patronage Bormann's name carried no weight with even the lowliest of Reich officials. Over the past several months Bormann had been pouring a steady drip of poison into Hitler's ears about Speer. In the circumstances he was surprised to find Speer returning to the bunker of his own free will. Ironically, he realised that Speer might be the only hope he had now of saving his own skin. Sidling up to the armaments minister, he asked if he would plead with the Führer to leave for Berchtesgaden as soon as possible. Speer listened but had no intention of passing the message on.

When Speer entered the Führer's private quarters, Hitler was cool and distant. He neither shook his hand nor offered him a seat. But at least he wasn't in a homicidal mood. The conversation between the two men was icy. Speer wanted to explain why he had been countering his scorched earth orders. Hitler didn't seem to be listening. He was more interested to know what Speer's opinion was of Admiral Dönitz. It was the first indication Speer had that Hitler was considering the Admiral as his successor. Hitler asked Speer whether he felt it would be better to end his life in Berlin or Berchtesgaden. Speer told him if he must end his life, it would be preferable to do so in Berlin, rather than at 'the weekend bungalow'. Then Hitler told Speer about Eva Braun and her desire to die at his side. 'Believe me, Speer,' he said, 'it is easy to put an end to my life. One brief moment and I am freed of everything.'

Albert Speer would spend the next eight hours saying his own farewells to the remaining members of the bunker community. He visited Magda Goebbels, who was now bedridden in her room in the upper bunker. He had wanted to discuss with her the possibility of spiriting her children away to safety. He wasn't alone in being horrified at the thought of what Magda and Joseph Goebbels planned to do with their children. But Joseph Goebbels was in the room with them and refused to leave. In the brief time Speer was there, many things went unsaid. Speer also visited Eva Braun. She produced a bottle of champagne and they chatted away while Hitler slept in the room next door.

In the early hours of the morning Field Marshal Keitel had found Wenck not far from the American Front. Wenck thought Keitel an absurd figure but he listened to what he had to say. He had no choice but to agree to the Führer's order. He assured Keitel that his men would relieve Berlin. After he had gone, though, he told the exhausted men under his command another story. In almost apologetic terms he said that regretfully they were going to face tough action once more. The Twelfth Army would advance towards Berlin, but not, insisted Wenck, to rescue Hitler, the Nazis or the Third Reich. Instead Wenck's plan was to create a corridor between the Elbe and the city to give soldiers and civilians a means of escaping to the west. Wenck told them that one force would head towards Potsdam to create one corridor. The other would race towards the east to link the Twelfth Army up with Busse's Ninth Army, which was encircled by the Russians. Their mission had nothing to do with saving Adolf Hitler, he emphasised to them, it was all about saving soldiers and civilians from further needless bloodshed.

Of all the departures from Berlin that night, the one that would prove to be most precipitous was that of Karl Koller, one of Hermann Göring's liaison officers in Berlin. Koller had not been in the bunker when Hitler had had his near-breakdown the day before. But General Christian had told him what had happened. The Führer's hysterical rage. His denunciation of all the armed forces. His avowal to die in Berlin. And his apparent suggestion that Göring should open up peace negotiations with the Allies. Koller decided this particular development was too important to be conveyed over the telephone. He got on a Luftwaffe plane to Munich and headed for Göring's residence in Obersalzberg.

Göring was astonished at Koller's description of events based on General Christian's briefing. By a decree of June 1941 Hitler had appointed him his successor. It was clear that the Führer had abdicated his responsibilities as Chancellor, which must surely mean that his responsibilities had now fallen on Göring's shoulders? And his indication that Göring was better than he at negotiating must surely mean that the Führer wanted the air Reich Marshal to begin talks with the Allies. Nothing would delight Göring more. He had wanted for some time to strike a deal with the American commander-in-chief General Eisenhower. But Göring wanted to clarify the situation. He knew that his sworn enemy, Martin Bormann, would do anything in his power to prevent him succeeding Hitler, the sole source of Bormann's power.

He resolved to send a telegram to Berlin on 22 April. The message would be carefully worded so as not to appear disrespectful of the Führer. After consulting his legal advisers a format was agreed upon.

My Führer!

– In view of your decision to remain at your post in the fortress of Berlin, do you agree that I take over, at once, the total leadership of the Reich, with full freedom of action at home and abroad, as your deputy, in accordance with your decree of 29 June 1941? If no reply is received by ten o'clock tonight, I shall take it for granted that you have lost your freedom of action, and shall consider the conditions of your decree as fulfilled, and shall act for the best interests of our country and our people. You know what I feel for you in this gravest hour of my life. Words fail me to express myself. May God protect you, and speed you quickly here in spite of all.

Your loyal – Hermann Göring

Albert Speer was with the Führer when the telegram arrived. It was drawn to Hitler's attention by Martin Bormann, who appeared elated at its arrival. For despite the careful wording that Göring had gone to some lengths to formulate, Bormann had spotted some incautious phraseology. The phrase he drew to Hitler's eyes first was the one asking that a reply be received by ten o'clock. Göring was presenting the Führer with an ultimatum! Hitler was enraged. He seemed to have completely forgotten that he had specifically told Jodl and Keitel that Göring was the only senior Nazi who could negotiate a capitulation with the Allies. Bormann suggested Göring be shot on the spot for high treason. But after some thought Hitler decided instead to send a telegram back to the air Reich Marshal, advising him that his actions constituted high treason against the Nazi Party. Hitler informed him that the penalty for such a crime was death. But in view of the services rendered by Göring to the Party in the past, he would be excused the ultimate sanction if, and only if, he resigned all his offices immediately. Shortly after midnight on 24 April, Göring, Koller and the rest of his staff at Obersalzberg were placed under house arrest. Later in the day, it was announced that Göring had resigned from all his offices for reasons of ill health.

Albert Speer was faintly amused by the episode. His own real treachery had been far worse than Göring's perceived misdemeanour. Shortly afterwards he bade his Führer farewell for the last time. It was an icy parting. Once more, Hitler didn't offer a handshake. 'Auf Wiedersehen,' the Führer said and turned his back on Speer as he left the room. Speer emerged into the chaos of Berlin above, and made his way to the Brandenburg Gate for yet another hazardous flight, this time out of the city.

While the stage was being set for the final act of Hitler's Third Reich, Hannes and I continued to deliver messages across the city, from Axmann's command post in the Party Chancellery. All our courier missions were made difficult because the streets were clogged with apparently leaderless formations of civilians and their animals. Repeatedly, we ran into a congestion of soldiers and refugees; of homeless with their belongings reduced to what they could carry; of children, probably with many orphans among them; and of animals, most of them abandoned. But for me, devoted to animals, and especially dogs, what caused the greatest pain was how cruelly the war that man waged affected them. There were many grisly sights. Once my stomach turned at the sight of a horse being cut up when it was still alive. It had been wounded by shrapnel and was lying flailing about on the pavement. A couple of men were hacking away at it with knives and saws. They were so desperately hungry but they didn't have any weapons to put the poor beast out of its misery. I can still remember its squeals of agony. On another occasion I saw a woman draining the blood from a slaughtered dog to give to her children. This sort of sight was an everyday occurrence. One of the most common was of squashed bodies reduced to shapeless messes in their own blood, crushed by tank tracks. It is a memory that still churns my mind and my stomach.

Once, however, we came upon something that froze us on the spot. A boy – he cannot have been more than 13 – was dangling from a post, hanged with a clothes line, his right ear half torn off, with blood all over his right side. No poster explained why. He was wearing a Volkssturm uniform far too big for him. His neck had apparently been broken after the hangman had put his head in the noose and pulled the rope. His eyes were swivelled skywards in a ghastly vision of torment. His hands were tied behind his back; his legs were tied together at the ankles. There was no Hitler Youth armband on his sleeve. Perhaps it had been removed. If so the inference was that he was a coward. So boys were being hanged after all.

We could not help but gaze at this wretched soul. We stopped to look closer. Then Hannes and I found ourselves under suspicion. We were stopped by a young Waffen-SS NCO. He asked us for the password. Nobody had told us anything about any password. Behind him was an older man who appeared to be wearing a long coat without insignia. It might have been that of a police officer. However, on this coat, he wore an Iron Cross I (First Class). One didn't wear medals on an overcoat. It seemed so out of place, even to Hannes, who remarked: 'He probably swiped that from a fallen comrade.' There were no other medals on his coat and no Iron Cross II (Second Class) stripe. One had to be awarded the Iron Cross II (Second Class) before qualifying for the Iron Cross I

(First Class). Something seemed phoney about this old man and the way he behaved. There were white flags hanging out of windows all the way along the street. He kept shooting at them wildly and to absolutely no effect. He'd obviously never used a firearm in his life. Then he turned to us and said menacingly: 'From here you either end up on the gallows or you go back into battle.'

'We are couriers from the Reich Chancellery,' I explained.

The NCO gave me a push, saying, 'Don't lie to me!'

'I am not!' I replied emphatically.

He got angry and then our troubles really began. He was bigger than me and certainly better fed by the looks of things. And his uniform was squeaky clean compared to my soiled and dishevelled rags. I wondered where he had been spending the war.

Hannes didn't have a pay-book. He produced as identification a membership pass of the motorised Hitler Youth and his driver's licence. He explained how he was my driver attached to the Reich's Youth Leader Headquarters. But the NCO wouldn't have any of it.

'Retreating from battle,' he said sadistically. 'No doubt about it!'

Then he asked me for identification. I had two pay-books on me, one as a recruit from the Waffen-SS and the other one as member of the Volkssturm. The NCO's immediate conclusion: I was a deserter from the Waffen-SS, now pretending to belong to the Volkssturm. He decided that we did not have the proper papers and were not authorised to retreat on a motorcycle. I had a message clearly addressed to Artur Axmann. But it had no effect on him. Did he not know that Axmann was in charge of the nation's youth? What was the matter with this guy? Then it dawned on Hannes what was happening.

'He has his eyes on our motorcycle,' he whispered. Any form of transport in Berlin was valuable at that stage in the war. It was not we who were planning to escape. It was him. He was the coward.

The only weapons Hannes and I carried were pistols in our pockets but they had their guns trained on us. I had escaped the Russians twice. Now we were on an important mission with military orders from Axmann that might even have originated, for all I knew, from Hitler. And here we were, stopped by whom? An old police officer whose behaviour seemed questionable and a Waffen-SS Unterführer who did not appear to be disabled in any way. He should be fighting in the battle zone and defending the women and children of Berlin, I thought.

'Follow me!' the young sergeant ordered.

We were led inside a corner house and down into the cellar. There were several women and, behind a makeshift desk cluttered with records, a field telephone and a briefcase. Behind it sat a really fat man. That was odd. Overweight people were a rarity in Germany during the last years of the war. This one obviously hadn't gone without. Oddly, he had a facial expression similar to Bormann's. He was also dressed in what appeared to me a 'mystery' uniform of dark-grey trousers and a frock coat with the collar resembling those of Catholic priests. Was this a First World War uniform? Was this fat official a man of the law? Could he have ordered the hanging of the boy outside?

I told this officer what I had told the NCO. To my surprise and great relief, he used the telephone and apparently was able to get through to the Hitler Youth headquarters. They told him I was telling the truth. He was visibly astonished at this, but told us we could go. He warned us: 'The Russians are listening in and know that you are coming.' He appeared blithely unconcerned about the risk he had exposed us to. The NCO was reluctant to hand us our motorcycle back. After thinking it over, I suppose he decided that it wasn't worth the risk of upsetting Artur Axmann.

Perhaps I should not have been surprised at what we experienced that day. Both Goebbels and Bormann had issued highly publicised directives that made it quite plain what would happen to *anyone* who faltered in the face of the enemy. They made it clear that the defence of Berlin was the paramount responsibility of every man, woman – and child. There was a newspaper for fighting troops called the *Panzerbär* (literally, the Tank Bear). One excerpt was typical. 'Whoever, at this moment, doesn't fulfil his duty is a traitor, a traitor of our nation . . . And when the point is reached that the weak think the end has come, then the strong have to carry on . . . The fight has to go on and harder and more fanatical than ever . . . Where the Führer is, there is victory! There can be no more consideration of one's personal fate. Fight, die or be declared and treated like a traitor!'

Later, when I raised the possibility with Axmann that Hitler Youth were being executed, he was curiously obtuse. 'For sure none of our boys!' he said, not looking me in the eye. But I wondered who 'our boys' were? By law, all of Germany's boys and girls belonged to the Hitler Youth. Hannes and I had seen what happened to 'our boys' who faltered in the face of the enemy. And we had seen that the people who meted out this savage justice were the real cowards.

The following morning was the anniversary of Lenin's birthday. The Russians, disappointed that Berlin was still not taken, ordered a 24-hour-a-day, non-stop advance. Red banners were distributed among troops in anticipation of the victory celebrations to follow. The Russian generals wanted every prominent building in the city to have the Red Flag flying from its rooftop. Unbelievably, Tempelhof airport had continued to run commercial services throughout the siege. But that morning the last flight took off. It was a plane to Sweden and it carried just nine passengers. As it sped down the runway it passed row after row of wrecked Focke-Wulf fighter planes.

The Russians were now within sight of Kaiserdamm and I decided we should transfer the infirmary at night. There really was no other way. Had we attempted to do it in daylight none of the patients would have survived and I doubt whether any of us would either. There were about 14 patients and medical staff to transfer. None of the patients could walk or help themselves in any useful way. Some of the staff of the Reichsjugendführung had been assigned to help me out and none of them looked as if they were looking forward to it. They were much higher in rank than me so this gave me an additional feeling of responsibility. Of course there were no ambulances to be found anywhere. The best we could lay our hands on was an old delivery truck that ran on charcoal. Dr Gertrud asked us to take along the last remaining medical supplies but they consisted of little more than a few cases of bottles and bandages. We had to bring along a much larger supply of sub-machine guns and Panzerfausts. It was going to be a long operation.

The patients were prepared before dusk. They were all designated stretchers that were lined up by the exit at the rear of the building. Then when darkness fell we began the operation. We ended up doing six runs in two stages, transferring the patients first to Police Headquarters and then to the Party Chancellery. Everything went remarkably smoothly until the last two patients were due to be transferred. Then we hit a snag.

We had been promised a military ambulance. But it never turned up. Waiting for it cost us an hour and by then the situation had changed drastically and there were Russian troops practically outside the front entrance. We had to get the hell out of there. But we couldn't leave those poor souls. Hannes suggested that he lead the way across the city. I'd follow in the delivery truck sitting next to the driver. The patients and Lotte and the other girls were in the back. But we ran into a barrage of fire. We couldn't find a way out. We headed for the cover of a partially demolished house and carried the wounded to temporary safety. That's when our problems really began. I told the driver to stay with the injured and with the girls. Then, armed with a sub-machine gun and a bazooka, I crossed the street.

There were two Russian tanks in front of me. They were wide-tracked T-34s with sloping armour. Several infantrymen were following behind. It was a startling sight. I could see the first one was approaching a particular house. I ran like mad through the backyards of a row of houses and positioned myself in the cellar of that house. While I was doing so the tank let off a round directly into the building where the girls and the wounded were sheltering. I had no idea if they had been hit. I dived into the sub-basement of the house the tank was approaching. It had narrow windows at street level. The glass had been blown out. Just a few sharp edges remained in the frame. I could see the T-34. It would bang off a potshot, then roll forward and take another shot at another building. I couldn't see the foot soldiers. They must have been behind it. There was no German military in sight.

The tank started rolling towards the building I was in. It was heading straight for me. The cellar wall and the floors began to tremble. The noise of the churning chains was horrible. I was terrified. Soon the distance between the tank and me could not have been more than 20 feet. It was more than flesh and blood could bear. I had no time to calculate the odds of what I was about to do. My instincts simply clicked into action. I raised the bazooka using the cast on my arm. Fixing the turret into my sights I pressed the handle, closing my eyes for a fraction of a second and praying to God.

Boom!!!

There was no recoil. There was no explosion. There was just the sound of a somewhat innocuous burst as the exhaust from the bazooka bounced back from the wall and cauterised the skin of my neck and singed my hair. The smoke made me cough and my eyes tear. But when I cleared them I could see the Russian tank was engulfed in a black cloud. And it was no longer moving. I had hit it! I couldn't believe my eyes. It was the first time I had ever used a bazooka against the enemy and I had scored a direct hit. (I later learned that the Russians were terrified of these simple, hand-held devices. They changed their entire tank tactics to cope with them.) Flames were leaping out of it. I saw one soldier jump out and dash across the street. Oddly, my first feeling, after the elation of the moment, was sympathy. I saw the silhouette of the one soldier disappear into the smoke and flames. But no others. I had no idea how many crew a T-34 had. But surely there must have been three, four or maybe even five? It was such a big tank.

I cannot exaggerate how much it had been instilled in us to hate our enemy, in particular the Russians. But I felt no hatred for them. Even those young soldiers who beat me up and were probably going to kill me, I could never feel hatred for. I thought of them as human beings. Now, the boot was on the other foot. But as I looked at the burning tank, I could only think of the poor men who were inside it: of their mothers, their sisters and their girlfriends or wives. Burning to death was my own greatest fear. I prayed to God that the end for them would be quick rather than torturous. I was now shaking badly.

I ran back to the house where I'd left the girls to get another Panzerfaust. When I entered the house there was smoke and dust everywhere from the tank attack. I ran down into the cellar worried that Hannes and the girls were wounded or maybe even dead. I could hardly see a thing until I made out the silhouettes of the three girls. They had grabbed a bazooka each and were heading for the Russian tank column.

'No!' I shouted, suddenly worried. 'Back down into the cellar!'

But they ignored me. I turned to Hannes for help, but he turned his back on the girls. 'If they want to fight, let them fight!'

'They are nurses' aides!' I protested.

But Hannes made no response.

We climbed upstairs. I went ahead with an automatic assault rifle, navigating through heavy debris. Not all of the steps held up, several were loose and some were missing.

Hannes carried two bazookas, his and mine. Through a hole in the brick wall, I looked down the street. On the other side on the pavement, leaning against the building, a few Russian infantry soldiers could now be seen. They were firing wildly at the windows in the corner house. I aimed and shot at them. But suddenly they were out of sight. They must have found cover in a cellar shaft. Or were they retreating?

The answer was no. They weren't retreating. A second tank came into sight once more, passing the burning one, almost ramming it. The street was hardly wide enough for two T-34s to pass. There was a column of soldiers behind the tank, which wasn't yet within Panzerfaust range. But I signalled Hannes to bring me mine. Then something unexpected happened. I couldn't believe my eyes. Lotte suddenly appeared in view. She was carrying a Panzerfaust and she raced straight into the middle of the street.

'Back off!' I shouted as loud as I could. It wasn't loud enough.

She stopped for a second, standing directly in the firing line of the tank. I clenched my teeth in fear. But Lotte seemed to be as calm as she was in Dr Gertrud's infirmary. She took aim carefully and fired the bazooka. Then she ran to the other side of the street and disappeared as fast as she had appeared, without stopping to see if she had hit the tank. I wasn't looking either, concentrating instead on the slight slip of a girl dashing across the rubble and debris. Only after I had followed her disappearing figure did I look back at the tank and realise she had scored a direct hit! The second tank was now ablaze just as the first one had been. Yet again I saw the dark silhouettes of Russian soldiers dashing for cover. But this time I did not dwell on the fate of those inside the burning tank. My thoughts were entirely on the stupendous bravery of Lotte.

It was almost daybreak by the time we had finished the move. Dr Gertrud's new medical treatment centre was next door to Axmann's new command centre in the bunker or cellar of the Party Chancellery. It was space in an air-raid shelter, unfurnished except for some wooden benches. We had brought along some stretchers, plank beds, chairs and the table new arrivals were treated on. The medical aid Dr Gertrud could supply was only very primitive. By military standards it barely passed as a *Hauptverbandsplatz* (major first-aid field-station) and couldn't be compared to the *Notlazarett* (emergency hospital) underneath the New Reich Chancellery. In the Notlazarett, they had an operating table with a bright light above from what appeared to be a sun lamp usually used for tanning. It was a small but fully equipped clinic. But then again they had several hundred wounded and only two physicians to attend to them. In comparison, Dr Gertrud and her aides had essentially brought along only first-aid supplies. She had what looked like a vanity case with a Red Cross emblem on it. The instruments in this bag appeared to be the only ones at her disposal. For the first two days we had carried some patients who required surgery but she was unable to do anything for them, either through lack of supplies or lack of expertise. There was a constant flow in and out of the centre. And as the Russian advance progressed, the number of patients went rapidly upwards as artillery fire increased above and grenade fragments showered upon those outside like hailstones.

Borman had left the Party Chancellery to be in the Führerbunker with Hitler. He was not alone. Several high-ranking military and Party officials decided they would rather rough it on the Reich Chancellery side of the street. The danger of crossing Wilhelmsstrasse was just too much for them to risk. The air-raid shelter of the Party Chancellery then became Axmann's command post and my new home. I shared Axmann's quarters with him, along with his adjutants Heinz Boldt and Günther Weltzin.

I, of course, felt close to the centre of power. Yet I had my moments of depression. Periods of total numbness. Instances when I felt dragged down, ready to collapse. Usually, it was Axmann who pulled me up again. Only years after the war would I know for sure that there had been no new miracle weapon ready to be deployed, that since the end of March even the production of the so-called vengeance weapons, the V-1s, the 'buzz bombs', and the V-2s, the first and only ballistic missiles in action, had ceased. These were manufactured underground, mostly by slave labourers and by concentration camp inmates and the advancing Allied Forces had ended production at least three weeks prior to Hitler's birthday when he had talked of a life-saving medicine for a dying patient.

By the time Axmann moved his command post into the cellar of Bormann's offices, Bormann was functioning as Hitler's right-hand man. He was Hitler's chief-of-staff, in charge of his secretariat and, most of all, his appointment schedule. He was the Führer's all-important protector from bad news. He decided who had direct access to Hitler and who did not. He also slanted incoming and outgoing messages, at times altering the meaning for Hitler, so that he would react in a certain way. He had indeed become 'the grey eminence' and advanced over his rivals, Göring and Himmler included. But not Axmann. Axmann had gained the Führer's ear by promising that the Hitler Youth would fight courageously and defiantly to the end. 'Unconditional allegiance to the Führer!' had become Axmann's motto.

∽ CHAPTER TEN ∽

Into the Führerbunker

THURSDAY, 26 APRIL BEGAN WITH AN intensive artillery and katyusha bombardment. I awoke to the sound of repeated katyusha barrages landing on the Wilhelmsstrasse. I was sharing Axmann's command centre with his adjutants Major Günther Weltzin and Heinz Boldt in the air-raid shelter of Martin Bormann's Party Chancellery. To describe it as a command centre was rather grand. Our quarters were cramped, nothing more than a poky cellar with low, arched ceilings. There were only two military cots and we took turns using them to get some sleep. Few of us had changed out of our uniforms in days, or shaved. Dr Gertrud's medical centre was next door and filling up by the hour. There was a nauseating smell of decomposing and charred human remains coming from the corridor outside where we stacked the dead bodies. The noise of the katyusha strikes was incredible, even below ground. Every so often there would be a massive crash as a rocket strike tore into the crumbling city above us. One could almost feel the foundations swaying under the assault. With every pounding a cloud of dust floated down on me from above. The lights flickered on and off. The smell of phosphorus and gas seemed to seep through the cellar walls. There was a four-barrel anti-aircraft gun on the Party Chancellery roof and we could hear it rattle off a few furious rounds from time to time. We could hear the sounds of bullets whizzing through the upper floors.

As Hannes said, this really was hell. My life was a fog of exhaustion in which night melted into day. I had no time to think. My clothes were covered in dust and soot. My diet was absolutely appalling. We lived out of boxes of tinned food piled up in a little kitchen area presided over by a motherly woman we called '*Mutti*' (Mum) Lehmann (who was no relation of mine). Most of the tins didn't have labels on so the only way we could find out what was in them was by opening them up. Mostly it was liverwurst and bloodwurst with cubes of bacon in it, or *schweineschmaltz* (salty lard). There was even tinned *Kommissbrot* (black bread). None of this food tasted of anything. There had long ceased to be any fresh water but there was no shortage of alcohol in the Party Chancellery's pantry. Bormann had made sure of that. There was a constant supply of crates stuffed with wine, champagne and hard liquor. The stocks were fast being plundered by his officials, who were now mostly sleeping across Wilhelmsstrasse in the more spacious Chancellery cellars. But there was no sign that the supplies would run out. So not only would we boil our tea in wine and champagne, we'd wash our faces in it too.

Fortunately Mutti Lehmann had a few small stocks of little luxuries, particularly sardines and *zwieback* (French toast), but these were rare little treats. She would let us eat in her small canteen with two or three tables pushed together. Once Hannes turned up with a rucksack full of fresh bread from the bakery that served the Führerbunker. We didn't ask him how he got it. But Mutti Lehmann cut it up into equal pieces so that we could all have our fair share, including the Russian patient in Dr Gertrud's medical centre. But it is hardly surprising in the circumstances that I and practically everyone else suffered diarrhoea. There was hardly any medication left to deal with it. I chewed zwieback and had some schnapps, thinking it might kill the germs. It didn't have the desired effect.

The toilets in the Party Chancellery were filthy and stinking. They were blocked up with excrement and vomit. This was particularly unappetising because they were close to the kitchen and the odour filtered through. It was not a pleasant experience eating in such conditions, but then eating wasn't such a pleasant experience by then anyhow. The cause was probably over-use and lack of flushing water. Only the Führerbunker had running water and clean washing facilities by now.

Ostensibly Bormann had moved into the Führerbunker to be closer to Hitler, but partly, I suspect, it was because he couldn't stomach facing the journey across Wilhelmsstrasse. He wasn't the only one. Of the SS and Nazi Party officials who had not managed to get out of town, many had chosen to decamp to the New Reich Chancellery cellars and dozens of the other air-raid shelters, bunkers and other refuges around Berlin rather than risk working in the comparative danger of their offices above ground. The lucky ones got into some of the quieter bunkers reserved for army officers. In these at night the corridors were lined with officers stretched out in their uniforms, exhausted from the day's exertions. The

Chancellery cellars were full of Nazi officials who had drunk themselves into a stupor and simply slept it off all night and all day long while the mayhem continued around them.

Today was going to be a momentous one for me – the first day I went into the Führerbunker itself. It was not just the Führerbunker. It was the *Führerhauptquartier* (the Armed Forces High Command), as it happened, the last Armed Forces High Command of the Third Reich. The first I knew about it was when Axmann ordered me to accompany him across Wilhemsstrasse. I was in a daze, not knowing whether it was night or day. Time had come to be a meaningless concept. I was too tired to think mostly, simply reacting to Axmann's orders instinctively. When thoughts did cross my mind they were cross-currents of faded memories and half-remembered dreams. I just picked myself up out of the cot and followed him. The two of us dashed across the street wearing handkerchiefs soaked in wine across our faces. Wilhelmsstrasse was under an almost ceaseless barrage of Russian katyushas and by now the Russians were so close we ran the additional risk of sniper fire. It was fast becoming a shooting gallery. Red Army snipers picked off anyone who raised their heads above the parapet.

I ran with a blind fury, not knowing whether I was going to be picked off by a sniper or blown to high heaven by a rocket strike. Miraculously we made it. We went through the Reich Chancellery main entrance, which was now bereft of any outside guards at all. Everybody was inside taking shelter. An LAH guard met us inside and accompanied us down a labyrinth of corridors. It seemed like an endless maze of twists and turns before we got to the entrance, a small room that was the office of Johann 'Hans' Rattenhuber, who commanded Hitler's personal bodyguard. Rattenhuber and Axmann knew one another well. He signed and handed me a runner's pass. He then took me to his weapons chamber and presented me with a Walther pistol. I slipped it into my pocket and that is where it remained. Then we continued on our way to the kitchen pantry and to what I would soon know was called the *Kannenberggang* – the steps to the tunnel that led to the large, reinforced door at the opening of the bunker. There were a couple of FBK guards still dressed smartly in their uniforms but in field-grey rather than smart black. They looked at my pass and waved us through without so much as a second glance. I was surprised that there were no other checks. I had my pistol in my pocket but nobody searched me. I have been told since that the security surrounding Hitler's bunker was so tight that even staff officers were searched and their side arms confiscated. Nobody was supposed to carry a gun near the Führer! That was not true by the time I first arrived. The place was in chaos by then. The doors were often left ajar to help the ventilation below, and after my first visit more often than not the guards simply waved me through.

Thereafter I would usually enter the bunker using the emergency door in the garden, mainly because it was half the distance from the Party Chancellery and so half the risk.

I have often been asked over the years whether I regret not shooting Hitler. I certainly had the opportunity. On several occasions I was within metres of the Führer. But the answer is no, I do not regret not trying to kill him. The reason is simple, but I realise why people today find it hard to understand. The fact of the matter is that the thought never crossed my mind. I was a 16-year-old boy growing up in Nazi Germany and had been utterly brainwashed by the Nazi system. To me it was the purest political system in the world. I didn't dream of questioning it and I idolised Hitler as most of Germany did. Even at that late stage in the war when it should have been obvious to anyone that everything he stood for was at best a sham and at worst thoroughly evil, I didn't realise it. You may ask, 'But surely you heard about the Jews? You heard about concentration camps?' And the answer is that I never heard anyone in the bunker or outside the bunker talk about either. I thought that the purpose of concentration camps was entirely different to what they turned out to be. It was only many, many years later that I began to realise the full horror of the evil of which I had been born into.

On a more practical level, I can answer honestly that no, I don't regret not having shot Hitler, because if I had done I most certainly wouldn't have been here to tell the tale. If I hadn't been shot on the spot, I would have been strung up in no time at all. And I suspect a meat hook would have been the slow and painful method of my strangulation rather than the more charitable option of a bullet in the head.

The first room I encountered on entering the upper bunker was what most of us called the *Gemeinschafsraum* (common room) although I've heard it called other names such as canteen corridor and dining passageway. It was a small room with a low roof and one strong oak table. It served as a dining-room for most of the junior bunker staff, the FBK guards, the orderlies and sometimes the secretaries. It was often laden with fresh food from the pantry that was immediately to the left as one entered from the tunnel. By the time I arrived there it served as a play-room for the Goebbels' children. There were books littered on the table-top and the floor. The children sat around the table like any other family would sit around their kitchen table, laughing, crying, teasing one another and the guards. It was usually a scene of complete domestic harmony. Some of the younger ones would play on the floor. Others would run in and out of the rooms playing hide-and-seek. At first I thought Traudl Junge was their nanny because she spent so much time feeding them and playing with them. It was only later that I discovered she was Hitler's secretary. The Goebbels' family suite was to the right when one entered the upper bunker. The senior members of the bunker had their food prepared for them upstairs and delivered downstairs.

Magda and Joseph Goebbels were now ensconced in the bunker *en famile*, if not an entirely happy family at that. According to some accounts they could barely tolerate one another's presence but whenever I saw them in the bunker they seemed to be perfectly pleasant to each other. But it seemed a cold and calculating relationship. Whatever their personal differences, they were both united in their dedication to the Nazi cause. And Magda Goebbels was infatuated with Hitler.

The Propaganda Minister had an office in the lower bunker where he also slept, while Magda and the children had their quarters in the upper bunker, up the concrete stairs. The six children shared one room, sleeping in three sets of bunk beds. Magda had a room to herself. The children played in the corridors of both bunkers, at ease with their 'Uncle Adolf'. He for his part made sure that Constanze Manziarly always provided them with plenty of sweets and cakes and freshly made sandwiches from the kitchen. To Helmut, who was ten, the whole experience was a big game. He was not the brightest of the brood and was a noisy little child who liked to play at being a soldier. Every time the bunker trembled with the crash of an explosion outside, he shouted with excitement. Heidi, the youngest, aged four, was so sweet everyone in the bunker loved her. The others were Hilde, aged eleven, Holde, eight, and Hedda, six. All sweet, innocent little things. Finally, there was Helga, the oldest, intelligent and appearing to be much older than her 12 years. She was her father's favourite.

Joseph Goebbels adored his children and played with them at every opportunity he could find in those last few days. Their arrival in the bunker had produced a strange mixture of emotions. One was pity, because it was quite clear what their parents had in store for them and it was abundantly obvious that they had no idea at all. The other was relief. It was nice to have a happy brood of children around after having to put up with the all-pervading gloom of endless bad news and the masculine atmosphere of Hitler's entourage. Traudl Junge seemed to have been most enlivened by their arrival. Playing nanny to the children must have been an enormous relief compared to having to listen to Hitler talk about the evils of international Jewry for the hundredth time.

It seems horrendous that any mother can have contemplated what Magda Goebbels was now considering. But she had already rationalised the situation in her mind. She confided to a friend: 'In the days to come Joseph will be regarded as one of the greatest criminals Germany has ever produced. The children will hear that daily, people will torment them, despise and humiliate them. We will take them with us, they are too good, too lovely for the world which lies ahead.' Magda Goebbels was no docile, easily impressed girl like Eva Braun. She was a woman with her own mind. He nevertheless trusted and adored Magda Goebbels and, of course, presented her with his gold Nazi Party badge in honour of her moving into the bunker to be with him.

But in these last few days of the Third Reich there was a slightly more ambiguous relationship between her husband and the Führer. He had demonstrated his loyalty to Hitler by moving into the bunker with his family while so many others were fleeing Berlin. Hitler had been best man at Goebbels' wedding to Magda in 1931. But there was a coldness between them now. Hitler rarely looked him directly in the eye and never had dinner alone with him. Presently, Hitler would even refuse to take calls directly from him. They would have to be channelled through Martin Bormann. This was a curious situation because Goebbels' room was only the other side of the conference corridor from Hitler's suite. So his calls had first to be directed to the small telephone switchboard next door, then to Bormann's office, then across the corridor to Hitler.

We went through the canteen corridor and down the concrete steps to the lower bunker. There were two further FBK guards at this door, but again, this was not always the case. Sometimes I would walk down the stairwell to find the door open and not a soul around, as would others. The first room we entered would be the one in which I would spend much of my time in the forthcoming days. The waiting-room, or *Vorzimmer Lage* (ante-situation room) was usually full of adjutants, their orderlies and secretaries, waiting to be summoned into the conference corridor beyond. There were also couriers, although most of them were not boys like me but senior officers. Invariably, when the door to the conference corridor opened we would get a glimpse of one of these men, Hitler often hunched over the table in front of him, Goebbels and Bormann pacing up and down, somehow finding the space to do so even though it was a tiny room. Hitler always wore his uniform, although I couldn't help notice as the days went by that it began to look as if he had slept in it the night before.

One day I was waiting in the conference corridor with several other couriers and some military officers. On both sides were several doors. Unexpectedly, Hitler entered. He stepped into the hallway from what was called the map-room. It was crowded with people on this occasion. I noticed that they were packed in as tight as sardines. When Hitler emerged into our midst he seemed to be in deep thought, no longer taking notice of anyone. He was by himself. Somehow this startled me. He just walked into the room where most of the dispatches were issued and received. And then he disappeared again as quickly as he had come.

There was an intense feeling of claustrophobia about both the upper and lower bunkers but at the same time it could be quite cool inside. The rooms were not big and the ceilings were low. The constant artificial light and almost permanent humming of the ventilation generator frazzled the mind. It wasn't a pleasant experience being there. Once I saw a group of generals emerge from the small map-room. How long had they been in there, I wondered? When they emerged they looked as if they were on the verge of suffocation. Their suffering was increased by the fact that nobody was allowed to smoke anywhere in the bunker complex on the Führer's orders.

I was relieved on my first visit to the Führerbunker to find that directly to the left of the concrete staircase was a row of toilets that were spotlessly clean. I suppose it was for the senior officers and Party officials who had to spend so much time hanging around the waiting-room. I used it whenever I could and nobody ever stopped me. The other great redeeming feature of the bunker was that there was fresh water available from an artesian well 20 metres beneath the surface. Virtually all the water supply to the rest of the Chancellery complex was by now either cut off or contaminated.

The aspect of the Führerbunker that I occasionally found hardest to stomach was the sight of the trolley-load of food that was almost a permanent feature in the waiting-room. The sandwiches were always made from fresh bread rather than the unspeakable canned composite we had to suffer. There was a bakery on Wilhelmsstrasse that, unbelievably, was still operating. And there were always fresh ingredients: salami, roast beef, fresh cheese and pickle. I desperately wanted to help myself to a handful of them but I never dared risk it. Most painful of all was the sight of Martin Bormann who would come into the waiting-room at regular intervals and scoop up as many of the sandwiches as he could before stuffing them into his tunic pockets and returning to where he came from. I was beginning to nurture a severe distaste for Bormann.

The wires between the Führerbunker and the navy radio dispatch room in the cellars of the Party Chancellery across Wilhelmsstrasse had by now been completely severed. Consequently any messages that needed to be sent from the Führerbunker had to be first taken physically by a courier over Wilhemsstrasse. (Some messages went via the radio room of the Propaganda Ministry, but only the navy radio room in the Party Chancellery had access to the navy and Party ciphers.) As a result I would spend the next few days running across Wilhemsstrasse a dozen or so times a day. It was a nightmare.

It was a game of Russian roulette and those who stepped out from cover were taking their life in their hands. At best they would get a mouthful of the constant cloud of phosphorus smoke and poisonous petrol from the incendiaries; at worst they would be sliced down by a Russian rocket. By then Wilhelmsstrasse stank with the smell of scorched bodies which had usually been incinerated by flame-throwers. It was a particularly nauseating, sickly sweet smell that I can still remember today. If a katyusha strike hit anywhere near where one was, it often produced sudden blindness and a terrible disorientation. That was the most dangerous moment. One had to find one's feet straight away otherwise the next strike could be for you.

The stretch we had to use for crossing had become an open-air burial pit. It was littered with the dead, some maimed beyond recognition. On the other side of Wilhelmsstrasse the Chancellery Garden had also become a graveyard. Small fires generated smoke that concealed some of the corpses and twice I stumbled over stiff bodies that had not been buried. Whenever we thought that the enemy firing must have reached its peak, it increased still further. The rain of metal caused incandescent specks on impact, creating carpets of sparks. Some bullets or shrapnel must have exploded upon impact and when they hit people, they tore them to shreds. We pulled several of the badly wounded to safety and treatment in Dr Gertrud's sick bay. Some she could not save. It was really only a first aid centre. Axmann wanted us to avoid exposure to this shooting gallery as much as possible, but in the brief four or five days I was there, I knew at least 20 who died, including Otto Hamann, Hitler Youth leader of Berlin.

Whenever I made this run I was surrounded by a thick cloud of suffocating smoke. The smack of a direct hit would make such a deafening sound that my eardrums almost burst. But far more devastating was the constant series of impacts, a hellish hallelujah that shredded my nerves.

There were never any guards posted outside the emergency entrance. They always stayed safely behind the door. There was a small canopy over the entrance that gave one some degree of shelter from the shelling outside. Whenever I arrived there, usually out of breath and always with my heart racing, they would greet me with the most mundane comments. 'Lucky boy! You made it again.' Or: 'What, you again, boy! You're still with us?' The FBK guards were scathingly called 'bunker soldiers' by the assistants in Constanze Manziarly's kitchen. 'Why don't you go out and fight instead of letting these boys do your job for you?' one of them once said.

One of the guards I became most familiar with and liked very much was Master Sergeant Erich 'Harry' Mengershausen. He seemed to work 16-hour shifts. Once, I remember running across Wilhelmsstrasse in a blind panic and arriving at the emergency entrance. The steel door was shut tight, which was unusual. Usually it was left slightly ajar. I banged and banged and banged on the door trying to get the attention of somebody inside. It was to no avail. The noise of the shells exploding outside drowned everything out. In the end I had to run around the front of the Chancellery and risk another hailstorm from hell before entering the bunker through the Kannenberggang. When I complained about this to Harry, he was very funny. 'It's a secret bunker, for Godsakes,' he said. 'Do you expect me to give you a latch-key?'

During the last days and nights Harry and I even shared bits of information, such as how close the Russians were. A constant topic of conversation was how long it would take Wenck's Twelfth to get to Berlin to relieve us.

Hitler's Third Reich had now been reduced to a few square kilometres of central Berlin. The focus of the Red Army's artillery barrage was now almost entirely on the *Regierungsviertel* (government quarter). This was the area known as '*der Zitadelle*'. And this citadel was going to be the site of Hitler's last stand. It embraced all the government buildings in the Regierungsviertel but the centre of it all was the Chancellery complex, which was becoming the vortex of the whirlwind that was sucking Hitler into oblivion. This was a compact square bounded by the Old Reich Chancellery on the Wilhelmsstrasse on the east, and the barracks of the LAH on the west. Connecting the two along Voss Strasse in the south was the New Reich Chancellery. There were important adjuncts to the citadel, such as the *Tiergarten* (zoo) to the west, the 'green lung' of Berlin and now home to an important military hospital in the Zoo flak tower and an underground supply of fuel for Erich Kempka's garages underneath the Chancellery.

Beneath this entire complex was a labyrinth of cellars and bunkers, most of them linked to one another by a warren of tunnels. (There were also another five separate bunkers for various government offices in the Chancellery area of Berlin and dozens of air-raid shelters and refuges. Joseph Goebbels had abandoned a particularly sumptuous bunker at his official residence on Hermann Göring Strasse to be with the Führer in his.) Much of the activity now in the Chancellery was underneath the long façade of Speer's building along Voss Strasse where a series of cellars-cum-air-raid-shelters were full to bursting point with fraught-looking SS men, wounded soldiers, nurses, doctors and civilians sheltering from the madness outside.

In these cellars was the command post for the SS general and military commander of the citadel, and the quarters for him and his adjutants. There was also an air-raid shelter that had originally been intended for 200 pregnant women, but by the time I arrived there were nearer to 500 civilians crowded into it and the conditions were appalling. At the centre of this complex was an emergency hospital. It had originally been the

Chancellery dispensary, but in the last few weeks it had been transformed into a primitive surgery and operating theatre. The conditions of utter degradation would soon come to resemble the cellar next door.

I would become very familiar with the layout of the emergency hospital because part of my job was to ferry medical supplies from it to Dr Gertrud's sick-room in the Party Chancellery. It was presided over by two surgeons. Professor Werner Haase had been Hitler's first personal physician. He had left the Führer's service in the Reich Chancellery some years ago to resume his private practice near the city's renowned Charité Hospital. But in these last days he would become close to the Führer once more and Hitler would trust Haase more than he trusted any of the other doctors. By this time Haase was dying of tuberculosis and he found himself out of breath much of the time, having to take rests at 20-minute intervals. His partner in the emergency hospital, or casualty station as it was also called, was Professor Ernst-Günther Schenck. Professor Schenck was not a surgeon but a nutritionist. He was not professionally qualified to operate and had to be guided by Professor Haase much of the time. The conditions were appalling. There was a constant lack of bandages, anaesthetics and basic medical supplies. Sometimes bandages had to be salvaged from the bodies of the dead whose corpses were piled up outside. At one stage the doctors between them completed 370 operations, many of them major, in seven days. 'I was up to my elbows in entrails, arteries, gore,' Schenck once said.

In the Chancellery complex there were other underground shelters, bunkers and cellars. There were underground garages for armoured personnel carriers and a vast 1,500-square-metre bunker for all the top Nazi Party officials' drivers and limousines, including Hitler's Mercedes. The German word for driver is *Fahrer* so naturally it became dubbed the *Fahrerbunker*. In the middle of these buildings was the Chancellery Garden where I had been presented to the Führer and where the only visible sign of the Führerbunker, the concrete pillbox emergency entrance, was. The pillbox was covered with *Zeltplanen* (patterned ground-sheet covers) and by now had an SS emplacement on the roof, complete with a machine-gun nest and spotlights.

Increasingly the only way to get in and out of the citadel was via a small landing strip hastily laid out near the Brandenburg Gate. The Brandenburg Gate airstrip would witness many hair-raising landings and take-offs as military commanders and high-ranking Nazi officials made the perilous journey to and from Berlin. Mostly they came in as Albert Speer had done in the light Fieseler Storch training aircraft that were among the few that could land in the small space provided. It took all the skill and bravery of the pilots to fly in, often at tree-top level, and drop onto the little strip. Many of them died in attempting to do so. Defensive fires blazed on the approach to the runway. Russian troops were virtually at the end of the runway.

Hitler had charged SS Brigadeführer Wilhelm Mohnke with the responsibility for the defence of the citadel. Mohnke was a highly decorated SS general who at only 34 was one of the youngest in the German army. He would later be accused of war crimes, though none were ever proven. By now too, Hitler had forgiven General Helmut Weidling his supposed 'cowardice' and had put him in charge of Berlin as a whole. Both men had an impossible task. The LAH that Mohnke had at his disposal was no more than 1,200 strong. Weidling was slightly better off. He had 45,000 regular army soldiers and 43,000 Volkssturm. Axmann had taken over responsibility for the 2,700 Hitler Youth who were mostly deployed holding the two bridges across the Spree and the Havel that were the only (land) escape route out of the city, the Weidendamm across the Spree and the Pichelsdorf across the Havel. Weidling also had 5,400 navy cadets provided by Admiral Dönitz. But these young seamen were proving to be hopelessly inadequate for urban warfare. They accounted for more than their fair share of casualties in Professor Haase's emergency hospital. Perhaps it was all academic. The German defenders faced an overwhelming enemy force of 2,500,000 men that their generals had appropriately called 'Shock Troops' as well as the Red Army's formidable tank battalions.

Just as Hitler's bunker wasn't really a bunker at all, but a reinforced air-raid shelter, the citadel could hardly be described as an impregnable fortress. (In Breslau, Karl Hanke had created an impregnable fortress. Hanke was a ruthless Nazi. He was determined that Breslau would not fall to the Russians. He had ordered all the older women and children to flee the city. Thousands of them froze to death. In the city itself ten-year-old children were put to work maintaining the defences. Defeatism was met with arbitrary execution. It was no secret to anyone with eyes that the defences of Berlin were wafer-thin.

The three most visible signs of any sort of defensive arrangements were the enormous 'flak' towers located to the north, west and east of Berlin. 'Towers' is a misleading name for them. They were more like massive, squat, concrete boxes of brutal design by Speer and intended to resemble medieval fortresses. The flak tower at the zoological gardens, just referred to as Zoo (a large area of Berlin, taking up more than just the zoo itself), was the biggest and it would be the one I would soon visit. I called it a bunker rather than a tower, because that was the function it served towards the end of the war. The Zoo bunker had five large storeys above ground level, but they were tall storeys, rising some 40 metres above the treetops of the gardens. Its walls were made of reinforced concrete 2 metres thick, and its few windows were protected behind stainless steel shutters that could be opened and shut depending upon whether it was under attack or not.

The Zoo bunker was a solid square shape and at each corner, just like a medieval castle, rose four towers. On top of each were a pair of 128-mm anti-aircraft guns, eight in all, capable of projecting a deadly wall of shellfire into the paths of enemy bombers in the sky above. In the 'battlements' below these fearsome guns, facing in all four directions, was a battery of 12 cannons that could take on low-level aircraft. The five storeys below contained, in descending order: a barracks for the gun crews; a hospital that included two surgeries and beds for almost 100 patients; a reinforced store-room containing treasures from the city's museums; and a two-storey air-raid shelter capable of accommodating 15,000 civilians. Below ground there were a further three storeys containing kitchens, toilets, power equipment and the ammunition for the guns.

The other two flak towers, one to the north of Unter den Linden near the Humbolthain subway station, and one to the east at Landsberger Allee, were not quite as big but they were formidable structures. These flak towers gave General Weidling's commanders a panoramic view of the encroaching Russian invaders. And they were rapidly filling up with civilians seeking shelter. All of them would find their air-raid shelters and hospitals accommodating far more people and patients than they were ever intended to. Men, women and children would exist for days on end, squashed side by side like sardines, along every corridor and in every room. The lavatories would very quickly cease to function, clogged up by overuse and impossible to flush because of lack of running water. The passageways of the hospital units became make-do mortuaries for the dead, the nurses and doctors fearing death themselves if they dared venture outside to bury the corpses. Buckets of severed limbs and other putrid body parts lined the corridors.

The flak towers were about all that the defence of Berlin amounted to as far as I could see on my outings from the Party Chancellery. At virtually every major intersection, bedraggled groups of Volkssturm had built makeshift tank barricades out of burnt-out cars, oil drums full of cement and any other debris they could lay their hands on. But if they seriously thought they were going to be of any use against the Red Army's T-34s then they had another thing coming. The most effective weapon against the Russian tanks continued to be the deadly Panzerfaust, mainly deployed by Hitler Youth from the basements of buildings. Even those natural features that might have presented barriers to attack were to prove hopelessly inadequate. When the Russians finally did come, the Spree, the Havel River and the Tetlow Canal were all breached in a matter of minutes rather than hours.

CHAPTER ELEVEN

The Mad House

ON THAT FIRST DAY IN THE Führerbunker I returned to the Party Chancellery and stopped at the sick bay. Dr Gertrud was naturally curious to know what my impressions of the bunker were and if I had seen Hitler. I had to say 'no', I had not on that occasion, although I would have glimpses of him, and several close encounters, in the days to come. But even when he was not visible the Führer managed to exert a kind of ghostly presence over the bunker. Then Gertrud said something that completely took me aback.

'Did you see Eva Braun?'

I had never heard the name before. (Nor had the vast majority of Germans at that time.) I had no idea who she was. 'Eva Braun?' I asked. 'Who is she?'

'You don't know?' she said. 'The Führer's lover.'

'Impossible!' I looked into Dr Gertrud's eyes. 'The Führer doesn't have a paramour!'

It came as a complete surprise. It just didn't fit my perception of this all-powerful, virile leader. It had been impressed upon the German people time and time again that the Führer's energies could not be diverted from the national cause by anything as trivial as a wife or a family. I even remember my mother once telling me, 'The Führer can't afford to be married!'

Now Dr Gertrud confessed it had been as big a shock to her as it was to me. 'I didn't know it either,' she said. But Dr Gertrud portrayed Eva Braun as a great heroine, telling me that she had come from

Berchtesgaden to be at the Führer's side. I wasn't entirely sure whether to believe this. We had been so conditioned to believing that the Führer was dedicating every ounce of his energy to the fate of the Fatherland and that alone. Later that day I asked Axmann if it was true and, of course, he too knew all about Eva Braun. I was astonished.

Inside the bunker I usually got a friendly welcome from the officer on duty I handed my messages over to. *'Machs gut, junge mein Junge! Ich verlass mich auf Dich.'* ('Cheers, my boy! I depend on you.') But not once was I offered a glass of water or a sandwich. Not all my runs were regarding military communications. Several involved missions to Professor Haase's emergency hospital in the New Reich Chancellery cellars to get supplies for Dr Gertrud. I tried to combine the two. But the priority was always clear. Messages first, medical supplies second.

That day I had entered the bunker through the emergency entrance and was surprised to encounter Hitler inside the ante-room. He was leaning against the wall listening to Bormann, who was making expressive gestures to emphasise his point. On the other side was an SS officer. Some guards passed by carrying out boxes. This was going on all the time in the last days of the bunker. Several cartons of sensitive documents were being taken out into the Chancellery Garden to be burned on bonfires. But the conditions were not terribly favourable for such a method of destruction. The garden was strewn with loose pages which had been wafted away in the wind.

Later on that day I was in the passageway from the Reich Chancellery to the air-raid shelter. The corridors were now crowded to bursting point with civilians and military people. There were many women in uniforms, but most of them were indistinguishable from one another, their uniforms dirty and their features hidden beneath grime and filth. But I immediately recognised one of them. Hanna Reitsch looked less like the glamorous test-pilot of legend and more like an exhausted soldier who had just emerged from a fox-hole. She was covered in mud and grime, grease and dirt. She looked vaguely hysterical too. The cause for her concern was an air force officer on a stretcher by her side. Although covered by an army blanket, he was still in his uniform. I noticed right away that in front of his collar, partly visible, was a Knight's Cross of the Iron Cross with oak leaves and swords covering the Pour le Merit, the highest order for bravery awarded in the First World War. He had a Bismarck-like face and a huge nose. It was obvious he had been badly wounded. The lower part of the blanket was drenched in blood and folded over by a physician or medic who, with a splint and bandages, was attending to his right foot. I couldn't tell if the foot was still firmly attached to the leg or if he would lose it. The injured man's eyes were closed. He could have been unconscious.

There were two SS guards with them. One of them commented: 'The little doll won't leave his side.' She was still holding the injured man's hand and frequently stroked his forehead. I pushed my way through the crowds and made my way towards her. As I approached I could see that she was almost hysterical. I saluted and said: 'Frau Reitsch, I met you in Hirschberg.' (My grandmother had known Reitsch's parents and she had taken me to their house many years earlier when I met the pilot briefly.)

Indignant, she sharply interrupted me. 'I am not Frau Reitsch, I am Air-Captain Reitsch!'

What could have made her so angry?

She looked ragged, but didn't we all who came from the outside? Close up, I noticed some grease on her hands and face. She wore a plain leather jacket that might not have been hers since it looked oversized and loose on her petite figure. Her white blouse underneath was smudged where visible and partly torn. I was a little taken aback by her response and I didn't dare to say anything further, let alone ask questions.

In fact the injured man was one of the most important men in the German military. Colonel-General Robert Ritter von Greim was commander of the Luftwaffe on the Eastern Front. Hanna Reitsch was his mistress. They made an extraordinary pair, he a huge, ageing, statesmanlike figure, she a petite, beautiful and dazzling woman. Both were fanatical supporters of Hitler and the Nazi regime. No wonder she was so concerned about him. The arrival of Hanna Reitsch and Ritter von Greim in Berlin was one of the most extraordinary episodes of those last days of Hitler. It was also an episode that was to demonstrate that despite Hitler's belief in his own military genius there was certainly no method to his madness.

The Führer was still raging at the perceived treachery of Göring. Axmann had been too, and thought that the air Reich Marshal should have been shot on the spot. But later, when he found out the full facts, he reversed his decision, realising that Göring had been the victim of Bormann's Machiavellian machinations. Hitler, nevertheless, was looking for a replacement and von Greim was an appropriate candidate. Not only was he one of the most highly decorated and respected officers in the armed forces, he was also a fervent Nazi. His mistress was an old friend of Hitler's and an equally zealous follower. Hitler had decided to appoint von Greim as commander-in-chief of the air force and promote him to Field Marshal. Hitler could have telephoned or telegraphed his orders. But instead he summoned von Greim on a highly perilous journey that was to risk his life and cost those of many other valuable airmen.

It was now practically homicidal to attempt to get into Berlin by air. The little Brandenburg Gate airstrip was surrounded by Russian forces. Albert Speer had been lucky to get through a few days previously. The story of how von Greim and Reitsch had got through was even more extraordinary. Von Greim's second-in-command, Karl Koller, chief-of-staff of the Luftwaffe, was now safely out of Berlin and in Munich. He begged von Greim not to go. The night before, Koller pointed out, an Allied bombing raid had practically flattened Hitler's home and southern command post at Obersalzberg. The Berghof had been badly damaged as had the Bormann and Göring residences. The war was all over, implored Koller. It was just a matter of time. But it was not in von Greim's nature to disobey an order from the Führer. Reitsch was an equally determined fanatic, not to mention fantasist. If the last act of the Third Reich was about to unfold, she wanted to be on the centre stage of it.

Together this bizarre couple made off for the Luftwaffe airbase at Rechlin, 60 miles north-east of Berlin. There they had hoped to use a helicopter that could land in the Chancellery Garden. But when they arrived it was too badly damaged to fly. Instead they found a Focke-Wulf 190 and the pilot who had flown Speer into Berlin. Now he was ordered to repeat his feat. There was one hitch. The Focke-Wulf 190 only had room for the pilot with von Greim's massive frame squeezed in behind him. But Reitsch refused to be left out. They discovered that there was an emergency exit in the tail with just enough space to squeeze in her own, more sprightly, frame. Reitsch was barely 5 feet tall. They took off, flying at almost hedge-top height and accompanied by a defensive flight of no less than 40 Luftwaffe fighters. These were fighters badly needed by the air force. And one by one they were shot out of the sky on this mission that remained a mystery to the main protagonists.

They arrived at Gatow airfield, their numbers badly depleted. Now the only aeroplane capable of taking them the remaining distance to the Brandenburg airstrip was a tiny two-seater trainer. Von Greim took the controls with Reitsch at his side. It was when they were approaching the centre of Berlin that calamity struck. Enemy fire from the street-fighting below ripped through the aircraft's thin fuselage. The bullets riddled von Greim's right foot. He was in immense pain and utterly incapable of controlling the aircraft. Hanna Reitsch leaned over him and in a very awkward position took the controls. In a feat of extraordinary flying she managed to land the craft at the Brandenburg airstrip. A car was commandeered and they were whisked to the Chancellery.

It was only when von Greim was taken to the Führerbunker that he was told what his extraordinary mission was about. He was having his foot patched up in Dr Stumpfegger's treatment room when Hitler explained he was to be the Luftwaffe's new commander-in-chief. Hitler was still agitated. Pacing up and down the small room, he embarked on a familiar denunciation of the German people, army generals, the SS and Hermann Göring. Shaking his fists in rage, at times he seemed on the verge of turning purple. 'Nothing is spared me. No allegiances are kept, no honour lived up to. There are no disappointments I've not had, no betrayals I have not experienced.' The German people were not worthy of the high ideals of National Socialism, he said. German soldiers were cowards who would rather run away even though they knew their wives would be raped by the Russians. Göring had thrown away the resources of the greatest air force in the world. It was a familiar litany.

It was a curious scene. Several fighter aircraft had been lost in the drama to bring von Greim into Berlin, along with most of their pilots. The new commander-in-chief of the Luftwaffe had been seriously wounded and would, in any case, be unable to leave the bunker for another three days. And several other planes dispatched to Berlin to take him and Reitsch to his command would also be shot out of the sky. At the end of his tirade, Hitler admonished his new Field Marshal and Hanna Reitsch. They really shouldn't have made the trip, he told them. Even soldiers, Hitler told the two of them, should disregard orders when they are futile. It was exactly the opposite of what the Führer repeatedly told everyone else under his command. For them orders must be obeyed, no matter how futile.

As von Greim was being treated inside the Führerbunker, the scenes outside were deteriorating rapidly. I will never forget the sight of the big container outside the Old Reich Chancellery building. It was a laundry tub, but it was full of amputated limbs, blood and putrefied dressings. It had obviously been used in the medical operating room. Someone had put it outside and had simply left it there. Either they didn't have time to dispose of this gruesome human garbage, or they didn't care to. Or perhaps they too had joined the dead, caught unawares by a Russian katyusha strike.

Care of the wounded was becoming increasingly hopeless. Back in the Party Chancellery, there were upwards of 30 patients now in a room barely capable of accommodating half that number. More were coming in by the hour. There was no more space in which to put them. There was a shortage of bandages and medications. What seemed to frustrate Dr Gertrud the most was the lack of water.

'Get water!' she would shout in desperation.

But water could only be got from the other side of Wilhelmsstrasse. For a while there was a temporary water-cart parked there. We started out using bulk jam containers, but their covers were not tight enough and they were too cumbersome for running fast across Wilhelmsstrasse. Eventually, we got hold of some 10-litre metal containers. I only carried water two or three times, thank God, as I had to deliver, ever more frequently, urgent dispatches. But right until the very end this deadly mission was accomplished hour in, hour out by young boys and girls. Many lost their lives.

There were no body-bags and no blankets to spare. The dead were simply stockpiled near the stairs of the cellar and taken into the backyard whenever the shelling subsided enough to make it safe. I remember once there was a lull in the shelling. A boy and a girl decided to risk it and take their young comrade outside to be buried. A mortar finished them off the second they moved outside the door. There is a bitter irony to that, isn't there? Killed, burying the dead. Once four or five of us were crowded by the exit, waiting for a pause. A courier made the sign of the cross and started running. Seconds later, in front of our eyes, he was hit.

'Straight into heaven!' commented one of the boys standing next to me.

'Let's get him!' I said. 'He might still be alive!' Three of us took off, two to look after the fallen comrade. But the boy was dead. I dashed to the emergency entrance of the Führerbunker. Once again, I somehow made it. When I told Axmann about the incident he was momentarily silent. But he made no comment. Axmann often brought to our attention the story of Richard Arndt, a legendary figure of the First World War in Germany. At the age of 15 Arndt had fought in the Battle of Verdun. He had written a book about his experiences and was something of an icon to Hitler Youth. But in the First World War, Richard Arndt was an exception. At the end of the Second World War, there were thousands of 15-year-olds fighting for the Fatherland.

In conversation we reassured ourselves that we would match Arndt's bravery. And naïve as we were, we thought we also deserved a glorious page in the book of history. As insane as this may appear today, we remained determined to live up to our Führer's expectations. Our mood was numbed but we kept going, still driven by blind faith and what we then thought of as idealism but which I now know was fanaticism and, yes, quite frankly, an evil fanaticism. But it was all we knew. As naïve as we were, I don't think any of us could help observing that while it was us in the citadel who appeared to be taking all the risks, the Nazi Party officials who had created this hell were all hiding in their bunkers or had disappeared altogether. We felt we were taking most of the risks. It came as something of an unwelcome surprise therefore to hear even more rumours about death squads roaming Berlin and hanging Hitler Youth who had deserted.

During all of this, there were little bits of bullet shrapnel under the skin of my finger. My left hand was in a cast and my little finger became infected. I really didn't notice it because of the intense pressure that I was under, seemingly never-ending days of exhaustion and danger at almost every moment. I was up at least 18 hours a day and sleep was something I captured whenever I could. I didn't think of my wounds. But Dr

Gertrud insisted that I get an injection from the emergency hospital in the Reich Chancellery. It was ironic. I had to make a dash across the alleyway of death just to get my little finger seen to. Unfortunately, they gave me an overdose of tetanus vaccine and I erupted in blisters all over my body.

By then we also realised that we were hopelessly short of medical supplies of all descriptions, not just Dr Gertrud's treatment centre but the emergency hospital under the New Chancellery also. The only place we were likely to find any was in the military hospital of the Zoo bunker. Renate, who was only a girl but was behaving like a senior physician, decided I should see if I could get something, anything, from there. The Zoo bunker was in the south-west corner of the Tiergarten. But getting there by now was, to say the least, an extremely hazardous exercise. It was a very, very long run through an area that was being pounded relentlessly by shells and for all I knew was being patrolled by Red Army troops.

'You can do it!' Renate said to me as if it was nothing more than a college challenge. It turned out to be a run through hell and back. The second I got out of the cellar I was under a thick hailstorm of exploding katyusha shells, the *Flammenmeer* (sea of flames) in the background, and, close to the bunker, blinding smoke. I was surprised I arrived alive.

When I did I discovered soldiers and civilians were jammed into the air-raid shelter. There was absolutely no discipline and the authorities had given up trying to impose it. I could hardly move. People were shouting, babies were crying – and I was greeted by the now familiar sight of men and women shamelessly making love in full view of everyone else. Fortunately, some of the supplies Renate requested were still on hand, but I had to wait. It occurred to me that Hannes might be there and I looked around for him, but only for a very short time because, even if he was, my chances of detecting him would have been very slim. The crowd was merciless. I had to push myself back down to the exit and was almost glad to be back in the hellfire of outside. It had been madness. But at least I was alive.

Renate rewarded me with an injection that relieved some of the pain and itching from the blisters. The zwieback and the schnapps didn't take care of my intestinal pangs. For a day I didn't eat. I drank only water. Had I not had access to the Führerbunker where drinking water was still available, dehydration might have taken its toll. Eventually my cramps subsided, but now I was a human wreck. It must have been more than mere willpower that kept me going. My instincts must have warned me that if I gave up it could be the end of me.

Later that evening in the Führerbunker Hitler asked Hanna Reitsch to join him in his study. He told her of his decision to commit suicide with Eva Braun, and how he wanted their remains to be incinerated afterwards. He then presented her with two phials of poison, one for herself and one for Ritter von Greim. Reitsch and von Greim were given rooms in the Führerbunker. She would spend much of the next three days tenderly holding his hand in the tiny bedroom. Hitler would spend a great deal of time with them too. He insisted that it was von Greim's duty to leave the bunker as soon as possible and assume his command. Neither Reitsch nor von Greim wanted to. They wanted to die in the bunker with Hitler. Peculiarly he now would not tolerate any disobedience despite his warm words a few hours previously. In those few days they agreed that they too would end it all when the time came by taking poison. But their own suicide pact had a neat twist to it. Instead of shooting their brains out at the same time, they would hold a heavy grenade each and pull the safety catch as they swallowed the poison.

Von Greim was an undoubted war hero and shrewd military tactician. Yet he too appears to have fallen under the Führer's spell. When Koller called him at the bunker he told his deputy that all would be well in the end. 'The presence of the Führer and his confidence have completely inspired me,' he said to Koller. 'This place is as good as a fountain of youth for me!'

Koller was incredulous. 'The whole place is a lunatic asylum,' he said.

The Führerbunker was indeed beginning to resemble a madhouse. Hitler spent much of his time raging about the treachery around him, pacing up and down his study or the map-room, sometimes falling into apoplectic fits of rage. Goebbels fumed at Göring's flight from the bunker. How dare he survive when those loyal to the Führer were prepared to sacrifice their lives for him! He spoke about the glory of dying for the Third Reich and savaged the delirium and treachery that surrounded the Führer in the last days of the war. With Göring effectively out of the way, Speer no longer in Berlin and Himmler branded a failure, Bormann had now become the most important aide to Hitler, with the possible exception of Goebbels and Axmann.

Axmann, like the Führer, believed that Providence had selected Hitler to be the leader of Germany, that he was an *Übermensch* (a human above all humans, a superman). That day Axmann got his reward for such fanatical devotion. The Führer bestowed upon him the highest decoration of the Reich: the Golden Cross of the German Order. Hitler personally awarded it to Axmann, who came into our room in the Party Chancellery cellar flushed with excitement. The Führer had told him: 'Without your boys, the battle could not be continued, not just here in Berlin, but in all of Germany.' Axmann said that he replied: 'Those are your boys, my Führer!' When he returned Axmann said to us: '*Für Treue! Für uns alle!*' (For loyalty! For all of us!) Axmann had become part of Hitler's inner circle and would be spending more time there. His motto now was:

'*Bedingungslose Treue zum Führer!*' (Unconditional allegiance to the Führer!)

That day General Weidling's headquarters on Hohenzollerndamm came under such an intensive katyusha attack that he decided to move it nearer to the Reich Chancellery. His new command post was in the cellars of the old army headquarters where Colonel Count von Stauffenberg had been put to death after the July assassination plot: not the greatest of omens. By 26 April Russian troops would be in Alexanderplatz and only a mile away from the citadel. Soon there would be Russian tanks on Wilhelmsstrasse.

∽ CHAPTER TWELVE ∽

The Final Betrayal

ON THE MORNING OF 27 APRIL once more I had arrived in the ante-room and was out of breath after having crossed the usual barrage of shellfire and suffocating smoke. Through my smoke-filled eyes I could make out the forms of three women in front of me. How shabby I must have looked to them. My uniform was torn. My face was dirty and unkempt. I was not the most decorous of sights. Since we had moved into the cellar of the Party Chancellery, I had not had a change of tunic and trousers, let alone of underwear or socks. I must have appeared crusty to say the least. My physical appearance and the state of extreme anxiety I was in obviously shocked the women, because one of them reached into her pocket and gave me a neatly folded silk handkerchief. Gratefully, I wiped my eyes with it. As I was doing so she handed me a cold drink. I was about to say thank you, when I looked into her eyes and the moist glass slipped out of my hand.

It was Eva Braun. One of the other women I immediately recognised as Magda Goebbels. The glass fell to the floor and shattered. I blushed. I was so embarrassed I just wanted to get out of there. But Fraeulein Braun reached out for a fresh glass of water from the food trolley and offered it to me. 'Calm down!' she said quietly. 'Calm down!'

As I accepted the drink I noticed Magda Goebbels put a hand on her own forehead as if she had a headache. The third woman in the background remarked: 'Isn't it horrible how these boys have to fight?' Magda Goebbels kept her right hand on her forehead without saying a word, while Eva Braun continued her efforts to comfort me. She even dipped the handkerchief in water and dabbed my stinging eyes. 'Calm down,' she repeated, once more.

Later, I told Dr Gertrud of my encounter. Dr Gertrud was still curious about Eva Braun. 'How old do you think she is?'

I was never good at guessing people's ages. '*Mitte Zwanzig?*' (mid-20s?) I replied, guessing. I was wrong. In fact Eva Braun was in her mid-30s, which was a surprise to me because in her manner and demeanour she appeared much younger: more of a girl than a woman. She had a definite girlish quality about her. She always seemed cheerful. I never once noticed her looking concerned, no matter how bad the news was. To my young eyes, she had all the poise of a movie star.

On that first day I met her she was wearing a dark dress with a golden brooch on it. I was to notice that Eva Braun was always smartly turned out in elegant and sometimes pretty dresses. Towards the last days in the bunker she became even more glorified in her appearance. It was almost as if she was relishing every moment of her role, now at the centre stage of history and by the side of her Führer. On the occasions I saw her she appeared almost radiant. That's the only way I can describe her. Whenever I saw her she was always in the presence of other women, never Hitler himself.

In most historic accounts, Eva Braun is portrayed as a naïve woman, simple even, not entirely comprehending the scale of the wickedness she was surrounded by. To my mind, my meeting with her in the waiting-room confirmed this view and exposed the essentially sweet and kind woman she was. But Professor Shenck did not think Eva Braun was a naïve woman, nor did he think her a nice person. Having observed her at close range in the bunker, he certainly did not think her a very intelligent person either. On that morning of 27 April, an episode was about to unfold which revealed that Eva Braun could be as casually ruthless as any of the most murderous Nazis.

Eva Braun's younger sister Gretl was a prominent member of Hitler's 'court', that collection of old cronies, Nazi Party apparatchiks, servants and bodyguards, most of whom had been with him since his Munich days. On the whole they felt more at home in the rarefied atmosphere of his Alpine retreat at the Berghof overlooking Berchtesgaden than in Berlin. Gretl Braun had been part of this clique ever since her elder sister became Hitler's mistress in the early 1930s. But while Eva was quiet, reserved and shy, Gretl was playful, adventurous and engaging. She smoked, which infuriated the Führer, which in turn she found amusing. And she flirted outrageously with his FBK guards.

In 1944 Gretl had married a swashbuckling SS cavalry officer named Hermann Fegelein. Adolf Hitler was chief witness at the marriage ceremony. The union suited both Fegelein and the Führer. There had been a feeling that Hitler had always been a little embarrassed by Eva Braun's lowly Bavarian background. Fegelein came from a distinguished family and had served conspicuously on the Eastern Front. Eva Braun's social status could only benefit with his connection to her family. At the same time, Fegelein's career would surely not be damaged by his admission into the Führer's inner circle.

Fegelein was a calculating and utterly unscrupulous opportunist. He had an arrogant swagger that did not endear him to either his peers or his underlings and it only became more insufferable after he married the sister of the Führer's mistress. Fegelein was also a serial womaniser. From the beginning of his marriage to Gretl he kept a series of mistresses in his apartment in the Charlottenburg district of Berlin while she set up home in Bavaria, soon becoming pregnant with their first child. There was a popular rumour that Eva Braun was one of his mistresses. They certainly danced and went horse-riding together, and Fegelein made much of his association with Eva. However, he was such a Machiavellian careerist, it is unlikely Fegelein would risk the displeasure of the Führer by being caught in bed with his girlfriend.

Fegelein's career in the SS had benefited from Heinrich Himmler's patronage. However, since Himmler's abject failure as a military commander had left him with a blemished reputation in the Reich Chancellery, the SS leader was no longer so warmly welcomed in Berlin. He had appointed Fegelein as his liaison officer with the Führer. Once safely away from his master's sphere of influence, Fegelein quickly trimmed his sails to the prevailing wind in Berlin. He betrayed Himmler at every opportunity and ingratiated himself with Bormann. These two most unsavoury of men seemed genuinely to enjoy one another's company and became regular drinking companions. Fegelein's rise into Hitler's inner circle was assured. He became one of the Führer's closest confidants.

However, on the morning I ran into Eva Braun, her brother-in-law's fortunes were about to undergo a dramatic transformation. Since the Führer had moved into the bunker, Fegelein had been one of the regular visitors to the subterranean complex. He had attended most of the afternoon and evening conferences waiting, like all the other adjutants and liaison officers, in the ante-room in case his presence was required by the Führer in the conference or map-room. However, he did not live in the bunker. When he was not in his Charlottenburg apartment he lodged in one of the other air-raid shelters under the Chancellery.

As the military situation went from bad to worse, it became obvious to Fegelein that Hitler, the Nazis and Berlin were all doomed. It also might have been a source of alarm to him that, as practically a part of the Führer's family, he might be expected to commit suicide along with all the other fanatics in the bunker. Fegelein had no intention of going down with the sinking ship. As the day of doom came nearer, he began to engineer his escape from Berlin. Quietly, Fegelein absented himself. He covered his tracks by making frequent telephone calls to the bunker to foster the illusion of a presence of sorts. The ploy was successful for a while. But around about 27 April the Führer suddenly noticed that he hadn't seen Himmler's SS liaison officer for some time. Where was he? Hitler demanded Fegelein's presence promptly. There was a hue and cry for him throughout the Reich Chancellery. But it was to no avail. Fegelein was nowhere to be found.

It was then that Otto Günsche recalled that Fegelein had an apartment in Charlottenburg on the outskirts of the city. Without further ado a squad of FBK guards was sent to investigate. At the address provided they found Fegelein almost incoherent with drink and in the company of a beautiful woman. The couple appeared to be planning a getaway. In two bags were false identity papers and a bundle of Reich Marks and Swiss francs. It was an awkward situation for the FBK guards because Fegelein was a superior officer. Deploying what charm he could muster in his advanced state of inebriation, Fegelein attempted to persuade the FBK men to let the matter drop. They should let him get away, he reasoned, and get themselves away to safety too. The war was lost. Hitler was doomed.

The guards remained unmoved. Consequently, Fegelein was left with no option but to attempt to pull rank. He asked to be excused a moment while he telephoned his sister-in-law in the Führerbunker. They acquiesced and he got through to Eva Braun. Playing on Eva's emotions, Fegelein told her that he was only planning to fly to Bavaria to be at Gretl's side when she gave birth to their child. But on this occasion Eva Braun did not display the naïvety for which she was renowned. She was appalled that he should try to abandon the Führer and told him to return to the Chancellery at once.

Hanna Reitsch was in the bunker with Braun when the call came through. She later recorded Hitler's mistress bursting into a slightly theatrical lament about her brother-in-law's betrayal of 'poor Adolf'. 'Better that 10,000 others die than he be lost to Germany,' Eva Braun is supposed to have said of the Führer. Fegelein was taken back to the Chancellery. The imbroglio at his apartment had one unintended consequence. While the FBK men were distracted, Fegelein's mystery woman escaped. It has long since been presumed she was a spy, probably a foreign diplomat's wife introduced to Fegelein unwittingly by Joseph Goebbels. (It has also been claimed that she was responsible for several security leaks from the Chancellery that had infuriated the Führer. If so, her flimsy connection to Goebbels might have explained the odd cooling off of relations between Hitler and Goebbels in the last days of the bunker.) When he arrived at the Chancellery Fegelein was thrown in a cell near the cellar air-raid shelters to await his fate.

By then the stink of dirt and decay clung to my clothes. I hadn't changed for days on end. Berlin was now a smouldering scape of rubble and ruins. Thick, black smoke wafted across the rooftops. The streets hissed to the sound of broken mains. Corpses littered the streets and a peculiar, almost sweet, stench of decomposing remains mixed with burnt flesh filled the air. Every major street corner seemed to be blocked by some sort of makeshift barricade. What purpose these ramshackle barriers served was not clear. Every road now was so littered with fallen masonry, rubble and burnt-out vehicles that nothing but a tank could have made any headway down them and only a lunatic could imagine that the tank barricades would stop a Russian T-34 tank.

As Hannes and I had dashed back and forth outside the immediate environs of the Reich Chancellery we noticed that it was becoming an increasingly common sight to see white sheets hanging from apartment windows. Sometimes whole streets of them were in evidence. Now SS death squads were patrolling the streets, ready to shoot anybody who so much as dared suggest surrender. Whenever a white flag appeared in an apartment house groups of SS dashed inside looking for the culprit. 'Flying court martial' scoured Berlin looking for men who were not fighting. They had the power to put anyone on trial and order their instant execution. Identity cards were demanded of civilians, pay-books of soldiers. Any male who was not at the front line was pulled out from the crowd and interrogated. Anyone who couldn't come up with a plausible story risked the noose or a firing squad.

But even the prospect of facing these inhuman squads seemed to be having little effect on a population that faced death every day. The SS were beginning to come into more and more conflicts with regular army soldiers who were sickened by the random brutality of it all. Increasingly Wehrmacht officers were intervening when they saw some terrified soul being threatened with summary execution by an SS man. Some senior commanders had warned the SS to keep out of their zones. Many elderly Volkssturm were simply handing themselves over to the enemy. They would rather risk the whim of the enemy than the certainty of death at the hands of their own side.

For much of that day Hitler displayed his usual manic inconsistency. One moment he would march out of his office telling anyone who was prepared to listen how Berlin was going to be saved by General Wenck's Twelfth Army. Or how Busse's Ninth was linking up with the Twelfth to deliver a hammer-blow through the Russian lines and into the city. To illustrate the intricacies of the military manoeuvres involved in order to execute the operation, Hitler carried around with him a road map, increasingly tattered and torn and disintegrating with every opening. In more despondent instances he would stand in the map-room banging the table limply with his clammy fist and demanding to know why Wenck was taking so much time. Over and over again he would curse Steiner. At other times he seethed with rage at the traitors in his midst.

In his study on the other side of the conference corridor Goebbels was performing a passable imitation of his master's histrionics. Like Hitler he paced backwards and forwards manically, raging with indignation and despair at the treachery that was everywhere to be found around the Führer. He mocked the absent Göring for his incompetence and upbraided him for his cowardice in escaping from Berlin. He poured scorn on the abilities of the German general staff, dismissed German soldiers as cowards and condemned the German people as utterly unworthy of the National Socialists.

Like Hitler, Goebbels was demanding to know what was taking Wenck such a long time. Like Hitler, Goebbels would swing from moments of sober rationality to moments of hysterical anger. At times the bunker was beginning to seem like the madhouse that Koller had described. Sometimes the lower bunker was shrouded in a deathly silence. Then, perhaps with the opening of a door, the peace would be broken by an explosion of bitter invective and screaming recriminations before the door swung shut once more and silence reigned again.

Among the remaining residents of the bunker there seemed to be a philosophic acceptance that the end was approaching and probably a lot quicker than any of them had expected. The FBK guards had plundered the pantries for liquor and now as they drowned their sorrows in drink they would sleep it off hunched over the oak table in the upper dining corridor. When they were on duty they spoke of little else other than how they could escape Berlin. Many of the bunker people were now exchanging views on the merits of various forms of suicide. Many of them had been provided with Dr Stumpfegger's little glass ampoules containing prussic acid.

That afternoon Weidling gave Hitler the unwelcome news that his men were exhausted and demoralised and had virtually no tanks or other heavy guns left. He urged the Führer to evacuate Berlin westwards along the East–West Axis and across the Havel Bridge that was still being held by Hitler Youth units. His men would provide a protective force for Hitler's retinue that would punch a hole through the Russian lines and join forces with Wenck in the west. Once more Hitler declined his offer.

Suddenly, amid all the bleakness of Weidling's military assessments, there was some unexpectedly good news to distract the bunker people. Since von Greim had been appointed commander-in-chief of the air force, a dozen aircraft had been dispatched to extricate him from Berlin. Each and every one of them had been shot down. Now a pilot had finally managed to land at the Brandenburg Gate airstrip. It was the same pilot who had managed the miraculous feat of getting Speer. He was waiting at the airstrip in his Arado 96 light aircraft to take von Greim to his headquarters at Plön in Schleswig-Holstein. On hearing the news Hitler marched into Dr Stumpfegger's treatment room and informed the new commander-in-chief of the Luftwaffe. Von Greim was still laid flat out with his injuries. With him was Hanna Reitsch who, when she had not been reading adventure stories to the Goebbels children or teaching them to yodel, had spent much of her time faithfully sitting by his side.

Hitler informed von Greim that he must fly to his operational headquarters at Schleswig-Holstein immediately. It was vital for him to arrange for the Luftwaffe to launch an all-out attack on Soviet tank positions that were now infiltrating deep into central Berlin. Hanna Reitsch objected, saying she thought they should both stay by the Führer's side in Berlin. But Hitler would not countenance any disobedience of futile orders on this occasion. He instructed his old friend and chief pilot Hans Baur to accompany them to the Brandenburg Gate airstrip. However, since the airstrip was under intense enemy bombardment, they would have to wait until dusk before it would be safe enough to take off. The other bunker residents soon heard that the colourful couple were about to depart. There was no doubt in most people's minds that nobody else was going to make it after them. Some began writing letters to give to Reitsch to post to their loved ones.

During the afternoon Hitler was told of a foreign news report that claimed Heinrich Himmler had made an advance to the Allies via the Swedish Red Cross. He was furious, but also a little incredulous. Hitler had always assumed that whatever his manifest faults, Himmler was one of his most loyal followers – 'Der treue Heinrich' (faithful Heinrich), as he called him. Himmler himself had declared: 'I owe everything to Hitler. How can I betray him?'

But by this stage Himmler was being motivated by more base considerations. In common with most of the Nazi hierarchy, he had no intention of volunteering himself for a part in Hitler's own version of Valhalla. For weeks he had been making concessions to Count Bernadotte, sending some Jewish concentration camp victims to Switzerland and returning Swedish prisoners home, in the hope that it would improve his own personal bargaining position when the inevitable peace talks began.

That afternoon Himmler received a call from the Führerbunker. Hitler wanted to know whether there was any truth in the wire reports that he had been talking to the representative of the Swedish Red Cross. Himmler denied it outright. And that was the end of the matter – for a few hours.

That day Axmann was looking for me. I had no idea why. When I arrived at the Chancellery cellar, I found Lotte was there also, as were Axmann, Dr Gertrud and Weltzin. There was another military aide whom I was to be introduced to later. Everyone was smiling. One of Dr Gertrud's assistants had a small camera. Mutti beemed at Lotte and me and called us the young *Panzerknacker* (tank destroyers). Axmann announced that we were to be awarded medals. For me the Iron Cross (First Class). For Lotte, the Iron Cross (Second Class). We were each to be awarded a tank stripe too, for destroying a tank. I was also to get the Silver Wound Badge.

Lotte was presented with her awards first, by Dr Gertrud. The Iron Cross was attached by a ribbon to her nurse's uniform. Then it was my turn and Axmann stepped forward. He said a few words of praise. He couldn't pin my cross on me because of his wooden arm. So it was Dr Gertrud who did the honours. She pinned the Iron Cross on my breast pocket and replaced my Black Wound Badge with the Silver one. Axmann then presented me with my certificates signed by himself and a facsimile of Hitler's signature. Then Dr Gertrud's aide stepped forward and snapped a picture of the two of us.

I felt so proud and wondered what my father would have thought of his 'weakling son' now. There I was, 16 years old, wounded twice in battle and standing with my left hand in a cast and the Iron Cross (First Class) on my chest in Adolf Hitler's bunker. Everyone I came into contact with seemed to regard me as a young hero. My father had no war medals. He had never been wounded in battle. I was desperate for him to know that I had not only met his expectations but exceeded them. I felt so frustrated that he did not know. He might never know. After the award ceremony, Axmann left and Mutti served us all champagne.

Later that day in the waiting-room in the bunker Axmann introduced me to a legendary figure. Erich Bärenfänger, at 27, was the youngest of Hitler's generals and something of a self-made legend in the German army. He was, it was true, a highly decorated infantry officer, with Knight's Cross and the Iron Cross with Oak Leaves. But he was something of an idiosyncratic character who owed his reputation as much to his prowess on the battlefield as a refusal to take orders from anyone other than Hitler. On a whim Hitler had just promoted him from lieutenant colonel to major general. Axmann introduced me to him as one of the boys who had been presented to Hitler on his birthday. They were great friends. Axmann had been best man at Bärenfänger's wedding. It was an enormous honour to be introduced to such a heroic figure in such a manner. He called me 'fearless'. I was flattered to receive such a compliment by someone of his stature.

But I wasn't fearless. Anyone who says he is fearless is out of touch with reality. I had been able to conquer my fears to a certain extent. I was miserable but like a good soldier I didn't buckle under the heart-breaking cries and agonising screams that were a perpetual encore to the pain, danger and horrible sights that had become a part of my daily existence. I coped by parting with those horrors inside me and maintaining as optimistic a state of mind as possible. But it was difficult. I never knew until after the war that Hitler had told Axmann that the best had sacrificed their lives on the battlefields already. Those who survived, said Hitler, were the inferior ones who did not deserve to survive. What an insult to all those who had lived through the horror he had single-handedly created.

At about seven o'clock that evening, Heinz Lorenz was monitoring the foreign radio broadcasts in the Propaganda Ministry on the Wilhelmsstrasse. Lorenz was effectively Hitler's press officer or communications supremo. Suddenly he heard a report on the BBC that had been picked up from Reuters in San Francisco. The wire agency confirmed that Heinrich Himmler had been in talks over several weeks with the Western Allies through the offices of the Swedish Red Cross representative Count Folke Bernadotte. Sensationally the Reuters report claimed that Himmler had offered an unconditional German surrender. Lorenz ran across Wilhemsstrasse and into the bunker. Hitler was apoplectic. Once more the sound of his histrionics reverberated. He seethed at Himmler's duplicity, denouncing his secret negotiations with Bernadotte as 'the most shameful betrayal in human history'.

When he finally regained his composure, Hitler shut himself away in his study with Bormann and Goebbels. Nobody except those three men knows what happened in the privacy of his office over the next half-hour or so. But it appears that Himmler's treachery had distilled in Hitler's mind many wayward strands. He began to see the makings of an elaborate SS plot. Steiner had failed to launch his counter-attack not because his men were exhausted, bewildered or demoralised, but because Himmler had ordered him not to launch the attack. Fegelein's attempt to flee Berlin was not the act of a drunken coward, but obviously part of Himmler's intrigues. Shortly after the name of Fegelein was raised in the Führer's mind, the order went out to have him hauled out of the cells and brought before one of Hitler's most brutal henchmen.

At about this time, I was sent to find SS-Gruppenführer Heinrich Müller, the head of the Gestapo. I had never heard his name before and although the building I was sent to was Gestapo headquarters I didn't know it at the time. He wasn't there, so that is the only role I can claim to have played in the drama that unfolded. Some other courier must have found Müller. Fegelein was hauled out of his cell and marched into an interrogation-room where he was confronted with the chief of the Gestapo. What went on in that interrogation has always been shrouded in mystery. Given that Fegelein was practically one of Hitler's family, it wouldn't be surprising if the Führer ordered the exact details to be hushed up. (And it would not be the first time that Müller had helped cover up an embarrassing personal situation for the Nazi leader. It had been he who had been responsible for the investigation into the mysterious death of Hitler's niece, Geli Raubal, when she was found dead in his Munich apartment. It was rumoured since that Bormann paid Müller off.)

When Müller confronted Fegelein it is conceivable that Fegelein may have confessed to knowing about the talks with Count Bernadotte. That would certainly have been enough to condemn him in Hitler's eyes. But there have been suggestions that he confessed to also knowing about a plan of Himmler's to have Hitler assassinated. It is unlikely however that there ever was such a plan, at least not by Himmler. For it appears that at that stage of the war Himmler presumed it was only a matter of hours before Hitler would shoot himself. And he assumed that as Reichsführer he would succeed him, regardless of Göring's other claim to the succession. (In fact most of the Nazi hierarchy, including Speer and Goebbels, thought Himmler the natural successor to Hitler and Himmler already had his own shadow government.) Like Göring, Himmler had taken Hitler's 'breakdown' in the bunker on 22 April as an abdication of responsibility. He saw no need for secret plots or assassination attempts.

Whatever happened between Müller and Fegelein, the interrogation furnished Müller with the pretext that Hitler needed. A reluctant Artur Axmann was dragged in to chair a panel to sit in judgement on Fegelein. The panel condemned the SS man to death. Within minutes Fegelein was goose-stepped into the Chancellery Garden and stripped of all badges of rank and his Knight's Cross. Gone was the languid swagger of the arrogant SS officer; in its place there was a look of fear and apprehension. Fegelein was stood against a wall and, without further ceremony, shot. His wife Gretl was pregnant with their first child at home in Bavaria. But if the Führer had any regret about the impact his actions may have had on his mistress's sister, he did not show it.

In the bunker von Greim and Hanna Reitsch were still waiting for darkness to fall. As Fegelein was being dispatched in the garden above, Hitler marched into their room. He now had further instructions for the new commander-in-chief of the Luftwaffe. Von Greim was to do everything he could to see that Himmler was called to account for his treachery. He must be arrested and tried before a court. Under no circumstances was Himmler to be allowed to succeed the Führer should Hitler be killed within the next few days. 'A traitor must never succeed me as Führer,' he said. The news of Himmler's treachery was greeted with somewhat theatrical cries of indignation by Reitsch. And as the Führer embarked on a familiar denunciation of all the traitors who had let him down, the test pilot nodded enthusiastically at his every word.

With Hitler's angry tirade still ringing in their ears, the odd couple prepared to take their leave, he in his full uniform displaying a chest of medals, she in her battered flying jacket now complemented by a black turtleneck sweater presented to her by Eva Braun. Before they could leave Eva Braun handed Reitsch a letter for her sister Gretl. In it she did not mention that her husband and father of their child had just been shot and was currently being unceremoniously tossed into a rough grave in the Chancellery Garden. The omission didn't really make any difference. The letter never reached Gretl. Reitsch opened it and, discovering the contents were banal beyond belief, ripped it up and threw it away. (It was 'vulgar, so theatrical and in such poor, adolescent taste' that it was not a fitting testimony to the Führer's last hours, Reitsch said later.)

To Hanna Reitsch, Eva Braun had never been anything but a silly little girl from Bavaria. Magda Goebbels' letter to her eldest son from her previous marriage to Günther Quandt would have been much more to Reitsch's taste. In it she said: 'Our glorious ideas are approaching the end and therewith everything beautiful and venerable, noble and virtuous I have known in my life. The world that will succeed the Führer and National Socialism will not be worth living in.' Magda could not have reflected any better Hanna Reitsch's view of the Third Reich.

There was a brief flurry of fond farewells as von Greim and Reitsch left the bunker with Hans Baur. She was in floods of tears, declaring through her sobs never-ending loyalty to the Führer and the Fatherland. He was on two crutches, his features distinctly yellow. When they arrived at the Brandenburg Gate the Arado light aircraft was waiting. So much for waiting for darkness. The whole area was alight with the flames of defensive fires lit along the East–West Axis. There was close-range gunfire and shelling in every direction. But once more their pilot performed the impossible. The plane hopped into the air and rose precariously close over the heads of the Russian troops below. It took them so much by surprise that they could hardly muster a response. The little plane just managed to clear the golden statue of the Quadriga, the golden chariot-rider and her four horses, on top of the gate. As they rose slowly above the city, the plane was buffeted roughly backwards and forwards by scores of explosions from shellfire. At 1,200 metres it reached the safety of cloud cover.

Above the clouds, Hanna Reitsch later recorded, they found the sky bathed in moonlight. Beneath them through the occasional break in the clouds all they could see was a sea of flaming fire that stretched far into the distance. Countless villages were being put to the torch by the avenging Red Army. When von Greim and Reitsch reached the aerodrome at Rechlin, he ordered every available aircraft to assist in the relief of Berlin. It was around midnight when they arrived at Admiral Dönitz's headquarters in Schleswig-Holstein.

∞ CHAPTER THIRTEEN ∞

Marriage

IT WAS LATER IN THE NIGHT when Traudl Junge settled down to grab a few moments' sleep on the army cot outside the Führer's office. Fully clothed, she pulled the sleeping bag up around her. It was her habit to sleep in the conference corridor outside the Führer's suite. Like everyone else in the bunker she was exhausted. Earlier in the day, sitting in Hitler's study she had been upset to realise that she could smell her own body odour. Everyone, she reflected, smelled. She had fallen into a deep sleep immediately and had been asleep for about an hour when an orderly shook her awake. The Führer needed her to take some dictation, she was told. Reluctantly but obediently Junge straightened out her clothes and made her way to the map-room where Hitler was waiting. She couldn't help noticing that the table was laid with silverware and champagne glasses as if for a reception. Hitler said nothing but inquired solicitously after her well-being as he always did and settled her down before the table. Then, pacing backwards and forwards, he began to dictate to Junge.

Hitler was reading out his last political testament. Junge began writing. Now she realised the end really must be near. She wondered whether in his final hours on earth the Führer would at last reveal some tantalising clues to events perhaps long since buried in his boyhood that had shaped his extraordinary world-view. Would he reveal the demons that had driven him to his murderous madness? But no, as Junge scribbled as quickly as she could to keep up with him, all she heard was the familiar litany of complaints ranging from the evils of international Jewry to the dangers of Bolshevism. Over the next hour he reeled out a list of his usual *bêtes noir*, which Junge had heard time and time again since she first worked for him. But when Hitler turned to his own private testament or will, Junge's ears pricked up.

Pacing back and forth, Hitler dictated:

> During the years of combat I was unable to commit myself to a contract of marriage, so I have decided this day before the end of my earthly life to take as my wife the young woman who, after many years of faithful friendship, has of her own free will come to the besieged capital to link her fate with my own. She will, according to her wishes, go to her death as my wife. For us, this will take the place of all that was denied us by my devotion to the service of my people.
>
> My wife and I choose to die in order to escape the shame of flight or capitulation. It is our wish that our bodies be burned immediately, here, where I have performed the greater part of my daily work during the 12 years I have served my people.

And shortly after dictating these words, in the very early hours of 29 April, Hitler married the sister of the woman whose husband he had just had executed. The ceremony took place in the map-room. Hitler, having despaired of every last traitor in his midst, was making a declaration of gratitude to the one person in the world who had demonstrated that her devotion to him was without qualification. Time and time again in his endless ramblings, Hitler had contrasted Eva Braun's simple and deep-seated loyalty to the rank disloyalty of the likes of Göring and now Himmler, Steiner and Fegelein.

It was a sign of his strangely distant feelings towards Goebbels in these last few days that the Propaganda Minister appears to have been kept entirely in the dark about Hitler's plans to marry Eva until the very last moment. More than anybody else Goebbels had been responsible for keeping the name of Eva Braun out of the public domain. It was part of his mythmaker's strategy to create the illusion that Hitler was a superman unlike any other human being whom no woman could possibly aspire to marry. But as the last days of Hitler would show, Goebbels' vision went far beyond the grave. He was determined the images he had created would live on, one day perhaps to be resurrected in a glorious new Reich that would owe its origins to the one he created. Undoubtedly, he would have preferred Hitler to have gone to his grave as the singular human being he was. And if the Führer insisted on marriage, Goebbels would have preferred a beautiful film star actress rather than a simple and slightly plump girl from Bavaria. But presented with a fait accompli Goebbels had no choice.

When he was told of Hitler's intentions he called on a local municipal official to preside over the proceedings. Walter Wagner had the authority to perform a civil wedding ceremony. He turned up wearing a brown Nazi uniform and Volkssturm armband, looking a little bewildered to be surrounded by the most senior Party officials of the Third Reich. The only other people present at the ceremony besides Hitler and Eva Braun were Goebbels and Bormann, who acted as witnesses. Hitler wore his usual black trousers and tunic. Eva wore a black taffeta dress that the Führer liked. It is not recorded whether Wagner had the temerity to ask the happy couple to make the required Nazi declarations about their Aryan ancestry and whether they were free from any hereditary diseases. After the brief formalities, the happy couple signed the marriage certificate, Hitler in his usual crabby scrawl. Eva Braun made the usual mistake that new brides invariably make. She began by writing 'Eva B...' but then changed the second name to Hitler. It was the early hours of 29 April, just after midnight. Finally Eva Braun was Eva Hitler, the new First Lady of the Third Reich.

After the brief marriage ceremony the newly weds emerged into the corridor to be congratulated by the other senior occupants of the bunker. Walter Wagner was allowed to remain among their number for a while. Again, he must have been astonished to now find himself actually sipping champagne with the most senior members of the Third Reich. He was sent on his way after he'd had a couple of glasses. Within the hour he would be dead, caught in the street-fighting on Wilhelmsstrasse. Shortly afterwards Hitler invited some members of the bunker community back into his living quarters to join them for their wedding breakfast. A table was covered with crisp white linen and laden with cakes, sandwiches and bottles of champagne. A gramophone played the same schmaltzy hit that had played in the Old Chancellery on Hitler's birthday, only nine days ago, but seemingly an eternity away. As the gramophone scratched out the lyrics of 'Red Roses Bring You Happiness', there were no red roses to hand, but there was clearly a lot of happiness in Eva Hitler's heart. Gerda Christian commented that her eyes were full of tears – but they were the tears of radiant joy.

By bestowing his hand in marriage on Eva, it must have counted as some sort of reward for the loyalty she had displayed over the years, in the face of frequent humiliation at the hands of Hitler himself. But how much of a reward it was difficult to read in her girlish, simple features. All those present at the wedding breakfast attested to her obvious happiness. But a few hours later, Professor Schenck was sitting amongst a gathering of bunkerites in the upper bunker dining corridor. He was surprised to be told that the blonde, rather simple woman happily knocking back wine at the top of the table was the new Frau Hitler. He like many others had never known Hitler had a mistress. On that evening when he saw Eva Hitler she appeared happy and curiously relaxed considering she must have known her own death was only hours away. But it was Professor Schenck's professional judgement on observing her at close quarters that she was not a happy woman at all. Rather, she was suffering from repressed hysteria.

Among the guests at the wedding breakfast were Magda and Joseph Goebbels, Bormann, Gerda Christian and Constanze Manziarly. Later, Axmann arrived with Krebs and Burgdorf. With her girlish insouciance Eva Braun, or rather Eva Hitler, looked content and entertained her guests with small talk about the Berghof and better times. Traudl Junge could not enjoy this welcome respite from the hysteria of the rest of the day for long. She was taking shorthand in the room next door as Hitler intermittently left the party to dictate his last will and political testament to her.

Hitler had acquired a great many paintings during his rise to power. But, he explained in his private will, he had accumulated them for the good of the nation, not himself. He expressed a desire that all his works of art be left to an art gallery in Linz. He appointed Martin Bormann, 'my most faithful Party comrade', as his executor and charged him with the responsibility of dividing his estate among relatives, friends and former secretaries. It was at Bormann's discretion to give them gifts of valuables and financial support that would maintain them at the comfortable standard of the 'petit bourgeoisie'. In particular he asked that Eva Braun's mother should be provided for.

Then Hitler dictated his political testament. It was to be as banal, tedious and utterly untruthful as anything he had said over countless boring dinner conversations with his entourage at the Berghof; in endless speeches of meaningless rhetoric on the Reich Radio network or at Nuremberg or Munich; and in hundreds of pages of *Mein Kampf*. 'It is untrue that I or anyone else in Germany wanted the war in 1939,' he declared. 'It was desired and instigated exclusively by those international statesmen who were either of Jewish descent or who worked for Jewish interests . . . Centuries will pass away, but out of the ruins of our towns and cultural monuments the hatred will ever renew itself against those ultimately responsible whom we have to thank for everything: international Jewry and its helpers.'

Hitler vowed that he would stay in the nation's capital and choose the time and manner of his own death rather than fall into the hands of his enemies. And he blamed the overwhelming force of the enemy for Germany's failure, although he also hinted that equally to blame were the German people and the German armed forces who had proved too weak and cowardly for the noble ambitions of the National Socialist cause.

Nevertheless he prophesied that the struggle would go on and that National Socialism would prevail. The six years of the war would go down in history as 'the most glorious and valiant manifestation of a nation's will to existence'.

A key passage in the first part of this political testament might be held up to lay bare the claims that Hitler knew nothing of the 'Final Solution'. It related to the fulfilment of the 'prophecy' of 1939.

> I also left no doubt that, if the nations of Europe are again to be regarded as mere blocks of shares of these international money and finance conspirators, then that race, too, which is really guilty of this murderous struggle, will be called to account: Jewry! It further left no one in doubt that this time millions of children of Europe's Aryan peoples would not die of hunger, millions of grown men would not suffer death and hundreds and thousands of women and children would not be burnt and bombed to death in the towns, without the real culprit having to atone for his guilt, even if by more humane means.

The political testament was divided into two parts. The second dealt with the succession, though whether he really believed there would be a succession is a matter of conjecture. If he did then he was as deluded as Göring and Himmler, neither of whom could comprehend the sheer scale of the world's opprobrium at what the Nazi regime had done. The new head of the state and the armed forces would be Grand Admiral Dönitz, whose title would be Reich President. He would not have the title Führer. There would only ever be one Führer. Goebbels would become the Chancellor of the Reich. Bormann would be Party Minister. Karl Hanke, the Gauleiter of Breslau, replaced Himmler as chief of the police and Reichsführer of the SS. Also in the second part of the testament Göring and Himmler were unceremoniously expelled from the Party. Speer was icily overlooked. There were dozens more political appointments that Hitler, Bormann and Goebbels kept bringing to Traudl Junge throughout the morning to add to the list. The testament concluded with the chilling words: 'I charge the leadership of the nation and their subjects with the meticulous observance of the race laws and the merciless resistance to the universal poisoner of all peoples, international Jewry.'

By 4 a.m. the documents had been typed up and were ready for Hitler's signature. Shortly afterwards he retired to his rooms. In the meantime the Führer's actions had spurred a frenzy of activity from Martin Bormann's office. He began sending messages to Nazi Party outposts across the country. Bormann was in an unenviable position. He might have been declared as the future Party Minister, but he knew that the moment Hitler was gone, all his authority was gone too. It was vital for him to shore up his power base wherever he could across the country – and finally liquidate his enemies wherever they were. One of the mass of telegrams he sent out that night was to the Berchtesgaden fortress where Hermann Göring was being held. He ordered him to be executed. (The commander failed to obey the order.)

Goebbels too was not in the happiest of positions. Goebbels, like Bormann (but in a significantly different way), derived all his power from Adolf Hitler. Bormann depended on Hitler, whereas to a certain extent Hitler also depended on Goebbels. Although the Führer had specifically ordered him to survive and escape from Berlin, Goebbels knew that once Adolf Hitler was gone, there was no future for him either. Goebbels was as much a part of the illusion that was Nazism and the Third Reich as Hitler was. Once Hitler had gone, there was nothing left for Goebbels to be. He now had no alternative but to make his own excuses and depart the world stage on which he had so briefly strutted with a mastery that even his detractors could not help but admire.

As Traudl Junge typed up Hitler's testaments, a wistful Goebbels came into the office and asked her if she would attach his own coda to the Führer's. 'If the Führer is dead,' he told her, 'my life is meaningless.' He began dictating to Junge: 'For the first time in my life, I must categorically refuse to obey an order of the Führer.' He continued: 'In the delirium of treachery which surrounds the Führer in these critical days of the war, there have to be at least a few who stay unconditionally loyal to him even unto death.'

I was in the bunker in the very early hours of Sunday, 29 April. I had no idea of the momentous events that had happened. Nor can I recall why I was waiting in the ante-room. But it must have been for an important message for me to have been there at such an hour. All that night until shortly after midnight there had been intense activity between the radio unit and Hitler's situation-room. It had probably been caused by Bormann sending out messages all over to military and Party leaders.

When I picked up the message from our radio station next to Axmann's command post, one of the dispatchers told me there was still contact in the east with fortress Breslau and in the west, to my great amazement, with the Channel Islands, which sounded reassuring. But then when I entered the Führerbunker and handed the message over to a duty officer, it must have been shocking news, judging from his reaction: 'This on top of everything!'

I was told to stay and an immediate reply would be forthcoming. He retreated and seemed to be gone for the longest time. Utterly exhausted physically, I dozed off sitting on the bench. I was not alone. There were several officers and orderlies asleep along the corridors and in the canteen. Oddly, Bormann was not among them. Rumour had it that he had last been seen disappearing into the night with a bottle of cognac under his arm.

It would become a long night of criss-crossing thoughts, cross-currents of abnormal duress. I was dead tired but unable to find restful sleep. My mind kept overflowing with anticipations, imaginings and reflections, resulting in questions upon questions upon questions. Earlier, when I had crossed Wilhelmsstrasse, someone standing in the doorway observing the hail of metal said: 'Boy, it's just insane!'

In war, insanity becomes a common occurrence in all its forms – the battle that was fought, the actual street-fighting from house to house. By having to run through heavy shellfire and seeing so many of my comrades killed and wounded, I, too, must have been in shock. It's difficult for me now to assess the condition I was in.

In the early morning hours an officer tapped me on the shoulder. It startled me and I became embarrassed. From the corners of my mouth, spittle had dribbled down my chin. 'Only a few minutes more,' he said. I wiped my mouth and now made an even more determined effort to avoid catnapping again.

Then suddenly Hitler appeared like a ghost.

Now no one awake was in sight, except him. Coming out of his private quarters into the ante-room, he walked towards me without looking up. I was so stunned I didn't salute. At last he glanced up, gazing, as if lost in deep thought. He almost stepped on one of the officers sleeping on the floor. It appeared as if he looked right through me.

At this very instant, a tremor shook the bunker. Hitler lifted his right arm, visibly shaking, and stretched it out until his hand touched the wall to find support. Was it a hit above the bunker's ceiling? A shower of dirt, dust and plaster filled the room, sprinkling down on the Führer. He looked more like a Charlie Chaplin figure than our once great Führer. But he didn't seem to notice anything. He muttered something to himself, something like: 'Another hit!' Then he turned and disappeared into his rooms again.

Hitler's condition had deteriorated even more than I remembered from ten days earlier at the birthday reception. It might have been caused by the bunker light, but he struck me as being yellow with jaundice. His face had looked sallow and the white of his gleaming eyes appeared to have turned yellow. Nor was his uniform as crisp as before.

⤜ CHAPTER FOURTEEN ⤛

Götterdämmerung

⟨THE TWILIGHT OF THE GODS (*GÖTTERDÄMMERUNG*) was fast approaching. I returned to the Party Chancellery just as Axmann was heading in the opposite direction to the Führerbunker. After he had gone I collapsed asleep without taking my clothes off or bothering to wash or clean myself up. I must have got two or possibly three hours' sleep before Axmann returned to the room. He had a horrified expression on his face.

'The Führer and Eva Braun have married!' he said.

I couldn't believe it. But my reaction was as naïve as it was possible to be. 'Then we'll include her in our midst, too, when we break out!'

Axmann had told me that if Berlin wasn't relieved by Wenck and Busse, then we Hitler Youth were going to break out with the Führer in our midst, providing him with a human shield. In my head we still kept on fighting for the 'patient' to survive until the 'miracle cure' could be administered to save us all. I still believed the Hitler Youth would provide the Führer with protection to break out of the Russian iron ring. The news spread, however, that Hitler had written his will. Again, in my youthful mind I didn't grasp the full implication of this. I certainly didn't think he would take the coward's way out. Hitler often referred to suicide as a cowardly act. Famously, when the Mayor of Leipzig had shot himself and his family, Hitler described it as a 'cowardly evasion of responsibility'. I presumed that the Führer was writing his will because he was concerned that he might be killed in the break-out bid, even if the Hitler Youth provided a human shield. A successor should be lined up. And this was even truer now that Göring and Himmler had emerged as traitors.

Never in my presence did Axmann address Hitler's chances for survival. It was our job to hold out. Generals Wenck and Steiner were still expected to slash open the encirclement and to get him and us out of Berlin. If they didn't succeed, the bodies of Hitler Youth boys would provide the Führer with a barrier to spearhead through the Russian front and reach our troops. They expected to take their leader to the Alpine fortress. At no time did Axmann or anyone in his entourage ever mention that Hitler might commit suicide.

Later that day I took the incoming telegram from Karl Hanke, Party *Gauleiter* (district leader), to the Goebbels family. It may very well have been his response to his new appointment. The Goebbels family had quarters in both the upper and the lower bunker. It was up to me to decide where to deliver the telegram and I decided on the upper bunker. As it happened, Dr Goebbels was just coming up from the lower bunker as his wife approached me with the two eldest girls at her side. I saluted and handed the envelope to Dr Goebbels.

Hanke's telegram was sent from Breslau. My father knew Hanke who now, as political commander of the fortress, was constantly in the news. Standing next to Magda Goebbels, I became aware of how short Dr Goebbels was. He ripped open the envelope, took out the telegram and remarked: 'Ah, from Hanke.'

Frau Goebbels looked over his shoulder, saying: 'Poor Karl, New Year's Eve all of us were still together.'

That evening the Goebbels family said their farewells to their staff. They chose one of the cellars of the New Reich Chancellery to hold an informal party. The six children were all seated around an oak table. There were around 40 staff present. A 15-year-old Hitler Youth sang old German lullabies and everyone joined in tearfully. This sweet scene was surrounded by pandemonium inside the New Reich Chancellery. The first floor was a sea of regular army soldiers in their soiled and dirty greenish-grey uniforms or SS rushing backwards and forwards barking what sounded like increasingly futile commands. The air-raid shelter in the basement was full to overflowing. There were women screaming and babies crying. There were the dreadful scenes of depravity that were becoming commonplace now – couples making love to one another in full view of mothers trying to feed their children, while grandfathers clung on to the tiniest morsel of food that they could find. The casualty station was full to overflowing with wounded soldiers quietly crying in agony. Dr Schenck was running to and fro. New casualties were being rushed in by the minute.

That day Axmann ordered Hannes and me to get a message to SS-Gruppenführer August Heissmeyer, who was in charge of a unit at Spandau. It consisted of students from elite Nazi schools in Spandau and

Potsdam. Their fanaticism, degree of bravery and willingness to sacrifice themselves for their leader and the nation seemed identical to that of my old Karl Gutschke unit. Once again Axmann expected the elite of the German youth to be instrumental in repelling the Russians.

Gutschke had managed to repel the Russian forces south-east of Breslau at Wansen and Weigwitz. Now Axmann wanted Heissmeyer to do the same at Spandau. Word had it that the city was already totally encircled by the Red Army. Axmann envisaged a major battle. And so did Heissmeyer. Shortly before we left to find him, he had given his boys a rousing speech. 'Never give in! Keep fighting to the last man!' What neither Axmann nor we knew was that this fearless warrior had then jumped on one of the last planes out of Gatow to join his wife fleeing from the Russians. He had told his driver: 'Should we lose the war, all the boys will be shot anyway.' Such was the breathtaking cynicism of our Nazi leaders.

Both Hitler and Axmann kept pinning unrealistic hopes on what the Hitler Youth fighting units could accomplish. The situation in Berlin was quite different from that in Breslau. The Silesian capital had been turned into a real fortress by Karl Hanke. Nobody was allowed out. Nobody was allowed in. Every entrance to the city was barricaded. The Reich capital instead had remained an open city, engulfed in flames and smoke, crowded with refugees and exhausted soldiers in need of sleep, food and ammunition.

When a body is exhausted and starved, the mind eventually succumbs to a similar state. Hitler didn't see it that way. He believed in mind over matter regardless of circumstances. I felt I was being put to the test. I was exhausted, though we still had sufficient food and a cot for the few hours of sleep available.

When we returned from our futile mission, Hannes and I were in urgent need of petrol. Axmann ordered us to take some from the underground motor pool facing Hermann Göring Strasse. When we arrived we found Hitler's personal chauffeur Erich Kempka presiding over the pool. Kempka was one of those closest to Hitler. He, like Bormann, treated me with disrespect or simply ignored me altogether. He declared brusquely: 'We are out of petrol! Period!' Our pleadings came to nothing. We were told that there might be some fuel left at the Tiergarten. Hannes said he would go and get it. He never returned. I don't even know if Hannes arrived there. Or whether or not he received petrol and where he went from there. Did he have one final *schluck* (drink from his flask) to warm his soul and then decide, like so many others, that the war was over?

I would never get an answer to that question. I would never see Hannes again, though I was soon to find out that Kempka did have petrol. But not for us.

That day, 29 April, news of Mussolini's fate would have reached Berlin. The Duce had been caught by partisans in northern Italy with his mistress Clara Petacci. The two of them had been killed and strung upside down in a Milan market-place where crowds desecrated their bodies. Whether this news was conveyed to Hitler is doubtful. Whether it would have had any effect on him was doubtful too. Mussolini had been a brutal ruler and was quite well aware of the retribution that was in store for him. As the day progressed, more and more people were leaving the bunker, and as they left, Hitler began to contemplate the exact time of his own departure.

Some people had received orders to leave. Others devised plausible schemes that would provide a compelling excuse for their departure. After Hitler's testaments had been typed up, he had ordered a group of four officers to carry copies to Admiral Dönitz at his headquarters at Lake Plön, and to Field Marshal Schörner, who had been chosen to be commander-in-chief of the army. The group chosen to be the couriers were Heinz Lorenz, Hitler's press officer, Bormann's aide, SS Colonel Wilhelm Zander and Major Willi Johannmeier, Hitler's army adjutant. That morning they left on their dangerous mission.

Shortly afterwards another group left. The adjutants to Krebs and Burgdorf sought their commanding officers' permission to try and find Wenck's Twelfth Army in the south-west. Freytag von Loringhoven told Krebs that he did not want to die 'like a rat' underground but would rather fight in the open. Krebs insisted it was up to the Führer. Surprisingly Hitler agreed. He was curious to know how von Loringhoven planned to get out of Berlin. When the adjutant said he hoped to find his way to the Havel lakes and get a boat, the Führer's interest was raised. He recommended finding an electric boat of the type used as pleasure crafts on lakes, so that the Russians wouldn't hear it.

Von Loringhoven understood Hitler well enough to know that the Führer could become bogged down in detail. He had obviously become obsessed by the idea of an electric boat. Not wanting to become distracted, von Loringhoven agreed to obey his orders unquestioningly. He would go by an electric boat and only an electric boat. That afternoon, Freytag von Loringhoven, Colonel Weiss and their own Rittmeister Gerhard Boldt left the Chancellery complex on their self-imposed mission.

These departures of military figures left a growing sense of isolation in the mind of Colonel Nicholas von Below. The Luftwaffe adjutant had been with the Führer for eight years and had a certain sense of loyalty to his master. But he was not entirely enthusiastic about joining his Führer in the Valhalla he was orchestrating for himself and the rest of Berlin. He summoned up the courage to ask Hitler for permission to escape and was surprised and relieved when the Führer acquiesced to the request without a murmur. He made only one condition: that von Below wait until after the evening conference. He had a message he would like von Below to deliver to Keitel. For a brief moment I was in line to serve as his guide, but I was turned down when I appeared with my cast.

That afternoon Hitler summoned Professor Werner Haase from the emergency hospital to the bunker to stage a dress rehearsal of his own suicide. Hitler no longer trusted the SS and he wanted an assurance that the poison capsules he had been provided with by the SS doctor Ludwig Stumpfegger actually worked. The guinea pig chosen for this experiment was his beloved Alsatian Blondi. The dog was led into the toilets off the waiting-room at the foot of the steps to the upper bunker by Hitler's dog-attendant Sergeant Fritz Tornow. Inside, Tornow forced Blondi's jaws open and crushed the capsule with pliers as Haase watched. The dog collapsed on to the ground instantly and didn't move. Tornow was visibly upset. Hitler couldn't bear to watch the scene himself. However, he entered the room shortly afterwards and, seeing the results for himself, departed without saying a word. Tornow was further mortified to be given the task of shooting Blondi's four young puppies. The Goebbels children were understandably upset when their sprightly little playthings were wrenched from them. Tornow took them up to the Chancellery Garden where they were put to death along with several other pets of the bunker inmates. Later, Hitler met the medical staff to thank them in the lower bunker. As Professor Schenck records in his memoirs, one of the nurses became hysterical.

That afternoon too, Hitler had a touching meeting with Hans Baur. He gave him further instructions. Once Hitler had killed himself he wanted Baur to get Bormann to Dönitz. First overland to the aerodrome at Rechlin. Then on to the Baltic by plane. Baur detested Bormann as much as anyone in the bunker did. But he was devoted to Hitler. He had tried to persuade him to fly out of Berlin. He had access to six prototype Junker 390 long-range planes that were reputed to have a flight range of nearly 10,000 kilometres. Since the Führer refused, Baur had said he would stay there at his side to the end. But if the Führer's orders were to get Bormann to the Baltic then that's what he'd do. Baur, as Hitler's pilot, had been responsible for organising the Führer's travels from one headquarters to the next as he crossed Occupied Europe. It had been Baur's job to see that Hitler's beloved portrait of Frederick the Great arrived unscathed at each new destination. Before the two men parted for the last time, Hitler presented him with the painting as a parting gift.

In the upper bunker common-room a small number of Hitler's entourage were drinking and eating. Among them were Axmann, Rattenhuber, Hans Baur and Kempka. Many of them were relics of Hitler's Berchtesgaden days and there was much talk about 'the good old days', some of it maudlin, some of it not. At one stage the Führer's new wife turned up with Traudl Junge and Else Krüger in tow. There was much wine and liquor drunk by the assembly. At one stage an SS officer emerged from the lower bunker to ask that none of them retire until they received further orders. The Führer wished to say 'goodbye' to them all. There was a silent communal sigh of relief tinged with sadness.

Hitler held his usual conference and at about midnight he emerged to hand von Below the message for Keitel. It was yet another testament, this time evaluating the performance of the armed forces in the war. The text was destroyed. But von Below later recalled it from memory. The army general staff were excoriated for their failure of leadership and outright cowardice. The Luftwaffe, perhaps in deference to its new air Reich Marshal Ritter von Greim, was excused and all its failures were blamed on the incompetence of Hermann Göring. Only the navy, under the loyal Admiral Dönitz, a Nazi to the end, was praised, although, in truth, the German navy had not had a glorious war. Von Below bade his master goodbye.

Shortly afterwards an SS officer emerged in the upper bunker to say the Führer was now ready to bid his final farewells. The news that he was finally about to go had spread around the Chancellery. A party atmosphere had broken out among the civilians and soldiers in the Chancellery cellars leading off the bunker. There was a gramophone and singing and dancing and much merry-making. The party had become quite raucous by the time Hitler made his way up the steps to the upper bunker and the noise was seeping in through the pantry, so much so that the bunker telephonist, Rochus Misch, was sent to ask them to be quiet. He was rudely ignored. When an SS officer went back to ask the revellers to be quiet, his pleas also fell on deaf ears. The party went on. Hitler finally arrived at the doorway of the upper bunker accompanied by the ever present Martin Bormann. The shouting and partying from above were audible to everyone in the small enclosure.

Assembled were a score of servants and guards. Hitler made his way along the line of secretaries, orderlies and officers and they all said goodbye to one another, most of them for the last time. Few could recall what he said, other than a few mumbled platitudes. But then addressing them all, he released them from their oaths to him and wished them luck escaping from the Russians. He told them there was no option but for him to die in Berlin. He didn't want Stalin putting him on show in a museum. With that the Führer disappeared back into the lower bunker. It was about 3 a.m.

At noon Hitler received the military report. The Russians were everywhere. There were snipers 300 metres away from the bunker. There was no hope. The Führer took the news with no visible show of emotion.

He summoned Bormann and told him he would kill himself that afternoon. Then he asked his adjutant Otto Günsche to oversee the cremation arrangements. Hitler instructed Günsche that there was to be nothing left of his remains for the Russians to get their hands on. Then he retired to his sitting-room for lunch with Gerda Christian, Traudl Junge and Constanze Manziarly. Eva Hitler, who would normally have been there, was not present. Perhaps as the Führer's wife she felt herself a little above his secretaries now.

At lunch Hitler thoughtfully presented each of them with ampoules of poison and apologised that he had nothing more valuable to offer. Both Christian and Junge accepted the little glass ampoules, but secretly vowed never to use them. While they were quietly having lunch, Günsche sent an order to Kempka at the underground garage to send over 200 litres of petrol. Kempka didn't think he had that much. (He didn't.) But eventually four of his men managed to find 180 litres and carried it across the Chancellery Garden in jerry cans to the emergency exit of the Führerbunker. There was an altercation between them and the FBK guards who wanted to know what it was for. Eventually Heinz Linge emerged and dismissed both the guards and Kempka's men. Shortly afterwards instructions went out to lock all the other entrances to the bunker and any doors leading from the Chancellery buildings into the garden. There were to be only a few carefully selected witnesses to what was to happen next.

Hitler dismissed his luncheon guests and remained in his room for a while. Then at about 2.30 p.m. Günsche summoned them back to the conference corridor. When they arrived they found Martin Bormann and his secretary Else Krüger; Magda and Joseph Goebbels; Generals Burgdorf and Krebs; Johann Rattenhuber; and Heinz Linge. Hitler emerged from his rooms with Eva Hitler at his side. He was wearing his usual black trousers and uniform tunic with a white shirt. She had on a blue dress with white trimmings. They moved around the room silently shaking hands and Hitler muttered a few indecipherable words to each of those gathered. He was even more hunched now than he had ever been. His skin was a deathly yellow pallor. Traudl Junge thought Eva mumbled something like: 'Say hello to Bavaria for me.' Magda Goebbels was nearly hysterical at this meeting with the Führer. After a few minutes, Hitler retreated to his rooms without a word.

While this had all been happening the Goebbels' children were playing games in the upper bunker blithely unaware of what had been going on just a few metres beneath them. They must have noticed as their mother rushed past them in tears alongside Eva Hitler. The two women ensconced themselves in their suite of rooms. What they said to one another will never be known. The younger woman had usurped the title of First Lady of the Reich. Magda Goebbels was bright, witty and independent. She had never had a great deal of respect for the docile, simple and easily impressed Eva Braun. Traudl Junge had realised that in her hysteria Magda Goebbels had forgotten to get the children lunch. She went in search of something for them in the Chancellery kitchens.

What she discovered shocked her. As Traudl approached Kannenberg's pantry she could hear drunken laughter and shouting from the Chancellery air-raid shelter beyond. When she explored further to find out what was going on she witnessed an orgy in full flight. 'An erotic fever seemed to have taken possession of everybody,' she recorded later. 'Everywhere, even in the dentist's chair, I saw bodies locked in lascivious embraces. The women had discarded all modesty and were freely exposing their private parts.' The jollity that had disturbed the Führer's final farewells in the early morning had given way to a fully fledged orgy. The dentist's chair was, apparently, a particularly favourite location for love-making because it could be adjusted to a number of positions.

Everywhere in the warren of cellars and air-raid shelters underneath the Chancellery men and women were making love in one last desperate bid to find some happiness before the horror they knew was to come. They were indifferent to the elderly people and young mothers with crying babies, indifferent to the wounded dying in Professor Haase's emergency hospital, indifferent to the crashing of shells in Voss Strasse above. Many SS soldiers charged with shooting deserters and fighting to the death had given up on their oaths already. Having plundered the Chancellery pantries for champagne, chocolates and delicacies, they had used them as trophies to entice women into their arms.

Presently Eva Hitler and Magda Goebbels reappeared in the lower bunker corridor. Magda Goebbels asked Otto Günsche if she could speak one more time to the Führer. Hitler agreed and emerged to talk to her. It is not known what she said to him. Some accounts say she begged him to leave for Berchtesgaden. But whatever Magda Goebbels said had no effect. The Führer retreated into his rooms and Eva followed him. Upstairs Traudl Junge had returned to the upper bunker with some sandwiches and fruit juice for the Goebbels' children. They chatted and played with her as if they hadn't a care in the world. It was just before 3.30 p.m.

There was an air of impatient anxiety in the lower bunker corridor. It was broken momentarily when Artur Axmann came running down the four flights of stairs from the emergency exit. Günsche was standing outside Hitler's rooms with his Luger drawn. Axmann desperately asked Günsche to let him see the Führer, but the nerve-wracked adjutant could not tolerate any further delay and refused his request. The small audience outside Hitler's rooms were steeling themselves for the moment. But the expected shots never came. Ten minutes had passed. Unable to bear it any more, Heinz Linge gingerly eased open the door.

Axmann and Goebbels went alone into the room first. As they entered, they saw the Führer sitting on a small couch, Eva at his side. Eva was slightly slumped forward, obviously dead. Her head was resting on her husband's shoulders. There was an acrid smell of bitter almonds emanating from her body, the distinctive smell of prussic acid. Her lips were puckered by the poison. Her Walther 6.35 pistol lay on the small coffee-table in front of them. It had not been fired.

Next to her, Hitler leaned heavily, with his jaw hanging loosely. A Walther 7.65 pistol lay on the floor near his feet where it had dropped from his hand. Blood was dripping from both his temples and was smeared around his mouth. But there was hardly any blood splattered around the room. At the time Axmann thought Hitler had shot himself through the mouth and had created such a blast as to cause the blood on the temples. (In fact, when the Russians subsequently found Hitler's skull, they disproved this theory. Had he shot himself in the mouth the air pressure would have been such as to blow his jaws apart. His jaws were intact.) A small vase of flowers had somehow fallen off the table. Linge picked them up and replaced them where they should have been.

Goebbels and Linge left the death scene and Axmann remained alone with the corpses and his thoughts for a short while. Presently Linge came in with another SS man and wrapped Hitler's body up in a rough army blanket. They took the bundle out into the corridor. Hitler's unmistakable black trousers were sticking out in an ungainly fashion. They handed the corpse to two other SS officers who manhandled it up the four flights of stairs to the emergency exit. Then Martin Bormann went in and picked up Eva Hitler's body. He handed it to Kempke who took it to the stairwell. Kempke handed it to Günsche who threw it over his shoulder and made his way up to the garden.

Thereafter the mourners and supposedly sole witnesses to the funeral moved into their positions. They were Bormann, Generals Krebs and Burgdorf, Joseph Goebbels, Kempka and Linge. Günsche presided over the ceremony. The two bodies were laid side by side in a shell crater close to the emergency exit. The petrol was then poured over them and in the face of Russian artillery bombardment the mourners were forced to retire to the safety of the emergency exit's porch. Joseph Goebbels struck a match to light the pyre. The flame failed to catch. Eventually someone lit a petrol rag and was finally able to get a good blaze roaring. The mourners then offered one last 'Heil Hitler' before retreating from the heat of the flames and the explosions of the Russian shells. Günsche did not fulfil the Führer's order to the letter. He delegated the responsibility for seeing that the bodies were completely destroyed to two of Hitler's SS bodyguards. In the meantime the residents of the bunker hastily prepared for their evacuation from the city. According to one report an SS guard stumbled upon the scene of the burning bodies by accident. He had been one of the SS men drinking in the Reich Chancellery canteen. He rushed down into the bunker to find the telephonist Rochus Misch. 'The chief's on fire,' he is said to have said. 'Do you want to come and have a look?'

The most noticeable sign that the Führer was no longer with them was that the bunker now stank of the intoxicating smell of cigarette smoke. The Führer had banned smoking and now that he was gone virtually all the occupants lit up in relief. Weidling came over at one stage for his usual afternoon conference. Nobody had told him of the afternoon's key event. When he was told the Führer had chosen the coward's way out, he was disgusted. He went back to his command post with the intention of releasing his men from their oaths. Finally, at about 11 p.m., Rattenhuber ordered the skeletal remains to be buried.

In the early afternoon of 30 April, I returned from the Führerbunker to Axmann's command post. I had no idea of the drama in the Führerbunker. Axmann didn't turn up for about two hours. When he did, he was visibly distraught. With a cracking voice, he said: 'The Führer has shot himself!' I was stunned. The Führer dead! It was beyond belief.

Almost immediately the question 'What about the miracle weapons?' crossed my mind. I felt as panic-stricken now as I had 13 years before when my father had left me on the pavement and driven off. Now I didn't cry. With Axmann visibly crushed, I did not dare to ask it out loud. He reached for paper and, with his left hand, jotted down some notes.

I recalled that just months ago, we had been told that Divine Providence had saved the Führer's life after he had survived the 20 July 1944 assassination attempt. If guided by Divine Providence, how could he have taken his life? Nothing seemed real any more.

Axmann sent me to get Dr Gertrud. She sensed immediately that something terrible must have happened. She grabbed my arm and held on to it as we walked to Axmann's desk. I left the room. After a few minutes, I saw her come out sobbing.

She seemed even more devastated than I was. But our jobs continued. With newly wounded still arriving she needed additional medical supplies; so once again I was off. On this last mission, I ran through bursting flames, choking smoke and a hail of metal. It must have been about midnight, less than 24 hours after my last close encounter with Hitler. Mass groupings of Russian tanks had been reported and we expected them to approach on Wilhelmsstrasse and Hermann Göring Strasse. As a result, I reversed my route and went through the garden to the emergency entrance and via the lower and upper bunkers. I continued underground to the air raid shelter below the new Chancellery.

The cellar underneath the New Reich Chancellery where the

emergency hospital was located had become a squalid place. The toilets were overflowing and people had to make do with whatever corner they could find. There was only a little fresh water to go around and there wasn't enough space for the hundreds of people who had now squashed into it. Order had completely disappeared. I had to go to many of these shelters in the course of every day. They were like zoos. Babies were crying and people were shouting angry recriminations at one another. All of them stank to high heaven: of urine, excrement and sweat.

I then witnessed the scenes of depravity in the cellars. Everywhere couples were embracing one another. An apocalyptic mood, *Weltunter-gangsstimmung*, was in the air. The fear of death – and possibly a very violent death at that – could almost be smelled. There was the sound of quiet sobs and urgent whispering. More and more people were beginning to be aware of the Führer's betrayal. There were frequent gasps and it was difficult to distinguish whether they were prompted by the pain of some injury or the realisation of what Hitler had done. There were the sounds of sweet curses and subdued crying. Everyone from the oldest man to the smallest child seemed to be aware of the terror that was enveloping the city.

I noticed two children alone and with nobody to look after them. What had happened to their mothers? Would they ever see their parents again? What chance would they stand in the coming onslaught? In another corner I heard a young girl say: 'We will get out of here. The Führer won't leave us in the lurch!' She was maybe eight or nine years old and she looked younger than my sister Dörte.

'The Führer is dead,' her mother replied, in a whisper mixed with fear and anger.

'The Führer is dead?' replied the child, uncomprehending.

'He left us to the Communists,' her mother seethed. 'The Führer abandoned us. The war is lost. The enemy will finish us off.'

None of the supplies Dr Gertrud needed were on hand any more. I left empty-handed and returned the same way I had come. I checked at the ante-room of the Führerbunker to see if dispatches were to be picked up. Two officers whom I had never seen before were there. One of them yelled at me to leave and then asked the other officer, 'Who permitted this lad to enter?' (The German word he used was '*Kerl*', a bad sort of a fellow.)

Volkssturm Hitler Youth uniforms were not common in Hitler's bunker and not even my decorations legitimised my presence as far as this officer was concerned.

I left through the emergency exit, passing sentries for the last time. No name-tags were worn and I never knew any of these guards by their names. Whenever I had talked to one, I addressed him by his rank. For most of them I was the 'Junge'. Nobody had ever called me a Kerl as this officer did. It had a derogatory connotation. I was without military rank. Earlier I had been addressed as Melder, which I preferred above all.

Harry Mengershausen came up to the emergency exit on this occasion while I was waiting for a break in the shelling. Now I had an opportunity to make some inquiries. Dr Gertrud wanted to know how the Hitlers were buried and where their graves were.

'There, I believe!' he answered without hesitation, pointing to a place in the garden that looked like a shell-crater.

'We didn't bury them!' he said. With 'we' he must have meant the regular guards. I didn't think of it as important to know who did and didn't lay the Hitlers to rest. (Subsequently Mengershausen, on his release from Soviet Russia, claimed he had dug the grave and buried the bodies, 3 feet down on three wooden planks. He also said they had not been completely destroyed by the fire and were easily identifiable.) Later, upon my return, I told Dr Gertrud that there was just one grave for both, a shell-crater, unmarked and still smouldering.

Once again, she seemed visibly shaken but continued to go about her work.

I didn't tell her that, through the rising smoke, I had seen what I thought was a bone, from an arm or a leg sticking out. Not having viewed it close up, it could have been a metal pipe or for that matter anything that didn't burn down. It had looked as if the soil was steaming. Obviously dirt had been shovelled upon the burned corpses, but not enough to eliminate the smouldering.

The surroundings of this historic grave looked more like a junkyard than a garden. Clutter covered the area, fragments of explosions, debris, bits of stone and metal and several corpses yet to be buried. I also remember a cement mixer and a burned-out car, both full of bullet holes. No actual man-to-man fighting had taken place in the Reich Chancellery Garden. The dead soldiers and civilians must have been victims of bomb or grenade hits.

∾ CHAPTER FIFTEEN ∾

Murder in the Bunker

IN MY YOUNG MIND I WAS STILL unable to grasp why Hitler had committed suicide. My belief structure had collapsed. But there was no time to think. First, I had to save my own life.

'Why did the Führer kill himself?' I asked Axmann.

'Because we are near the end.' He said the words as if in a trance. (After the war Axmann would publish his memoir, entitled *It Can't be the End*.)

I would not give up. 'Where are the miracle weapons we are waiting for?'

'Not yet finished,' he replied hesitantly.

This also proved to be nonsense. There were no miracle weapons. Even the V-2s were no longer being produced. The much-vaunted V-3 rocket had never gone into production. There was talk of Hitler's fabled Amerika rocket – which could reach New York City. It didn't exist, except on paper, or in the dreams of a few Nazi scientists. In the United States, on the other hand, the atomic bomb would very soon exist. Its development was almost complete. At that time, none of us had ever heard of an atomic bomb and I doubt that Axmann knew anything about this catastrophic weapon either.

For the first time during the war, I was beginning to feel betrayed and bitter. Curiously though, I did not direct my anger at the Führer. He still had some sort of strange hypnotic hold over my youthful mind. Adolf Hitler was dead and buried, but such was his influence over me that I still didn't dare invoke his name.

'Now there will be no more heroes' deaths,' I said to Axmann bitterly. 'Now God will just let us perish!'

'We have no alternative but to break out,' was all Axmann would say.

But the possibilities of breaking out of Berlin were becoming slimmer with each passing moment. The city was entirely encircled by the Russian armies. The most popular escape route was out of the Chancellery and across the Tiergarten, along Kantstrasse and then on to the Heersstrasse westwards towards the Pichelsdorf Bridge – still held by the Hitler Youth. This was the route the officer couriers had taken before Hitler committed suicide. Another possible route was north across the Weidendamm Bridge, which was also being held by the Hitler Youth. But the Red Army was quickly tightening its grip on both areas and it would only be a matter of time before the enemy would be on the north and west sides of both bridges.

Axmann, though, still held out the hope of breaking through and joining forces with the remnants of Hitler Youth groups north of Berlin. There was, he emphasised, one crucial element to the plan. It was vital to keep the death of the Führer – and the manner of his demise – a secret. The truth would be utterly demoralising. The only reason our troops had been fighting so valiantly was that they were under the impression that Wenck's Twelfth Army and possibly Busse's Ninth Army were about to relieve the city. Everyone had been told the Russians were being repelled in the east and that they were falling out with the Western Allies. Once these fictions were exposed chaos would ensue.

But it soon became apparent to me that it would not be possible to keep the Führer's death a secret. It was already dawning on those outside the higher echelons of the citadel that Hitler was gone. I discovered this when I had to deliver a message to the Chancellery. (It was the news that a Hitler Youth fighting group at Neukölln had been wiped out by a Russian tank attack. Those of my brave young comrades that were not killed outright would be prisoners of the Red Army by now. It would not be long before they would perish too, death by disease in Soviet labour camps.)

In the cellars of the Reich Chancellery the looming catastrophe was prompting a further orgy of last-minute love-making fuelled by alcohol. A young girl in the uniform of a signal auxiliary approached me and grasped me in an embrace. She babbled: '*Ach du kleiner Süsser, von Dir möcht ich auch noch ein baby.*' ('You sweet little one. I want a baby from you too.') She put her hand over my Iron Cross. When I felt her tongue in my ear and her hair in my face, I told her: '*Ich bin im Dienst!*' ('I am on duty.') I slipped from her embrace as inoffensively as possible. Then she sobbed. '*Ich will den Russen nicht in die Hände fallen.*' ('I don't want to be captured by the Russians.')

But what could I do? I felt sorry for her. I felt her pain. But I also felt helpless. There I was in a crowd of soldiers and civilians and an attractive young girl wanted to make love to me. But I was committed to Anne-Maria. She might be pregnant with my child. Even if I did not survive in Berlin, the wellspring of renewal and of my life's continuation might survive where she was in Hof. My life might end and my body parch and turn into ashes, blown by the wind into eternal space. But my child might survive.

When I returned to the Party Chancellery, Dr Gertrud's nurses were also talking about becoming pregnant. They saw it as some sort of protection or precaution. Others thought of committing suicide and they talked about it without hesitation. Any thought of victory had now entirely dissipated. Everyone knew this was the end.

The break-out had initially been planned for the evening Hitler had committed suicide. But when Axmann returned to his command post at about 6 p.m. he told me our departure was postponed 24 hours. We would now be going out at shortly after 10 p.m. on the following day, Tuesday, 1 May. I wanted to know why. Axmann said that there was a chance of peace negotiations with the Red Army. Goebbels and Bormann had held a meeting to put together a peace proposal for the Russians. Axmann was present along with Generals Burgdorf, Krebs and Mohnke. It was agreed that they should urgently convey to the Russian leadership the news that Goebbels and Bormann were members of the new administration of Germany and that Grand Admiral Dönitz was the new Chancellor. If the Russians granted them safe passage north to Dönitz's headquarters in Schleswig-Holstein, they would convene the government and open peace negotiations with Moscow.

Martin Bormann was, of course, the single individual who had most to gain. Regardless of his new position outlined in Hitler's political testament, with his patron gone he had lost the only man who had any respect for him. All power now lay with the new Chancellor in Schleswig-Holstein. If Bormann could get to Dönitz before he realised Hitler was dead, he would at least have a slim chance of recovering his authority. But it was wishful thinking. There wasn't the slightest chance the Russians would let either Goebbels or Bormann out of their grasp and any peace negotiations would be held on Stalin's terms alone.

There was another good reason to delay the break-out though. We were all at the end of our tether. I had not slept for two nights and every minute of the past two days seemed to have been filled with a whirlwind of action. It was the same for everyone else. In our parlous state few of us were in any physical condition to run more than a couple of hundred metres. We were all ordered to catch as much sleep as we could.

So with our mortal enemies bearing down on us with the ferocity of a tiger about to rip its victim apart our orders were to sleep. But few of us could sleep. It was partly because of fear. We were all convinced that we would be dead soon. And it would not be a quick, painless demise for many of us. We all knew now how close the Russians were. At times the intensity of their barrage was incredible. Yet it continued to increase.

Mortar and shellfire, the whoosh of ferocious katyushas and endless machine-gun fire. Thoughts of survival were on everyone's mind. Thoughts of God too. How quickly we turn to the Creator when the chips are down! I'm ashamed to say that I began to stop thinking about my comrades and started thinking about myself. I wondered if there was any chance I could avoid the fate that surely awaited the rest of them.

I quickly put these thoughts out of my mind. To take off and try to reach the Russians with hands up was not an option I would have considered at that time. I had to follow orders, participate in the break-out and hopefully survive. I remembered my grandmother. As a little boy, when I prayed, asking favours of God, she had urged me to thank him instead of begging. For the rest of the night I still did not sleep, but I ended up praying: not asking for him to save my life, but promising to do something with it should I survive.

Thoughts of my childhood entered my mind. The beautiful forests of Silesia. Picking berries with my mother. Taking my dogs for a walk. My pet deer. My loving grandparents. The father whom I had so disappointed but whom I even now sought to please. Where was Hannes now? I longed for his company. He would get us out of this tricky little situation intact. I knew that for sure. But Hannes was missing now. And wherever he lay were my two last letters to my mother and Anne-Maria. They would never receive them. They would never read my last words to them. And they might never know what had happened to me. It was hard to see the point of sleeping when oblivion was so close at hand.

It was while I was lying exhausted on the cot with these thoughts going through my mind that it came to my attention that Martin Bormann was trying to engineer his own break-out group from the citadel. The request came to Axmann to provide him with a coterie of Hitler Youth as a human shield. I listened to Weltzin and Axmann discuss it. This was the very same human shield that Axmann had promised he would supply for the Führer. Bormann's reasoning was that as he was now Party leader, he surely should be entitled to the same offer. Other senior officers had broken through Russian lines with the protection of boy soldiers, so in many respects his request was a perfectly valid one.

But Axmann was flabbergasted. He suspected that Bormann had spent the last days in the bunker doing nothing other than engineer the downfall of his rivals and his own survival. After Hitler had killed himself Bormann had ordered Hans Baur to fly him to Dönitz's headquarters on the Baltic. But Baur told him there wasn't a plane available and absolutely no prospect of a quick escape for Bormann, the consummate coward. At one stage he was supposed to have said that he wished Hanna Reitsch hadn't left – as if her daredevil antics could save him, even without a plane. Bormann could hardly have relished the prospect of a break-out on foot.

But the thought of a group of boy soldiers to put themselves in the way of him and the Russian bullets must have been at least a little comforting.

For a moment I wished that Axmann would oblige. If he went along with Bormann's request then I, for sure, would have been one of the boys assigned to this task. If there were just a few of us we might stand a better chance of getting through than the massive break-out originally planned. I disliked Bormann intensely but would have welcomed the chance to break out with him ahead of the pack. I got up from my cot and encouraged Axmann to approve Bormann's plan. So did some of the officers present, including Boldt. But one objected that such an undertaking would have to receive approval from General Mohnke. Weltzin was sent to his command post in the New Chancellery to get his approval. We all waited. Back came the reply. '*Kommt nicht in Frage!*' ('Out of the question!')

There was to be no separate break-out, not even for Martin Bormann. There could be no more vivid illustration of how Bormann's power was slipping from his grasp than the way in which he was being ignored by everybody. He had no control over the military forces. Bormann was behaving like the Goldfasan my grandfather had always said he was. He had all the fine flummery of high office. But he couldn't fly. He was not a soldier-type. He was a bully, like many cowards. I know that's what Axmann thought of him. But he was discreet. All he would ever say of Bormann was: '*Er konnte viel vertragen*' ('He could hold his liquor'). After Hitler's suicide Bormann's state of intoxication became an embarrassment. Word went about that he'd raided the pantries for bottles of liquor and was handing spirits and cigarettes around to all his cronies.

I was disappointed that we weren't going to make a run for it. But I laughed secretly to myself. With his request denied, Bormann must have realised that, Party chief or not, he had no real power at all. So, Hitler had let his 'most loyal Party comrade' down too! His naming him Party chief amounted to absolutely nothing.

I asked myself, was I ready to die? And strangely, for the first time in the war, the answer came to me quite promptly that no, I was not. What would I die for? The Führer? He was dead. The nation? It was in tatters and couldn't be realistically described as a nation as such any more. My mother, my sisters and my brothers? No. They wouldn't want me to die for them. My father? Ha! He would definitely see my heroic demise as a badge of honour. But would it be heroic? Or would it be sordid and pitiful? Would I be crushed under a tank track, or scorched to death by a flame-thrower? And if my death was a heroic one, would my father ever know? Would anyone get to know? Would I make one last sacrifice to glory in spite of defeat? A noble example for future generations?

No. I had no intention of dying. I knew that Anne-Maria was waiting for me.

Late that night Goebbels and Bormann ordered General Krebs to leave the bunker and talk to the Red Army chief General Chuikov about peace terms. Krebs spoke fluent Russian and in an earlier incarnation as a military attaché to Moscow, he had once been embraced by Stalin. It was hoped the memory of earlier, happier times might oil the wheels of diplomacy. It would prove to be a forlorn hope. Krebs left the bunker waving a white flag. He carried a letter from Goebbels and Bormann explaining that they were members of the new government of the Reich and that Admiral Dönitz was the new leader of the country. Bormann requested safe passage to visit Dönitz at his headquarters in Schleswig-Holstein.

Krebs was not to return until later the following morning, about 6 a.m. When he did come back it was with the very clear message that the Russians would accept nothing short of a complete capitulation. They demanded a response by 4 p.m. It was 1 May, a special day for Russia, and Stalin was looking to celebrate it in a very special way. By now Bormann and Goebbels knew there was no chance whatsoever of a peace treaty. They instructed that the break-out go ahead. Goebbels said he would not be joining the escape, but would die in Berlin as the Führer had. Bormann, finally realising that there was no point now of keeping the truth from Dönitz, informed the new Chancellor that Hitler was dead.

In the Führerbunker Goebbels summoned his adjutant Günther Schwägermann to his office off the main corridor. He told him he would not be joining the break-out but would die with his wife in Berlin as the Führer had done. He asked Schwägermann to burn his remains as the Führer's had been. He also told him that they had decided the children must be murdered too. At the end of the conversation Goebbels presented Schwägermann with a silver-framed photograph of Hitler that had stood on his desk for many years. It was an encounter entirely devoid of emotion on either side.

That afternoon Axmann went over to the Führerbunker to tell Bormann that General Mohnke had turned down his request for a separate advance. Afterwards Axmann visited Goebbels in his office. Goebbels told him of his decision to kill himself and Magda. Later Axmann joined Magda and Joseph Goebbels sitting at the conference table in the lower bunker. There were several others at the gathering including Hans Baur, Hitler's pilot, and General Krebs. They shared a bottle of champagne and talked about old times. Magda puffed nervously on a cigarette. Goebbels wistfully recalled the pre-war days when he and Axmann had fought Communists and Socialists on the streets of Berlin.

Axmann must have told Dr Gertrud what the Goebbels planned to do when he returned because she was visibly upset. She came up with a plan to save them. Her idea was to use two assistants from among her nursing staff to take the children underground to the children's clinic near the Charité Hospital near the Weidendamm Bridge. She asked me what conditions outside were really like. What I had to tell her was not reassuring. I told her that given the current conditions there was little chance that they wouldn't be killed. The place was the subject of ceaseless bombardments and the streets whistled to the piercing sounds of flying bullets. The clinic was marked with a Red Cross and she thought that hospitals would be spared. But that wasn't the case of course. If anything we were to discover later that the Russians took great satisfaction in not only shelling hospitals, but raping the nurses when they finally got there.

Around about the same time I received an indication that the Goebbels were not the only Nazis planning to annihilate their children. I was directed to pick up a message from Bormann in the lower bunker. But he wouldn't give it to me. Despite the fact that he had seen me several times before, picking up dispatches, he asked: 'Is this the courier?' 'Yes,' said the staff officer present, who took the dispatch envelope from Bormann and handed it to me. I ran back to the marine radio room and handed it to the operator. I can still see the radio operator who opened this one shake his head in disbelief, saying: 'My God, these children too!' Bormann had directed his wife Gerda to kill all ten of their children and then herself.

Goebbels dictated his last telegram shortly after midday. It was to Admiral Dönitz, confirming that Adolf Hitler was dead. Then the Propaganda Minister retired with Magda to their rooms in the upper bunker. The children were playing in the dining corridor under the supervision of Traudl Junge. We will never know whether Goebbels and his wife discussed what was about to happen in the privacy of their rooms only metres away from the children. There is certainly evidence that in these, their last hours on earth, neither the Goebbels nor anyone else could bear to refer directly to the unnatural act that Magda Goebbels was about to commit. The issue had been raised repeatedly over the past months with both parents vacillating wildly. One moment Joseph Goebbels expressed the wish that they be sent west, preferably to fall into the hands of the British, whom he admired. The next, he would realise the hopelessness of the situation. Joseph Goebbels' children would never be allowed to lead a normal existence, no matter how benign the hands of the authorities into which they fell. It would be wrong to assume however, that it was primarily Joseph Goebbels who was the motivating force in his children's murder. Magda Goebbels also recognised the practical inevitabilities of the situation. It would not be an easy life after the war as Joseph Goebbels' children. But with Magda there was the macabre hint that the sacrifice of her six children was not just an act of mercy. It has been speculated that by offering her children at the altar of the Führer, she would confirm herself in the role of the First Lady of the Reich, above and beyond the last-minute pretender Eva Braun.

Later on that same afternoon, as the evening approached, Joseph

Goebbels summoned an SS dentist, Helmuth Kuntz, to his office across the corridor from Hitler's. Explaining that his wife had a special request of him, Goebbels then excused himself, leaving Kuntz alone with Magda. Kuntz was the family's dentist. He had a surgery in the basement of the New Reich Chancellery. It was his dentist's chair that had proved so popular with the revellers in the Chancellery cellars above the bunker. Kuntz had arrived in the Chancellery on 27 April when Magda had first approached him with a delicate topic she wanted to raise. Then she explained that the situation was such she felt she would have to kill her children. At the time he agreed that the killing of the children would be an act of mercy.

But now that the reality of the situation had arrived at its pressing conclusion, Kuntz appeared a little more squeamish. Magda Goebbels asked directly if the doctor would help kill their children. He tried to convince her that they could be taken to the Charité Hospital where they would be safe under the Red Cross's protection. She dismissed the idea out of hand. Shortly afterwards Joseph Goebbels returned and also brushed the idea aside. 'They are the children of Goebbels,' was all he said, summarising succinctly the curse that he had placed over his own children's heads. Once more Joseph Goebbels left the room and was not seen for another hour or so. With the situation still undecided, Dr Kuntz and Magda Goebbels then sat down to play a game of cards.

The Führer's death had left an eerie quiet in the bunker. Everybody knew what had happened except the Goebbels' children. Now, as their last bedtime approached, some of the children were playing in the corridor outside the suite of rooms where 'Uncle Adolf' had only hours ago taken his life. The others were playing in the rooms of the upper bunker where a small party of the remaining bunker adults had settled down to reminisce over drinks in the dining corridor. The noise from the party in the Chancellery cellar filtered down into the bunker. While Magda continued her game of cards with Dr Kuntz, Traudl Junge began preparing the children for bed. Joseph Goebbels entered, looking anxious. From the look on his face the Russians might have been on top of the bunker. They had to do something straight away or the whole family might fall into the Red Army's hands.

Quickly Magda Goebbels and Dr Kuntz made their way from the lower bunker up the concrete steps to the upper bunker and entered the children's small bedroom. All six children were in their nightgowns and ready to go to bed. There were three sets of bunk beds in the room. Magda picked a syringe off a shelf. It contained morphine. She explained that the doctor had come to give them all a vaccination that was being dispensed to everyone else in the bunker and all the soldiers. Tomorrow they would all be flying to join Uncle Adolf at Berchtesgaden and the children must prepare for the journey with a good night's sleep. Whether her eldest daughter Helga fell for this ploy will never be known, but there are grounds for thinking she did not. Over the past few days bunker inmates had witnessed with a mixture of emotions the heart-breaking scenes of the children playing innocently, unaware of the drama unfolding around them. But they noticed that Helga, aged 12 and by far the brightest of them, seemed to be aware that something sinister was in the air. After Hitler had killed himself her mother had been so overwrought with grief that it would have been impossible for Helga not to notice. Had she not noticed that the usually ever-attentive Uncle Adolf did not seem to have put in an appearance over the past few hours?

Nevertheless Helga obeyed her mother when Magda asked all the children to get into their beds and allow the SS dentist to administer the medicine. Magda could not face this initial phase of her plan. She left the room and waited outside for him to complete the task. It was some time after eight when Dr Kuntz emerged from the room. Nervously, he told her it would take about ten minutes for the drug to have an effect. The SS doctor also told her that he couldn't go through with what was required next. A more compliant physician had to be found quickly. Shortly afterwards Dr Stumpfegger arrived.

Dr Stumpfegger had a peculiar set of values for a physician. It is the normal instinct of a doctor to preserve life, but Stumpfegger had spent much of his time in the bunker distributing the small, blue-glass ampoules of prussic acid that would so efficiently take life. Professors Haase and Schenck had repeatedly asked for assistance in the Chancellery emergency hospital. But they had never received any from Stumpfegger. When, a few days previously, Dr Gertrud had asked him if he would operate on a Hitler Youth in her treatment room in the Party Chancellery, he had turned the request down, not wanting to risk his own life crossing Wilhemsstrasse just to save another's. The boy died of his injuries.

Now Stumpfegger entered the children's bedroom with Magda Goebbels. All the children were in a morphine-induced sleep, although some were more asleep than others. Magda Goebbels then went up to each of her children in turn. She forced each child's jaws open. Stumpfegger then placed one of his glass ampoules of prussic acid between the children's teeth. Then Magda crushed each of her children's jaws firmly shut. There may have been a tiny spasm, a brisk intake of breath. But death followed within a fraction of a second. Except perhaps for Helga. When Soviet troops found the children's bodies some days later, their doctors' autopsy reported 'several black and blue bruises' about Helga's face. It suggested that she awoke and realised something was amiss, before struggling with her mother as she attempted to force the child's jaws shut. It cannot have been the nicest of ways to say goodbye to the first daughter one had brought into the world. After Stumpfegger and Magda Goebbels had finished their deadly business they placed a sheet over each of the dead bodies.

The silence in the upper bunker now really was deathly. Within minutes the whole Goebbels family would be dead.

When Magda returned to the lower bunker her husband had reappeared and was pacing up and down looking very anxious. His adjutant Günther Schwägermann and General Mohnke were in the corridor with him. They looked at Goebbels with the same mixture of apprehension and impatience that Günsche had displayed before Hitler killed himself. The conference corridor echoed to the ghostly booms and bangs of warfare from above. Magda was smoking a cigarette nervously. She indicated to her husband that it was 'all over' with the children. She devoted no more words to the subject. Her husband did not register any emotion. 'Let's get this over with,' Joseph Goebbels said impatiently to Schwägermann. Magda stubbed the cigarette out and picked up a small bottle of champagne that had been left on the table. Pouring herself a glass, she took a few sips, replacing it and straightening her dress. She was prepared for this moment. She had Hitler's gold Party badge on her and a gold cigarette case that he had presented her inscribed 'Adolf Hitler, 29 May 1934'. Husband and wife then passed Schwägermann and Mohnke and walked quickly up the four flights of stairs to the garden above.

Exactly how they met their end is not known. Perhaps Goebbels shot his wife before shooting himself. Perhaps she sank her teeth into Stumpfegger's prussic acid ampoules as Eva Hitler had and then Goebbels shot himself. We will never know. But after leaving a discreet amount of time, Schwägermann ran up the stairs. He found the bodies of Magda and Joseph Goebbels just metres away from where Eva and Adolf Hitler were buried. The smouldering from the flames of the Hitlers' funeral pyre was still rising out of the ground like steam. Schwägermann may have administered a *coup de grace* to each body, but again we will never know. He then hurriedly splashed petrol over their remains and set them alight. There was not quite enough fuel, though, for the Goebbels. When the Russians arrived they were both easily identifiable. The cigarette case was not destroyed by the flames, nor was the gold Party badge. Joseph Goebbels' over-sized skull was immediately recognisable from Soviet propaganda cartoons, and his orthopaedic foot also survived the blaze.

Goebbels had genuinely loved his children. But before his demise he had made few explicit references to the manner of theirs. Perhaps he could not bear to think about it. The one reference he did make was a curiously clinical one. It was no more than a casual suggestion to some of the bunker staff that they might find a moment to bury 'the cadavers' of the children after Joseph and Magda had gone. In fact none of the bunker staff could bear entering the room where the unnatural deed had been committed. So the children's bodies stayed there, in their ghostly white nightgowns, until the Red Army soldiers stumbled on them several days later.

When Schwägermann returned downstairs Mohnke told him to set Hitler's quarters alight. There was not much fuel left. But the adjutant found a single can and poured it over the map-room floor. He flicked a match at it and it whooshed ablaze. Without waiting to see how it progressed, Mohnke and Schwägermann began the evacuation of the Führerbunker.

∽ CHAPTER SIXTEEN ∽

Break-out

IT WAS ALMOST 9 P.M. WHEN General Mohnke and Captain Schwägermann finally left the bunker. Mohnke now assumed the role of *Ausbruchskommandant* (the break-out commander). He immediately convened a meeting in his cellar command post with senior officers from the various military positions in and around Berlin. Axmann was one of those summoned, representing the Hitler Youth holding the Weidendamm Bridge and Havel Bridge and the 100 or so in the Reich Chancellery itself. The SS general began by outlining to everyone the sensational developments of the past two days. Few of those present knew exactly what had been going on in the Führerbunker, but they had all heard the rumours. Now Mohnke confirmed for them the marriage of Eva Braun and Adolf Hitler and the suicides of the newly weds and the Goebbels. The details were greeted with mild surprise but no discernible distress. What was more worrying was Mohnke's assessment of the military situation. There was no chance at all of Wenck's Twelfth Army and Busse's Ninth Army coming to the relief of the capital.

This revelation was received with quiet anger. Mohnke explained that the only option left now was for individual battle groups to try and punch through the Russian lines in the general direction of the northwest, with the ultimate hope of getting to Admiral Dönitz's Schleswig-Holstein headquarters. He said that on the stroke of 11 p.m. the order would go out to each battle group to cease defending positions and that the mass break-out would begin then. He asked that the truth about Hitler's suicide and Busse's and Wenck's 'ghost' armies be kept from their men until an

198

hour beforehand. With that, everyone left the command post and began preparing their own individual strategies for survival over the forthcoming trying hours.

Shortly after this conference, at 9.30 p.m., the Reich Radio station in Hamburg announced that listeners should prepare for a grave and important announcement. In the meantime the airwaves were filled with the maudlin melodies of Wagner's operas and Bruckner's Seventh Symphony. It was almost another hour and a half before listeners were told that Hitler was dead. Typically, the German people were still not told the unvarnished truth. They were told their Führer had died 'at his post in the Reich Chancellery, while fighting to the last breath against Bolshevism'. When the unfamiliar voice of Grand Admiral Dönitz came on he repeated the lie, speaking of Hitler's 'heroic death'. Dönitz revealed that he had succeeded Hitler, although he would not be called the Führer, but the Chancellor.

The broadcast was yet another Nazi lie, of course. Hitler had taken the coward's way out as so many other ardent Nazis now appeared to be doing. They had sent many millions of people to long, lingering deaths. They had brutalised many millions more across Europe. But now these men and women who were drenched in the blood of others were not prepared to wait for a taste of their own medicine. Dönitz had been as surprised by the news of Hitler's suicide as General Weidling. But that was where any similarity between the two men ended. At 10 p.m., Weidling was about to assuage his anger with Hitler by releasing the men under his command from their oaths. His order stated curtly and accurately: 'On 30.4.45 the Führer took his own life and therefore abandoned those who had sworn loyalty to him.' Weidling would tell them that to continue fighting was pointless and that they should lay down their arms. Dönitz was a Nazi right until the end. For him and his men, the fight would go on as Hitler had wished, until death.

Russian troops were now in position on the other side of both the Pichelsdorf Bridge over the Havel to the west of the city and the Weidendamm Bridge over the Spree to the north of the Chancellery building. With the two most obvious escape routes effectively blocked, Mohnke had devised an audacious strategy for the soldiers and staff of the Reich Chancellery. There was one possible way out: underneath the city. Despite the pounding the city had taken, Berlin's subway system was remarkably intact. The surface entrances had been reduced to rubble. But in the past 11 days of ceaseless bombardment thousands of Berliners had turned the subway tunnels into their homes. Incredibly some trains had been running until a few days ago. Mohnke's plan was to evacuate anyone who could still walk along the underground tracks and up as far as the northern suburbs of Berlin to emerge behind enemy lines.

The route would start at the Kaiserhof subway station, diagonally opposite the Chancellery on the other side of Wilhelmplatz. From there the evacuees would travel eastwards to the Stadtmitte station, from where they would turn north and head for the Friedrichstrasse station. At this juncture the subway went underneath the Spree. The groups would make their way under the river and emerge at the Stettiner station in the northern suburb of Wedding. There, they would hopefully link up with other German army groups and make their way to Admiral Dönitz's headquarters 120 kilometres to the north-west.

The plan was not without its risks. The most hazardous part might very well be the initial 100-metre dash from the Chancellery's underground garage, across Wilhelmplatz to the Kaiserhof subway station. Russian troops were within 100 metres of the Chancellery and every road around the building was a death trap. There were also rumours of Red Army riflemen in the subways, or even clearing them out with flame-throwers. And there was talk of both the German defenders and the Russian invaders flooding the subways. But it was, as General Mohnke said, their best hope.

Two groups would not be taking this precarious flight along the underground. The first were the hundred or so Hitler Youth who were still serving in the precincts of the Chancellery. Axmann had decided we would go above ground. Being a native Berliner, Axmann believed that he stood a better chance on the streets of the city he knew. But he was also a brave man. Hiding from the enemy was not the sort of notion he was comfortable with. Running away down the subway lines like a rat did not appeal. If he had to face the enemy, then he would face him head on. I think Mohnke also wanted above-ground activities to divert attention from the underground escape attempt. To me it made no difference. Underground or overground carried similar risks. I just wanted to get out of the Chancellery. It occurred to me to ask Axmann what the plan was if we did manage to break through the Russian lines.

'Keep on fighting as ordered by the Führer!' he replied simply.

'What about the wounded?' I wanted to know.

'They have to be left behind.'

This was the second group, who would not be escaping. There was nothing that they could do except wait for the enemy to arrive. There were some 40 or so patients in the first-aid station under the Party Chancellery. They would stay in the care of Dr Gertrud. There were several hundred wretched souls in the emergency hospital under the Reich Chancellery. They would stay under the care of Professor Haase. Hitler's old SS doctor was so ill he couldn't walk more than 20 metres without wheezing. Professor Schenck would accompany General Mohnke as his third-in-command. But Dr Gertrud was not happy to hear that

Axmann planned to leave her behind. She insisted that we take her along. At first Axmann was adamant. She must stay with her patients. It would be too dangerous for a woman.

'You will be needing me!' she insisted.

Eventually Axmann gave in. Dr Gertrud had once again demonstrated her bravery. She had also signed her own death sentence.

At this time I scribbled a quick poem.

> From an
> unknown grave, my burning soul
> And the winter wind
> reach an
> endless sea,
> with wondrous
> waves
> of eternity.

What urged me to write these poems under the most adverse of conditions, I still don't know. That I had the urge to write is as much a mystery as life is. Perhaps I felt that though I was facing death, my words would survive in the care of the wounded who we were going to leave behind. I left my poem with Dieter Shröder, a 13-year-old boy we were going to have to leave. Whatever happened to him, I never found out.

Everyone was ordered to assemble in the cellar of the New Reich Chancellery. From there they were instructed to make their way down to one of the underground garages that faced Wilhemsstrasse. It had once housed the Chancellery fire brigade but was now home to a fleet of shiny black government limousines, which very soon would be commandeered by the triumphant Red Army invaders. But for now the cars had been shunted in an untidy pile to the side of the vast garage to make way for the army of escapees. There were about 1,000 people to be evacuated in all. Most of them were members of Mohnke's SS LAH division, but there were 20 members of Hitler's staff and some 80 of Rattenhuber's men.

There were vast numbers of people assembled in all the underground bunkers and cellars in the Chancellery. As the night progressed more and more soldiers shuffled into the low-ceilinged rooms. Men and boys, civilians and soldiers, arrived one after the other, their clothes and faces caked in so much dirt that it was impossible to distinguish them from one another. The look on their faces was of dejection and defeat. But more than anything else it was a look of abject weariness. Their uniforms were torn and tattered. Like me they had slept and fought in them for the past two weeks at least.

The plan was to make their way in groups of 20 or so across

Wilhelmplatz and into the Kaiserhof subway station. Mohnke would lead the first group, which would include all of his staff officers, Professor Schenck, Otto Günsche and the remaining ladies of the bunker: Traudl Junge and Gerda Christian, and Bormann's secretary Else Krüger, as well as Hitler's cook Constanze Manziarly. Rattenhuber was the leader of group number two and they took up Mohnke's trail.

We were scheduled to be group three. There was some argument about which group Martin Bormann would be in. Since Hitler's death Bormann had been treated as a figure of ridicule by almost everyone. Mohnke could not disguise his contempt. Bormann was increasingly intoxicated and began to fall into loud-mouthed squabbles with Mohnke's junior officers. They too treated him with ill-concealed disdain. That night Bormann appeared so inebriated that Weltzin told Axmann, '*In diesem Zustand nehmen wir ihn aber nicht mit.*' ('In that condition we just won't take him along.') He was wearing an oversized leather coat that made him look even fatter than he actually was. General Mohnke also had civilian clothes with him. Two men who had spent the last several weeks insisting that others fight until the death were now planning their own cowardly getaway dressed as civilians.

Bormann was approaching the end of his life, with all the seediness and selfishness taking its toll. He was not alone. Many of his Party Chancellery staff had drunk themselves into a stupor, and all of them had abandoned the Nazi uniforms they had so grandly flaunted for the past dozen years.

Mohnke made it abundantly clear he did not want Bormann in his group. He was so drunk Dr Stumpfegger had to sober him up. Axmann was even less inclined to take him. In the end a group from the Propaganda Ministry agreed to take him. Ludwig Stumpfegger, Hitler's personal physician, would also go along in this group, as would Hans Baur, Hitler's pilot. Baur detested Bormann as much as everyone else did. But since accepting Hitler's order to accompany Bormann to Admiral Dönitz's headquarters, he felt honour-bound by his pledge to the Führer. That night Baur had the valuable oil painting gifted by Hitler rolled up in a knapsack. Stumpfegger appeared to be assisting Bormann to regain some semblance of sobriety.

There was some argument between our group and Bormann's as to who should go first. Bormann didn't want to wait as long as the 20-minute interval that General Mohnke had ordered between each group. He was in a panic to get out of the Chancellery as soon as possible. We could all hear the Russian snipers outside. In the end it became academic. Since Axmann had decided we were going to go overland we didn't have to fit in with the other groups' plans. Axmann was going to try and coincide our departure with Mohnke's.

At 11 p.m. General Mohnke led his group out onto Wilhelmsstrasse, gingerly looking left and right for any signs of Russian snipers. In groups of three or four they ran down the Wilhemsstrasse and over the Wilhelmplatz.

While Mohnke's group went across Wilhelmsstrasse to the Kaiserhof station, we were to head directly north up the street. As we were about to leave Axmann produced two heavy bags that he told me contained over half a million Reich Marks. I was to carry them. I couldn't, they were too heavy. So I took one and one of the other Hitler Youth district leaders took the other. Our group consisted of the remaining Hitler Youth fighting units left in the citadel, Axmann's adjutants Günther Weltzin and Heinz Boldt, and Dr Gertrud and two of her nursing assistants.

Axmann gave the word and we were all to go, one by one, walking single-file and as close to the walls as was possible. Some of the boys were given specific orders to keep an eye on the girls. I had not had sleep for three nights. I cannot describe the state of mind I was in. But whatever adrenaline I had left kept my survival instinct going. So did Axmann's orders. It was a great relief to me when we first emerged on Wilhelmsstrasse because it was quieter than I had thought it would be. In the background the noise from Stalin's guns rumbled on as much as ever, but Wilhelmsstrasse at that moment wasn't the shooting gallery it had been during the day. It was suspiciously quiet, thankfully. Nevertheless it was nerve-wracking when the odd shot did ring out and it made one duck involuntarily. Fortunately, none of us was hit.

When we reached Unter den Linden we encountered enemy troops for the first time. They were at the Brandenburg Gate cooking a feast over an open spit and seemingly entirely oblivious, or perhaps indifferent, to our shadowy forms. It was a surreal experience because we had been expecting ferocious fighting.

Then we made our way gingerly along Unter den Linden, in the opposite direction to the Russian troops. It is inconceivable that they didn't see us, but again, no shots rang out. It was only when we turned north into Friedrichstrasse and towards the Weidendamm Bridge that we could see trouble ahead. We were approaching what appeared to be heavy fighting at a tank barricade on the bridge. There were hundreds and hundreds of SS, Wehrmacht soldiers and civilians gathered at the bridge. There was one mammoth Tiger tank and a self-propelled assault gun. The group were trying to smash through the anti-tank barrier on the other side, but they came under heavy fire. We joined them. That's when all hell broke loose.

It seemed that we were fired at from every direction, even from behind. Didn't some of our own troops realise that we were ahead of them? Bullets hissed through the air. Vicious shards of shrapnel flew at me from every direction and great jagged pieces of metal rained down on us. I couldn't see anything except a blur of sparks and flashing fire. I had absolutely no control over what I was doing or what was happening to me. I really was in the vortex of the cauldron. This is it, I thought. This is the end.

An explosion ahead of us produced a huge tremor as flames spewed into the sky. I dived against a wall for cover. Thankfully we could see an entrance that looked as if it led to a cellar a few metres ahead. We crawled towards it but discovered it was a shaft full of thick, toxic smoke. We were shouting at one another to overcome the noise around us. Axmann conceded we'd never get across the bridge.

'We have to bypass it,' was his decision.

'Assembly point?' I asked, shouting as loud as I could.

'Over there!'

He pointed to the building on the opposite side of the street. It was the Admiral's Palace. It wasn't filled with smoke as yet, as every other building in the area was. Weltzin too pointed to the building across the street. 'There!' he screamed at me. In between myself and the palace it seemed as if the street was being subjected to a constant hailstorm of mortar, shellfire and rocket strikes. Bullets criss-crossed the place from one angle to the next. But there was no alternative. Off I went through this merciless hail of metal.

On the other side I found Dr Gertrud. She was with a line of BDM girls. Two of them had been hit and were covered in blood. Dr Gertrud seemed all right. Then Axmann ordered me back across the street once more to get the other Hitler Youth boys who were carrying the briefcases stuffed with the Reich Marks. Axmann told me to get them so that we could discuss how exactly we could bypass the bridge. I held my breath and ran. But halfway across the street I became hopelessly disorientated. I had lost sight of them. I didn't know which direction I was pointing in. I was hunched down low as far as I could bend in the middle of the street, desperately looking around me trying to make out where they were. There was no let-up in the maelstrom of fire and flame around me.

Then, suddenly, the end.

It was like a release. All I remember thinking was that it was something of an anti-climax compared to the inferno I had endured for the past hour or so. As if in a dream, I vaguely felt a few small fragments of shrapnel glancing off the top of my steel helmet. Then I felt a knock and heard the jagged sound of metal thwacking metal. I threw myself on the pavement, pushing ever more closely against the wall for minimum exposure. I assured myself that, even should my body be torn apart, my soul was bullet-proof and would remain whole.

Paralysis.

I remember bits and pieces of what happened next. I remember my shrieking.

I must have gone down.

A piece of shrapnel hit my spine.

Then: nothing but blankness.

I could see myself as in a dream, looking from above at my very own body, mutilated but still alive. As a young boy, I had visions of a twin brother. Now, in my apparition, I had become two. I didn't know if I was dead or alive.

I had been lucky despite my misfortune. Hit, but not killed, I had been dug out before dying. Whether by Germans or Russians, I don't know. Probably some poor German woman who had seen my young face and taken pity on me, because my pay-books and my dog-tag were gone. There were women we called 'rubble women' who went through the rubble looking for people who were still alive. They knew the Russians would have exacted terrible retribution on the SS and so they threw away men's dog-tags and ID. If a Russian found me he would have taken my decorations as souvenirs at the very least, but not the items that would have identified me. He might very well have put a gun to my head.

Now my first mental awareness was that of a Russian female officer. I was on a stretcher, I thought at the time outside the Reich Chancellery, but I subsequently learned it was the Charité Hospital. I was paralysed from the waist down. She must have been a physician. She spoke German and wanted to know my name and age. Then she asked me if I was a Fascist.

'No!' I answered, to my mind truthfully. At that time, all I knew was that Fascism was the politics of Italy's Duce. Had she asked me if I were a National Socialist or a Nazi, I would have said, 'Yes.' I was still a Nazi. I saw nothing to be ashamed of. I never lied to any of my interrogators over the next few months. I always told the truth. The odd thing is, none of them ever asked if I had served directly under Hitler. So I never told them.

I slipped in and out of consciousness. The extent of my injuries was not at all clear.

I was only able to move my arms and my head but not my legs. I had no control over my bladder or bowels. I was helpless and soiled, lying on a stretcher. I wore a shirt and nothing else, covered by a blanket.

At the time I did not know that my condition was caused by a spine contusion sufficient to produce temporary paralysis that would soon disappear. That was good news for me. Had the doctor known I would recover she would probably have assigned me to a Russian labour camp in Siberia. That was a prospect no German soldier relished. It might as well have been certain death. As it was she let me be, a poor hopeless cripple.

Of course I didn't know that I'd recover, almost entirely, either. Thinking I would forever be a helpless, horrible cripple, I developed a death wish, so much so that I pleaded with an old man to shoot me. It took my mind back to that awful day when an old man had asked me to shoot him.

'Boy, are you crazy?' he said, before adding with a shrug, 'where would I get a gun from?' The Berliners' famed sense of humour had not dimmed.

A woman heard this exchange and intervened. 'I'll clean you up. Be brave.'

The woman, a refugee, undressed and washed me, without soap and with an old rag. She dressed me in underwear and a uniform with all of the insignia removed. She must have taken the clothes from a corpse. Mine was so filthy and stank so badly, a corpse wouldn't be seen dead in it.

'Don't die on me,' said the old lady.

But I wanted to.

I drifted away again, and when I came back I sensed I was on a military truck. I could hear the screams of a girl and something told me she was being raped. I also remember hearing a baby cry. A Russian soldier had given me bread to eat and had handed me a cube of butter that was melting in my hand. Then he poured vodka in my mouth. Intoxicated himself, he poured the vodka all over my face. The alcohol stung my eyes like fire. My screaming infuriated him and one of his comrades. I remember feeling their boots stamping on me. And the next thing I recall was finding myself lying by the road. Some other kindly soul took me into their farmhouse. They fed me and cleaned me, and slowly I regained feeling below the waist, along with my sanity, and my will to live.

It was many years later that I discovered what happened on that fateful night that we broke out from the Chancellery.

∽ CHAPTER SEVENTEEN ∽

The Ghost of Adolf Hitler

THE REICH CHANCELLERY WAS FINALLY TAKEN, not on May Day as Stalin had hoped, but the day after. It was General Nikolai Berzarin's Fifth Shock Army that won the coveted prize. The Red flag was raised above the fire-blackened building. But although Moscow propaganda talked heroically about a bitter battle to gain control of the last redoubt of Hitler the truth is a little more prosaic. The last SS soldiers supposed to defend the Reich Chancellery had fled the day before, mostly in General Mohnke's break-out parties. Even the Hitler Youth had gone. The building wasn't even booby-trapped as the Russians had feared. After sappers checking for explosives announced the all-clear, the Red Army soldiers gingerly made their way through Speer's vast portals. All that the Russians found when they finally breached the threshold were several hundred wounded in the basement emergency hospital tended by Professor Haase, Dr Kuntz and two nurses. They were still desperately short of medical supplies. The Russians were amazed at the contrast with the pantries, which were still stuffed to overflowing with champagne and fine foods the likes of which they hadn't seen for years.

Berzarin had promised that the man who found Hitler's body would be awarded the gold star of the Hero of the Soviet Union. So it came as little surprise to his men when they discovered an elite team from Stalin's SMERSH counter-intelligence organisation had been ordered to complete a thorough search first. Picking their way around the shell-holes and stumps of uprooted trees in the Reich Chancellery Garden, the men from SMERSH quickly stumbled on two charred cadavers. They were grotesquely deformed and appeared to be half the size of an adult corpse. But the Russian agents immediately recognised Joseph Goebbels' over-sized head and club foot from his comedy caricatures in Soviet propaganda cartoons. By the side of the other corpse was a blackened Nazi Party badge and a gold cigarette case. It was inscribed: 'Adolf Hitler, 29 May 1934'.

They looked, but did not find the body of Hitler nearby. Inside the deserted bunker they found it much as it had been when Mohnke ordered it to be abandoned. The map-room was scarred by Günsche's failed attempt to incinerate Hitler's rooms. But there was no other damage. The rest of the complex displayed the typical signs of any building hastily deserted. Office paper was strewn across every desktop and drawers had been left half-open. The pictures hanging from the walls were askew and chairs lay overturned everywhere. On almost every surface there were empty bottles of champagne, cigarette stubs and plates displaying the crumbs of last-minute celebrations.

In Hitler's suite of rooms his tunics and black trousers hung in a modest wardrobe, as did Eva Braun's dresses in the rooms next door. Hitler's hefty leather-bound appointments diary was lying on a chair, though nobody noticed it for weeks. The portrait of Frederick the Great had gone, but there was a supply of silver-framed photos of the Führer that he kept in his office as presents. Eventually the Russians found Krebs, slumped over his revolver, a bottle of Cognac drained at his side. Oddly, it was a matter of some days before they found the six stiff corpses of the Goebbels children, ghostly white beneath the shrouds their mother had hastily thrown over them. They were told that Burgdorf had also vowed to kill himself but in the confusion of these first minutes they didn't find his body.

But did they find Hitler? The question is still raised today, not because there is any real doubt about the answer, but because for so long the Soviet leadership appeared to deliberately sew doubt in the minds of its own people and the rest of the world. Shortly after the Russians took Berlin, Red Army military commanders and diplomats were confidently telling their Allied counterparts that they had discovered Hitler's jawbone and positively identified it as his through dental records. But soon afterwards, they were furiously backtracking on these claims and said they had no idea what had happened to Hitler. Coupled with the incorrect statement of Admiral Dönitz about the time and nature of the Führer's death that accompanied his broadcast to the German people, it created an air of mystery that fuelled all manner of speculation.

Throughout the summer of 1945 stories that Hitler was still alive gathered pace. A German submarine that had escaped the Allied net to surface in Buenos Aires was swooped on by American and British

Intelligence. The story of *U-977*, or 'Hitler's U-boat', as it was called, has become something of a legend. Its escape to South America was motivated by nothing more than the crew desperately wanting to flee the squalor of what they knew post-war Germany would be like and try and seek a new life in South America. (Another U-boat crew made exactly the same voyage with exactly the same intention.) But after a South American newspaper reporter concocted a colourful story, *U-977* became the boat that had squirrelled Adolf Hitler and Eva Braun to a secret Nazi base in Patagonia, a kind of Antarctic Berchtesgaden.

The idea may seem fanciful viewed from the distance of more than half a century, but at the time it was taken seriously. The commander of *U-977* was interrogated by both American and British Intelligence for the best part of a year. About the same time a number of stories emerged placing Hitler, variously, off the Irish coast, in the south of France, living as a hermit in Italy and a croupier in a casino in Evian. Argentina in particular and South America in general have regularly featured in these fantastic scenarios mainly because of Nazi Germany's wartime links with the Peronist regime and the undoubted flight of several senior Nazis to those parts. The US occupation authorities also received reports that Hitler was living in a vast underground cave complex in a Scandinavian mountain.

Underground bases equipped with James Bond-style security gadgetry and housing not just Hitler but many other important Nazis who escaped the Allies at the end of the war are talked about. Many of these stories are fuelled by knowledge of some of the 'wonder weapons' that the Nazis were working on towards the end of the war, including Junker long-range planes that could fly 10,000 kilometres (such as the ones Hans Baur is supposed to have told Hitler about). And the German navy's fleet of extremely long-range submarines. Many intelligent people seem to have been taken in by these stories and have even written books about them. Perhaps we should not be surprised after all. For didn't Hitler exercise a peculiar hold over many intelligent people 60 years ago, people who should have known better but never gave up in believing his wonder weapons were just around the corner?

As ever with conspiracy theories, they thrive when apparently intelligent and motiveless people vent their spleen. Hitler's case was no different. A lawyer claimed Hitler was in Innsbruck. A doctor claimed to have treated Hitler at his casualty station opposite the Berlin Zoo bunker after the Führer had been wounded in fierce tank fighting on 1 May. Much of the misinformation can probably be laid at the door of Moscow's propaganda machine. It suited Stalin to keep the ghost of Hitler alive and preferably link his continued existence to the capitalist West. The Russian newspaper *Izvestiia* reported that Hitler and his new bride were living in a moated castle in British-controlled Westphalia. Not all of the doubts can be blamed on Soviet propaganda though. At times Stalin seems to have been genuinely reluctant to accept that Hitler was dead. German witnesses such as Linge and Günsche, who were kept in captivity for up to ten years, were repeatedly asked whether Hitler could be alive or dead. It was clear that the Russians were genuinely unsure.

This confusion prompted British Intelligence to commission a report from a young Oxford don. Hugh Trevor-Roper would go on to become the distinguished (and now late) historian, Lord Dacre. In 1945 he was a major serving in the British army. Trevor-Roper was ordered to meticulously reconstruct the last days of Hitler with the intention of getting to the bottom of what happened to the Führer. To help him, he was given access to an extensive and comprehensive dossier of the US Counter-Intelligence Corps that had been compiled over the duration of the war. (The report arrived at some conclusions that would have been embarrassing, given the Allies' successful campaign to demonise Hitler. It noted that he was fond and solicitous towards children, loved walking his dog, disliked certain fanatical people and was conservative and fastidious in his habits.)

Trevor-Roper began his inquiries in September 1945 and the result was a report and subsequently a best-selling book that was the first to meticulously detail the last days of Hitler. What is remarkable about both is that, although Trevor-Roper was denied access to many Soviet files on the subject and many witnesses in Soviet prisons, the young major's conclusions subsequently proved to be accurate in the basic details. His book *The Last Days of Hitler* has many small inaccuracies, the result of crucial Soviet files being denied to him, but it remains the benchmark for every subsequent work on this compelling issue, including this one.

Trevor-Roper interviewed dozens of witnesses in the course of his investigation, and as many people as he could get hold of who were actually in the bunker. Key witnesses such as Linge, Günsche, Rattenhuber and Baur were in Russian hands and unavailable. But of those witnesses he discovered, he found their testimony differed in minor inessentials (usually dates and timings, which was hardly surprising because in the upside-down world of the bunker, night merged into day and days merged into one another). Some of the witnesses, usually the minor ones, seemed to have embellished their stories (more for dramatic effect, or self-aggrandisement, than to cover anything up). Basically, they all told the same story. Trevor-Roper gave a press conference in Berlin on 1 November 1945. He said that Hitler had committed suicide after about 2.30 p.m. on 30 April 1945 by shooting himself in the mouth, and that his bride had died at the same time through cyanide poisoning (subsequently it was accepted that the poison was probably prussic acid) although she had been supplied with a revolver. Subsequently, both their corpses were set alight in the Chancellery Garden. They were burned to a lesser or greater degree, it was impossible to say, and an attempt was probably made to bury whatever bones remained. What subsequently happened to those remains, Trevor-Roper could cast no light upon. But he was certain about one thing: 'The above evidence is not complete; but it is positive, circumstantial, consistent and independent. There is no evidence whatever to support any of the theories that have been circulated and which presuppose that Hitler is still alive. All such stories which have been reported have been investigated and have been found to be quite baseless; most of them have dissolved at the first touch of fact and some of them have been admitted by their authors to have been pure fabrication.'

Over the years, as new evidence leaked out, most of it confirmed the essentials of Trevor-Roper's case. (In fact he discovered the first corroborative evidence only weeks later in the form of Hitler's will and political testament and other documents that confirmed most of what he had been told about Hitler's last days.)

Artur Axmann was one of the key witnesses that Trevor-Roper interviewed. His evidence was crucial both to Hitler's death and that of Martin Bormann. Axmann had entered Hitler's room immediately after the Führer committed suicide and claimed to have seen Bormann's dead body after the break-out. Unfortunately, nobody could corroborate the Bormann find at the time. However, Trevor-Roper noted that, in virtually every other instance, Axmann's evidence had been truthful and accurate. But in the absence of a body, he acknowledged that there was no conclusive proof that Hitler's deputy was not still alive and at large. This, of course, gave ammunition to those who believed Bormann had certainly survived.

Thanks to the recent opening of Russian archives, the nearest account of the full truth of what happened to Hitler's remains has now emerged. It too confirms the essentials of the Trevor-Roper thesis and cocks a snook at all the fantasists, conspiracy theorists and plain charlatans who, for whatever reasons of their own, would like to convince people that Hitler survived the bunker.

On 2 May, when the Russian SMERSH team found the charred remains of Magda and Joseph Goebbels, they discovered another gruesome find in the Chancellery Garden. An old water tank contained a putrefying collection of decaying corpses and body parts. Presumably they were the victims of shell-bursts or patients who had died in the emergency hospital and had been tossed into the tank. Among these remains was a body that could have been taken as being Hitler's. Admiral Voss confirmed it was Hitler and the Soviets immediately put it on display in the entrance hall of the New Reich Chancellery. (Just as Hitler feared they would do.)

Then on 4 May, a member of the SMERSH team stumbled on what appeared to be a pair of legs sticking out of a bomb-crater. They started digging them up and discovered that they were the bodies of a man and a woman. It didn't strike these investigators for one moment that they might have found the remains of Adolf and Eva Hitler because they already presumed Hitler's corpse was lying in the lobby of the Chancellery. It was only two days later that someone realised what the find might be. The corpse that the Russians had presumed was Hitler's in the Chancellery lobby would soon be removed.

Urgently, the remains were sent to a field hospital in Buch near Berlin for a preliminary autopsy on 8 May. It was impossible to take fingerprints because the skin had been burnt off. DNA hadn't been discovered at the time. But the teeth of the skeletons had survived. The male one had a distinctive crown-bridge. The Russians put the bridge in an old cigar box and mingled it with several others. Then they tracked down two technicians who had worked for Hitler's dentist, Dr Hugo Blaschke. Fritz Echtmann had designed the crown-bridge and Käthe Heusemann had helped Blaschke install it. (Blaschke himself had fled to Bavaria and was not immediately available.) The Russians asked both technicians to draw the layout of Hitler's teeth from memory. Then they were asked, separately, to select the correct crown-bridge from the collection in the cigar box. The results were unequivocal. Both technicians sketched drawings identical to the teeth the Russians had found in the Chancellery Garden. Both selected the same crown-bridge. Hence the mortal remains of the Führer had ended up not in Valhalla, but in a cheap, tin cigar box.

Echtmann and Heusemann soon found themselves detained in Russia. It would be many years before their stories would be revealed. It was claimed that the remains of the Hitlers, the Goebbels and possibly General Krebs too were buried in an anonymous plot near Magdeburg. A year after the first autopsy the Soviets held another investigation into Hitler's death and criticised the deficiencies of the autopsy. They concluded, 'We cannot just state: this was Hitler.' Subsequently, for whatever motivations of their own, the Soviet authorities insisted there was no positive proof of Hitler's death, although there was clearly an enormous amount of evidence, factual and circumstantial. After the Cold War ended the opening of Soviet archives produced other revelations, among them that Soviet leader Leonid Brezhnev ordered the KGB to disinter and burn the buried remains near Magdeburg on the night of 4–5 April 1970. Were they the remains of Hitler, Braun and the Goebbels? The chances are they were.

But what of the other members of the Führerbunker community who broke out on 1 May 1945? How did they fare?

Shortly after I last saw her, Dr Gertrud met her death. She was last seen trying to run across the same street outside the Admiral's Palace that I had been cut down on. She was hit by a shell or mortar fire and had both her legs blown off. After I had been knocked out, the rest of my group suffered such severe casualties at the Weidendamm Bridge that Axmann decided to join forces with Bormann's group, the number three group out of the Chancellery. It included Stumpfegger, Schwägermann and Kempka. Bormann still had the copy of Hitler's last testament in the pocket of his big leather overcoat and he was determined to get to Schleswig-Holstein. Stumpfegger's most useful possession was probably a cache of his poisonous ampoules.

The massive gathering of SS, Wehrmacht soldiers and civilians continued to attempt to break across the bridge. Shortly after a Tiger tank arrived, along with a self-propelled assault gun and a half-track. The plan was to crash through the tank barrier at the northern end of the bridge with a column of civilians and soldiers following in the armoured vehicles' wake. Axmann and Bormann's reformed group joined the first push just after midnight. They joined scores of civilians and soldiers following in the wave behind the Tiger as it progressed across the bridge. The Tiger easily smashed through the barrier on the northern side of the bridge but encountered stiff counter-fire beyond. It was hit by a wayward Panzerfaust and in the blast the whole group were knocked off their feet along with dozens of others following the tank. Axmann was badly injured but managed to pick himself up. Kempka was knocked unconscious.

There were a further three attempts at breaking through the north of the bridge in the space of two hours. Each effort was repulsed with even greater vigour than the last. But the group stayed together, following the railway line to the Lehrterstrasse station where in the confusion they were parted. Bormann and Stumpfegger walked east along the Invalidenstrasse towards Stettinger station. Axmann and the others walked westwards but were soon separated in the mayhem. Axmann ran into a Russian forward position. He retraced his steps to try and find Bormann and Stumpfegger. At the Lehrterstrasse station he stumbled across two prone bodies in leather coats lying flat on their backs. He could immediately see they were Bormann and Stumpfegger but couldn't see any immediate signs of wounds. Further inspection was out of the question though, and Axmann went on his own way.

I was to discover too that those who had chosen to escape in the subway tunnels had a much more easy time of it. They encountered no Russian riflemen in the tunnels after all, only many German refugees who had taken subterranean refuge from the bombs and were also hopeful of fleeing the Russians.

Mohnke's party crossed Wilhelmsstrasse without incident and arrived safely at the Kaiserhof subway station. In the bowels of the station it was a relief to them to discover that the muted sounds they heard came from German civilians and not Red Army soldiers. They walked in single file for hundreds of metres, edgily at first because, although the trains had stopped, they had no idea whether the electricity had been turned off. After a while they were reassured to realise it had. With General Mohnke in the lead, each group followed slowly through the tunnel. They emerged at Friedrichstrasse station and Mohnke and the other groups liaised and made their way towards the Spree. But Mohnke's group was the only one to cross the Spree. They wisely avoided the Weidendamm Bridge and found a footbridge 300 metres away. On the other side of the river Mohnke mounted the roof of a garage and witnessed the sudden violent firefight at the bridge. It might have been this sudden hail of bullets and shells that felled me. Or it might have been the other attacks that happened shortly afterwards and hastened the end of Martin Bormann and Ludwig Stumpfegger.

Mohnke's group managed to stay together and were the only intact group to cross the Spree. It included Günsche, Baur, Rattenhuber, Gerda Christian, Traudl Junge, Else Krüger and Constanze Manziarly. Having become the only break-out group to cross the Spree they made their way eastwards before finding themselves in the Schönhauser Allee district which had been overrun by Red Army troops. They hid in a cellar but were soon discovered. Resistance was pointless so they gave themselves up. The men were arrested but the women set free. Mohnke was kept in solitary confinement by the Russians until 1949 and remained in captivity until 1955. He was subsequently accused of war crimes in incidents that predated his Reich Chancellery service and that were never proven.

The women were soon separated from the cook. The last Gerda Christian saw of Manziarly was when she dived into a cellar after a barrage of shellfire hit the street they were escaping down. She saw the cook disappear into a passage. When she called after her, there was no reply. She was never seen again and it has often been rumoured that Manziarly disappeared into the night and adopted an assumed identity after the war. The other secretaries dressed up as men to avoid the attentions of the Russian enlisted men. They eventually made it to the British sector on a refugee train.

Otto Günsche was taken prisoner by the Russians and immediately handed over to SMERSH, Moscow's counter-intelligence group, as a key witness to Hitler's last days. Günther Weltzin and Hans Baur were also captured by the Russians. Weltzin died in Russian hands. Baur was severely wounded, but he emerged after a period of captivity to tell his story. The Führerbunker FBK guard Harry Mengershausen participated in the break-out but was captured. Linge was captured by the Russians and returned to Germany in 1955. Kempka eventually made it across the Elbe and ended up in American hands. Almost every single Hitler Youth on the Weidendamm Bridge was wiped out.

And what really happened to Martin Bormann? Was that really his body that Artur Axmann saw in the Invalidenstrasse in the early hours of 2 May 1945? Bormann's real fate, like that of Hitler, has been the source of great speculation ever since. It is no coincidence that both mysteries were fuelled by the absence of accurately identified bodies. But the circumstantial evidence in each case has been overwhelming and the various theories advanced about their subsequent whereabouts have never had the slightest basis in truth.

Bormann was sentenced to death in absentia at Nuremberg on 1 October 1946. His wife Gerda had never carried out Bormann's instructions to kill her ten children but in the same year she died of cancer. Subsequently reports of Bormann living in a north Italian monastery surfaced. It was alleged he had escaped like many others to South America, via Rome. He has been reported spotted in Chile, Brazil and Argentina. A recent theory (not yet published) is that he is one of several top Nazis buried at the bottom of the sea in a fleet of long-range submarines requisitioned to take them to South America.

In the 1960s, a Russian journalist published what he claimed was Bormann's diary, found in the pocket of an abandoned leather coat discovered exactly where Axmann had said he had stumbled across the bodies of Bormann and Stumpfegger. Its authenticity was disputed. But then, in 1972, in the course of routine construction work, builders unearthed two skeletons at exactly the same place. Bormann had the same dentist as Hitler, Professor Hugo Blaschke. A forensic dental examination confirmed that the teeth belonged to Bormann. It is assumed that both Bormann and Stumpfegger took their own lives by biting on poison ampoules. In April 1973 a West German court formally pronounced him dead.

Göring was captured by the Americans on 9 May. He was put on trial at Nuremberg the following year. He defended himself aggressively and frequently outwitted the prosecution. Nevertheless he was found guilty on four counts: conspiracy to wage war, crimes against peace, war crimes and crimes against humanity. He was sentenced to death by hanging on 15 October 1946. But he cheated the hangman. Two hours before the sentence was due to be carried out, he bit on a poison ampoule that had somehow managed to evade his captors' attention.

The demise of Himmler was perhaps the most bizarre of all the Nazi leaders. For days he continued to hold staff conferences and meetings at his Flensburg headquarters in northern Germany. They continued to be attended by heads of departments with portentous names that no longer existed or had the power to operate. Hanna Reitsch and Ritter von Greim had delivered the late Führer's excoriating verdict on his treachery after their amazing flight from Berlin. And Admiral Dönitz had written to him abolishing his role as Reichsführer. Himmler was unmoved but didn't know what to do. He sought advice from his former cronies and was puzzled to find them not returning his calls. He even wrote to Field Marshal Bernard Montgomery who also failed to reply. For two weeks Himmler led a meaningless and friendless existence. He finally walked out of his house in the uniform of an ordinary foot soldier and disguised with a preposterous eye-patch. It was so preposterous that he was immediately recognised when he reached a British checkpoint. Stripped and about to be given a body search by a British surgeon, he bit on the poison ampoule in his mouth.

Of all the senior Nazi leaders only one was prepared to face the Bolshevik enemy and fight, and only one did not resort to suicide. Artur Axmann was the youngest of Hitler's inner circle in the dying days of the war. And however the world might judge his twisted sense of values, it can never be said that he was not true to them. He never contemplated suicide and he was fearless in battle. Axmann was also the only senior Nazi to break out of the Russian iron ring. Despite his injuries inflicted at the Weidendamm Bridge, Axmann managed to find his way out of Berlin and eventually to the Bavarian Alps. There he joined a reconstituted band of Hitler Youth. They operated in Bavaria for six months after the war had ended.

Axmann was eventually arrested in an elaborate Anglo–American Intelligence sting. His interrogators found that the evidence he gave was accurate in almost every detail save for accidental errors of time. After the war I visited him and we had several long conversations. He made admissions – '*Fehler wurden gemacht*' ('Mistakes were made'). But he never said anything against Hitler. Axmann died in 1996.

Epilogue

What happened in Auschwitz is the greatest, most satanic mass murder committed in world history. I am guilty before God and this nation to have guided the youth to follow Hitler, whom I considered to be unimpeachable but who turned out to be a murderer of millions.

– Baldur von Schirach

THUS SPOKE BALDUR VON SCHIRACH, THE former Leader of the Hitler Youth. He was giving testimony before the Nuremberg tribunal on 24 May 1946. It was the day after my 18th birthday. I had just become an adult. And I was beginning to learn how my childhood had been stolen from me. Baldur von Schirach was the person I came to admire most in my post-war world. It was von Schirach who had encouraged me to write poetry before the war. It was von Schirach's words at the Nuremberg tribunals that launched me on the road to pacifism. I began, with the help of a Catholic university professor, to search for the truth of what had happened during Germany's immediate past.

With Axmann the situation was different. We looked back from different perspectives. He never lost his admiration for Hitler. I visited him twice and we also corresponded and spoke on the telephone several times. In matters he was willing to discuss, I always felt that he was truthful with me. Yet he always prided himself on his continuing loyalty towards his Führer. I am all for loyalty but loyalty must have its ethic too! It was Baldur von Schirach's admission of guilt and not Artur Axmann's demonstration of loyalty that propelled me to find non-aggressive solutions and to vanquish hate once and for all.

When the Soviet army doctors issued me with discharge papers they restricted me to the Russian occupied zone. Very soon afterwards I decided to try and make it across the Mulde River to get to the American side. Wading through the waters with a heavy knapsack, my paralysis returned. Fortunately I was rescued by a border patrol and taken to the medical facility of a reception centre where a US Intelligence officer interrogated me. While I was there I was also shown the documentaries that General Eisenhower had ordered to be made when Buchenwald and Bergen-Belsen were liberated.

I was so shocked. At first I couldn't believe what I saw. One old German soldier whispered in my ear: 'Hollywood.' Others shrugged it off as propaganda too. But I couldn't see it that way. There were heaps of skeletons and some of the bodies still moved. This couldn't have been staged, with so many bodies of skin and bone. I knew it was true. And others did too. One of the wounded German soldiers confided to me: 'It's true. That's what went on in the concentration camps.'

The officer who had interrogated me had still photographs as well, horrendous portrayals of destruction and death. This was before I was steady on my feet again. While paralysed for the first time, I had wanted to die. Now I wanted to vanish because the way these documentaries were presented made me feel that I shared guilt in these heinous crimes committed by Hitler, the Führer I had believed in and served. It affected me physically. I could neither eat nor sleep for three days and three nights.

Then I discovered that I was expected to share the guilt for what had happened. But as far as I was concerned, I obeyed and carried out what I had been taught was my duty. We were expected to be blindly loyal to the Führer. For how long I would have continued to do so, I will never know. I struggled for years with the concept of collective guilt and finally decided I could hold myself only responsible for my own actions. Nevertheless, I came to the conclusion that had Hitler won this war, I would most likely, without realising it, have become a criminal.

Because of my youth in 1945, I was exempt from having to face a court. I wasn't even called to appear before a *Spruchkammer* (literally: verdict chamber). The Spruchkammer was an invention of the Joint Allied Forces to identify and, when warranted, to punish ex-Nazi functionaries. My father, though, denied the truth about his past in the SS. He maintained that it was the 'smart' thing to do. I remember him telling me that he was honour-bound to keep his duties in the SS a secret. He had served the state and people like him could never reveal the truth about their activities. But to me to deny the truth was to lie.

When the de-Nazification process came to an end, I remained disturbed by my father's continued lies about his past. He, who had once beaten me mercilessly for having lied, never revealed that he had falsified his past. He seemed pleased with himself for having got away with it. We all remembered how proud he had been of his black SS uniform in Breslau where he never stopped boasting that he was a member of Hitler's elite.

We lived in Eberspoint, Bavaria, after the war. No one knew him except members of the family. Obviously we didn't turn him in and, fortunately, I was never questioned by any officials about his past. I raised the matter of the Jews with him once when I was 18 or 19 years old. He treated me as if I was still a little boy. 'If you knew how the Jews treated us, you would realise they have only themselves to blame for what happened to them!' he roared at me.

I was so shocked I choked. After all that had happened, how could his thoughts have been so demented, his mind so twisted? For me, nothing would justify the cruelty and slaughter. The 'Final Solution' was abhorrent beyond belief. By then, I had learned about the many additional concentration and extermination camps, especially Auschwitz and Dachau. I agonised physically and mentally over what had happened. My whole belief system crashed and only gradually established itself anew.

Although my father remained quiet about many things I was to ask him, the horror-night of Dresden was not one of them. At any occasion that presented itself, he would tell the story of his survival, over and over again, always emphasising that, among the hundreds of patients and nurses in the mountain hospital, he was one of only three that survived. 'Murder is murder and mass murder is mass murder whether committed in Auschwitz or Dresden. Never forget it!' Except for stating that 'one does not excuse the other', I didn't discuss this point of view with him. To my mind, there are no valid excuses for the deliberate extermination of human beings. The 'Final Solution' for the Jewish people and the killing of the people in Dresden were both terrible slaughters.

I never knew what exactly he had been doing in Dresden that night. After the war he explained that he had transferred confidential materials from Breslau to the radio station there. He didn't elaborate on what kind of records they were; neither did I find out why he, officially a war correspondent, once again, was on such a special mission. Curiously, a member of the Vienna Reich Radio station claimed that my father was sent there to investigate possible fifth columnists among the staff, and that he was responsible for dismissing several. It was also suggested that there were some executions in Vienna as part of a last-minute mop-up operation and that my father might have been responsible for that. I did undergo some extensive research into both these claims but could find no evidence for either. That doesn't mean, of course, that neither was true.

During the last years of his life, among old comrades, my father reminisced and shared memories of these past secret missions. One who initially belonged to this inner circle of old comrades, and who survived him, mentioned at his funeral that all who belonged to this informal group of veterans held my father in high esteem and considered his war record honourable. Right up until they died, these veterans rationalised that 'orders were orders' and had to be followed. Those who issued the orders were responsible, not those who carried them out. There was never any indication that my father suffered under psychological burdens. He was always good at explaining things away. He maintained that horrible things happen in horrible times. All participants in the war are responsible for its horrors.

I am certain he was a very intelligent man. But what had happened to his reasoning ability? I am sure that he was not a sadist by nature. With his fellow hunters, he had deplored the torture of animals. He had compassion towards fellow human beings. When we were children, he always demanded consideration and courtesy towards grown-ups.

Whether he knew about the 'Final Solution' and what went on in concentration camps, I am still not certain. I have always given him the benefit of the doubt. But, after the war, when the horrible deprivations, repulsive persecutions and abominable mass-murders came to light, he should have deplored what happened if he was repelled as most of us were.

He only countered with arguments that the enemies also engaged in mass killings, naming Hiroshima and, especially, Dresden. To his way of thinking, I remained naïve. He would ask me why I hadn't matured after I had served as a soldier as he had in just as much bloody combat, if not more? Why, he would ask, after I had seen this war of slaughter come to its end, could I not see that one side was no better or worse than the next? My answer: 'War causes but never sanctions crimes against humanity. Justifying terrors of the past would invite terrors in the future.' I could no longer abide my father's views. We were estranged for much of my adult life. There was one last family reunion, but only after he had agreed beforehand not to talk about his views. We all met for dinner, but as time progressed father began his familiar diatribe. I had to kick him under the table to make him stop. That was the last I ever saw of him.

Less than ten years after the war, my parents went their separate ways but never divorced. My father died in Germany in 1979. My mother died in France, in 1988, and that is where she is buried. My sister Ute, who cared for my mother during her last years, lives in France, tends her garden and is very creative working with wood and clay. My sister Angela also lives in France with her French husband. My sister Anje has become a well-known artist and lives in Switzerland. She has become a Swiss citizen. My sister Dörte lives with her husband in Germany. My brother Wulf, ten years my junior to the day, did not survive his first heart attack. (I am fortunate to have survived five.) Once a card-carrying member of the Communist Party, he had embraced Buddhism just prior to his death. My brother Ulrich lives in Turkey.

In 1948, I attended a six-month crash course in journalism arranged by the occupation authorities. It was offered to fill the many posts vacated by journalists as almost all of them had been Nazis. I became a reporter and travel writer. In 1951, I was cleared for a civilian position in the US army in Munich and went on to serve in the United States Armed Forces as a German teacher. In 1967, I was naturalised and was granted US citizenship. In 1969, I received a Community Leader of America award from the editorial board of Community Leaders in America. I've spent my professional career in the travel industry, promoting world understanding.

Before becoming a US citizen I made several trips to Israel and met with concentration camp survivors, planted trees and made whatever personal monetary contributions I could afford. I have contacted peace activists and humanitarians all over the world, including Dr Albert Schweitzer, Prime Minister Nehru of India and the followers of Mahatma Gandhi after he was assassinated. I have been active in peace groups such as Dr Linus Pauling's Campaign for Nuclear Weapons Disarmament. I have a distaste for all things totalitarian, hate-groups, fanatics and ultra-extremists, particularly groups that try to put Hitler on a pedestal. My own experience of war has created in me a passionate devotion to peace. Raised in an atmosphere of hate and prejudice, I've surmounted the teachings of my youth and risen to carry the words of peace around the world.

The Second World War was a liberation in body and soul for me as a human being. My greatest fear is that what happened in Nazi Germany will one day happen somewhere else in the world. The primal source of peace is the human mind. What has happened in the past is irreversible and cannot be revoked. The future, however, is for us to build and its foundation should be one of honesty. Problems solved by war recur. Only peaceful solutions have a chance to last. If we want to work towards prevention of acts of violence in any form we need to set minds straight from the moment our children begin to think.

I have been married three times. My first marriage to an American schoolteacher I met in Germany ended in divorce. Her name was Margaret Ransom and we have one daughter. My second wife Aila died after a courageous battle with cancer. I have two stepchildren from that marriage. I married my present wife Kim in a sunrise ceremony in Palisades Park in Santa Monica, California, on 25 October 1981.

As for Anne-Maria? In the late summer of 1945 after my discharge I was able to walk again. With the trains now working once more, I located Anne-Maria in Hof der Saale. She was pregnant. The father of the child she carried was an American GI who married her in time. They called their son Peter. My first wife Margaret and I met Anne-Maria and her first husband Bill once, in Greece. My wife Kim and I met her and her husband Jim in Munich in May of 2001.

Index

Adlerhorst 18
Adolf Hitler Schuler (Adolf Hitler School) 43
Ahnenpass 32
All Quiet on the Western Front 43
Almanach de Gotha 28
Anne-Maria 64–70, 86, 109, 113, 189
Arlosoroff, Victor 96
Arndt, Richard 152
assassination attempt 17
Auschwitz 220
Axmann, Artur 7–10, 39, 48, 70–3, 79–86, 102, 109–10, 113, 116, 124, 128–9, 132–6, 142, 152, 154, 163–5, 171, 173, 175–7, 179, 182–4, 187–93, 198, 200–4, 210, 213, 215–8

Baarova, Lida 96, 97
Börenfänger, Major General Erich 163
Baur, Captain Hans 120, 124, 162, 166, 179, 190, 192, 202, 209, 210, 214
BBC 43
Below, Colonel Nicholas von 178–80
Berchtesgaden 22, 78, 87–90, 93, 95, 97, 119, 124, 148, 157, 172, 179
Bergen-Belsen 218
Berghof 20, 78, 87, 92, 157, 171
Berlichingen, Götz 45–6

Bernadotte, Count Folke 83, 108, 121, 123, 162, 164–5
Berzarin, General Nikolai Erastovitch 208
Blaschke, Dr Hugo 213, 216
Blondi 24, 91, 93, 179
Blut und Boden (Blood and Soil) 32
Boldt, Rittmeister Gerhard 178
Boldt, Heinz 133, 135, 191, 203
Bormann, Gerda 26, 193, 215
Bormann, Martin 10, 21, 23, 26, 48, 70, 77–8, 88, 90, 92, 98, 116, 119, 122, 124, 129, 133, 135–6, 140, 150, 154, 158, 164–5, 170–3, 177–81, 183, 189–93, 202, 210, 213–15
Braun, Eva 8, 12, 24, 92–3, 97, 116, 119, 123–4, 140, 147, 156–9, 166, 169–71, 175, 181–3, 194, 196, 198, 208, 209
Braun, Gretl 116, 157–8, 165–6
Breker, Arno 16
Brezhnev, President Leonid 213
Buchenwald 219
Bund Deutscher Madel (BDM) 101
Burgdorf, General Wilhelm 7, 116, 124, 171, 178, 181, 183, 189

Busse, General Theodor 84, 111, 117, 125, 160, 188, 199

Chopin, Frederick 41
Christian, General Eckard 89, 91, 122, 125
Christian, Gerda 19, 89–92, 119, 122–3, 170–1, 181, 202, 214
Chuikov, General Vassili 192
Crystal Night *see Kristallnacht*

Dachau 31, 220
Deutsche Wochenshau 38
Dönitz, Grand Admiral Karl 90, 124, 145, 167, 172, 178–80, 189–90, 192–3, 198–200, 202, 208
Dresden 20, 60, 62, 219–20
Dunkirk 43

Echtmann, Fritz 213
Einstein, Albert 45
Eisenhower, General 125, 218
Elisabet Gymnasium, Breslau 38

Fegelein, Hermann 116, 157–9, 164–5, 169
Feuchtwanger, Leon 45
Final Solution 172, 219
Flossenbürg 67
Frederick the Great 24, 27, 179, 208

Freud, Sigmund 45
Friedlander, Richard 96
Führerbegleitkommando
(FBK) 19, 22

Galland, Adolf 42
Gandhi, Mahatma 222
Gestapo 31
Goebbels, Hedda 96, 139,
176, 179, 182, 193–7, 208
Goebbels, Heidi 96–7, 139,
176, 179, 182, 193–8, 208
Goebbels, Helga 96, 139, 176,
179, 182, 193–7, 208
Goebbels, Helmut 96, 139,
176, 179, 182, 193–8, 209
Goebbels, Hilda 96, 139, 176,
179, 182, 193–7, 208
Goebbels, Holde 96, 139, 176,
179, 182, 193–8, 209
Goebbels, Dr Joseph 10, 12,
18, 21, 24, 26–7, 30, 33,
38–9, 42, 48, 54, 70, 73–4,
76–8, 88, 92–3, 95–8,
106–7, 118–19, 123–4,
129, 138–40, 154, 159–62,
164, 169–73, 176, 181–3,
189, 191–3, 195–7, 209,
211–12
Goebbels, Magda 12, 17, 22,
36, 78, 92, 94–7, 118–20,
123–4, 138–40, 156, 166,
171, 176, 181–2, 192–7,
208, 212
Goethe, Johann Wolfgang von
45
Göring, Edda 88
Göring, Emmy 88
Göring, Hermann 15, 21–2,
43, 88–9, 91, 105, 111,
118, 123, 125–6, 149–50,
154, 161, 165, 169, 172,
175, 180, 184, 215
Greim, Colonel-General
Robert Ritter von 149–51,
154, 162, 165–7, 180
Günsche, Major Otto 77, 120,
123, 159, 181–3, 196,
202, 208, 210, 214
Gutschke, Karl 52, 55–6, 66,
69, 103, 108–10, 112, 177

Haase, Professor Werner 144,
179, 182, 195, 200, 207
Hamman, Otto 142
Hanke, Karl 36, 51, 96, 97,
145, 172, 176–7
Heinrich, Dieter 43, 57–8
Heinrici, General Gothard 83
Heissmeyer, Gruppenführer
August 176–7
Hess, Rudolf 78, 97
Heusemann, Kathe 212
Himmler, Heinrich 18, 25–6,
31, 48, 76, 78, 82–3, 88–9,
92, 99, 108, 120, 122–3,
134, 158, 162, 164–6, 169,
172, 175, 215–16
Himmler, Marga 25
Hitler, Adolf 7–13, 15–28, 30,
33, 36–8, 40, 42–3, 48, 54,
60, 69–94, 96–100, 107,
110–11, 117–26, 132–4,
138, 145, 150–1, 153–4,
158, 160–6, 168–90,
192–4, 196–200, 204,
207–12, 215–18
Hitler, Eva (née Braun) 170,
181–3, 194, 196, 199,
208–9, 212
Hitler, Klara 94
Hitler's Submarine see U-977
Hoffman, Heinrich 92–3
Horst Wessel song 33
Huhn, Dr Gertrud 101–2,
115–16, 132–3, 135–6,
140, 142, 144, 147, 151–3,
157, 163, 184–6, 189, 192,
194, 200–1, 203–4, 213

Jodl, General Alfred 77, 116,
118–19, 122, 126
Johannmeier, Major Willi 178
Junge, Gertrud (Traudl) 19,
90–2, 97, 119–20, 123,
138–9, 168–9, 171–3,
180–2, 193, 197, 202, 214
Junge, Hans 91
Jungvolk (young folk) 9, 12, 37,
49, 73
Jungmaedel (young maidens) 9,
73

Kannenberg, Artur 19

Karinhall 88
Keitel, Field Marshal Wilhelm
77, 107, 111, 116–19,
121–2, 125–6, 179
Kempka, SS Colonel Erich
91, 143, 177, 179, 181,
183, 214, 216
Kesselring, Field Marshal
Albert 90
KGB 213
Koller, General Karl 89, 111,
125–6, 150, 161
Kopernicus, Nicholas 41
Krebs, General Hans 77,
106–8, 110–11, 116, 124,
171, 178, 181, 183, 189,
191, 197, 208, 212
Kristallnacht (Crystal Night)
28, 39–40
Krüger, Elsa 119, 180–1, 203,
215
Kuntz, SS Dr Helmuth 194–5,
208

Last Days of Hitler 211–2
Last Testament 169
Lehmann, Aila 223
Lehmann, Angela 26, 50, 221
Lehmann, Anje 26, 50, 221
Lehmann, Armin Dieter 7–8,
12, 221
Lehmann, Dörte 26, 185, 222
Lehmann Family 25, 78, 222
Lehmann, Frederick Wulf 26,
38, 50, 221
Lehmann, Kim 222
Lehmann, Margaret (née
Ransom) 223
Lehmann, 'Mutti' 136, 163
Lehmann, Ulrich Georg 26,
40, 50, 222
Lehmann, Ute 26, 50, 222
Leibstandarte Adolf Hitler
(LAH) 17, 22
Leipzig, Mayor of 175
Linge, Heinz 18, 123–4, 181,
183, 210, 214
Linz 21, 88, 94, 171, 197
Lorenz, Heinz 164, 178
Loringhoven, Major Freytag
von 178

Machtergreifung (Day of Seizing Might) 11, 26
Mann, Thomas 45
Manziarly, Constanze 22–3, 92, 119–21, 123, 139, 142, 171, 181, 197, 202, 214
Mein Kampf 38, 97, 171
Mengershausen, Master Sergeant 'Harry' 142–3, 186, 214
Misch, Rochus 21, 23, 95, 180, 184
Mitford, Diana 95
Mitford, Unity 95
Mohnke, Wilhelm 18, 124, 145, 189, 191–2, 196–7, 198–203, 207–8, 213–14
Mölders, Werner 42
Montgomery, Field Marshal Bernard 217
Morell, Dr Theodor 17, 23, 98, 117, 122–3
Muller, SS Gruppenfuhrer Heinrich 164–5
Mussolini, Benito 178
Der Mythus des 20 Jahrhunderts (The Myth of the 20th Century) 38

NAPOLAs (National Political Training Establishments) 33, 43
National Socialists Workers' Party 11, 26, 28, 32, 101, 171
Naujocks, Fritz 36
Night of the Long Knives 30
Nuremberg Laws 32

OberKommando der Wehrmacht (OKW) 40
O'Donnell, James P. 197
Operation Sea Lion 43

Pauling, Dr Linus 222
Petacci, Clara 178
Polish Corridor 40
Prien, Captain 42
Prominenten 117

Quandt, Gunther 95, 166

Rattenhuber, Hans 18, 137, 179, 181, 184, 201–2, 214
Raubal, Angela 93–4
Raubal, Geli 93–4, 120, 165
Reich Chancellery 15–17, 21
Reich Radio 18, 26, 33, 36, 73, 106, 171, 199, 219
Reichssicherheitsdienst (RSD) 18
Reitsch, Hanna 95, 148–51, 153–4, 159, 162, 165–7, 190, 216
Reymann, General Helmut 107, 110
Ribbentrop, Joachim von 28
Riefenstahl, Leni 95
Rilke, Rainer Maria 55
Röhm, Captain Ernst 31
Rosenberg, Alfred 38

Sachs, Hans 40
Sachsenhausen 121
Schaub, Lieutenant General Julius 77, 120
Schenck, Professor Ernst-Gunther 144, 157, 170–1, 176, 179, 200, 202
Schiller, Frederick von 46
Schirach, Baldur von 11, 46, 51, 217–18
Schloss Ullersdorf 49
Schörner, Field Marshal Ferdinand 178
Schroader, Christa 90, 119–20, 122
Schulze-Kossens, SS Colonel Richard 97
Schutz Staffel (SS) 26, 31–2
Schwägermann, Gunther 124, 192, 196–7, 198, 213
Schweitzer, Dr Albert 222
Seraglio (Operation) 120
Seventh Symphony (Bruckner) 199
Shröder, Dieter 201
Sklodowska, Marie 41
SMERSH 207, 211–12, 214
Speer, Albert 15–16, 20, 30, 78, 88–9, 92–3, 122–4, 126, 143–5, 149–50, 162, 165, 169, 172, 207
Stalin, Joseph 54, 180, 191
Stauffenberg, Colonel Claus von 16, 155
Steiner, SS General Felix 110–11, 115–18, 164, 169, 176
Stumpfegger, SS Colonel Ludwig 117, 120, 124, 150, 161, 179, 195–6, 202, 213–15
Sturm Abteilung 30–1

Tornow, Sergeant Fritz 179
Treaty of Versailles 12
Trevor-Roper, Hugh 211

U-977 210

Volksdeutschen 41
Volksgemeinscahft (people's community) 37
Volkssturm 9–10
Volkswagen 37

Wagner, Siegfried 95
Wagner, Walter 169–70
Wagner, Winifred 95
Wandervogel ('back to nature' movement) 30–1
Weidling, General Helmuth 84, 110, 117, 124, 145–6, 155, 161, 199
Weiss, Colonel 178
Weltzin, Günther 133, 135, 163, 190, 202–3, 214
Wenck, General 121, 125, 160–1, 176, 178, 188, 198
Wolf, Johanna 19, 90, 119, 122
Wunderwaffen (miracle weapons) 10, 73, 76

Zander, SS Colonel Wilhelm 178
Zoo Bunker 107, 143, 145–6, 152
Zossen 21, 106, 108, 110